CAREERXROADS

career(cross)roads

Gerry Crispin & Mark Mehler

MMC Group
Kendall Park, NJ

CAREERXROADS

©1997 by **Gerry Crispin & Mark Mehler**
Published by MMC Group

Printed in the United States of America. All rights reserved. This book-specifically our database and our approach to reviewing job, resume and career management sites constitutes original research intended for the personal use of job seekers and company recruiters. It may not be reproduced in any fashion, however limited, for the purpose of creating, adding to or building another database without the prior written permission of the authors.

Second Edition

0 9 8 7 6 5 4 3 2 1

ISSN 1088-4629
ISBN 0-9652239-5-7

Trademarks
A number of words in which we have reason to believe are trademarks, service marks, or other proprietary rights have been designated as such by use of initial capitalization. However, no attempt has been made to designate as trademarks or service marks all personal computer words or terms in which proprietary rights might exist. The inclusion, exclusion, or definition of a word or term is not intended to affect, or to express any judgment on the validity or legal status of any proprietary right which may be claimed in that word or term.

Every effort has been made to obtain up-to-date and reliable information.

We assume no responsibility, however, for errors or omissions and reserve the right to include or eliminate listings as well as edit and comment on the sites reviewed based on our judgement as to what is useful for job-seekers and recruiters.

With the Internet's World Wide Web growing at a rate unlike any phenomenon known before, we have offered the purchasers of **CAREERXROADS** an option of registering with our site and receiving updates via e-mail.

We offer new job related sites the opportunity to be included in these updates at no cost based on our determination of their value to our audience. Please send new information, comments, corrections or any other correspondence to: **mmc@careerxroads.com**.

MMC Group
P.O. Box 253
Kendall Park, NJ 08824
mmc@careerxroads.com
http://www.careerxroads.com

REGISTER!

Keep **CAREERXROADS** up-to-date.

Register your e-mail address and changes will be sent to you each month.

Clip out and Mail this page to: **MMC Group, P.O. Box 253, Kendall Park, NJ 08824** or Visit us at **http://www.careerxroads.com**.

Name:_____

Company:_____

e-mail:_____

Address:_____

_____

Phone:_____**Fax:**_____

My interest in **CAREERXROADS**

jobseeker_____   recruiter_____

other
(please specify_____)

Thank you for purchasing our directory. We are interested in hearing what you think and we're always interested in any new sites or types you would like reviewed. Send e-mail to: mmc@careerxroads.com

Gerry Crispin & Mark Mehler

Authors' Note & Acknowledgments

Working with emerging technology to help companies and people find each other, you come to expect rapid change and steady growth. Even so, what has happened on the World Wide Web in less than a year has astounded everyone.

When we finished the first edition of CAREERXROADS in May of 1996, the search for sites that had job, resume or career management information was relatively easy until we hit the 150-200 mark and then we really began to struggle. We only wanted to include information that was useful, actionable, and that met our criteria for adding value to the job search or the applicant hunt. Even though we dropped out most international job sites (too few), placement agencies (self-promoting) and companies (too narrow), there were several that just made the grade.

During these last six months, while working on our second edition, we realized that the explosion of so many new sites related to the job marketplace necessitated that we change our approach. We became more selective. We've added numerous international sites that weren't even "under construction" six months ago. We've included a cleaner format, additional categories to review and an award to the "Best of the Best".

CAREERXROADS was inevitable from the day we met at a 7:00 AM meeting of the Princeton Human Resource Group, a local networking organization of human resource professionals looking for their next opportunity. Gerry and I have successful day jobs but we both felt a strong need to help others in transition (much too often at the request of their former employers). The Princeton group meets every third Saturday morning to share job leads and discuss strategy. The goal of each member is to become an "alumnus" of the group...and most do within several months. From the beginning of 1995, we saw a steady increase in the number of job leads available on the World Wide Web as well as the growing ability to research targeted companies, identify hiring managers and market yourself via e-mail. From this came the idea for CAREERXROADS...a guide to where the talented job seeker and cyber-savvy recruiter could connect on the Internet.

We quickly learned while researching the WWW that there was no "yellow brick road", and few signposts to show you which sites had what kind of job, resume or career management information.

In this edition, we added articles from professionals with insight into the job hunting and hiring process. While their tips about what works are important, we try not to forget that it's the job seekers who find the useful sites first and drive much of the interest in the web. They are the ones who see clearly where the sites that give them an edge are located.

We accept the responsibility for correcting any inaccuracies in our effort to share this information in the "real" world. Please contact us in cyberspace with any changes, additions, and suggestions and we will place that information on our web site as an update and e-mail it to all who register with us.

The following people deserve our thanks:

Our brides, Beth and Diane, with whom we would like to spend more time but understand that when it becomes crunch time on a project they may not see us for awhile.

Our children, Lauren, Dara, Jaime, and Gerry, who have gotten a kick out of seeing their fathers' names on a book (and in Lauren's case has even contributed to helping me become more computer literate).

To the members of the Princeton Human Resource Network both new and old, but especially those whose commitment to one another's success creates an environment that expands those possibilities. To Dick Stone, the group's founder who continues to make it happen.

To Marc Liebeskind, who has helped us get through the technical aspects of dealing with ISDN lines and teaching one non-technical individual how to use computers to get the most out of them. To Janet and Pat from Graphiti who designed our cover to keep us on track. To Carol Adelman for her proof reading. To Karl Mount who kept me going when the going got rough. To Teresa Taylor who convinced her organization IEEE to distribute our book and gave us the freedom to give you a quality product.

To recruiters, human resource practitioners and hiring managers the world over who have their feet to the fire to find the best talent at the lowest cost in the least amount of time. They are being asked to combine the skills of air traffic controllers, financial analysts and psychologists. They are learning the meaning of "just-in-time."

And to the adventurers, explorers, webmasters and cyberpreneurs who are building a new medium.

Mark Mehler & Gerry Crispin
December 1996
mmc@careerxroads.com
http://www.careerxroads.com

Contents

Register	iii
Acknowledgments	v
Introduction	1

Tips and Tools for Job Seekers & Recruiters

The Strategic Career Manager: Use the Internet to Your Competitive Advantage	6
Preparing your Resume For E-Mail	10
Internet Technology Will Re-engineer the Hiring Process for Companies and Applicants	12
Strategic Staffing Through Recruitment Automation	14
Notes on Designing Web Sites for Staffing	18

CAREERXROADS: The 1997 Directory

HOW TO USE THIS DIRECTORY	23
ALPHA LISTING	26
CROSS REFERENCE LISTINGS	279
AGENTS- Sites that do the work for you	280
CAREER HUBS- Megasites with everything	281
CAREER MGM'T- Offer a helping hand	282
COLLEGE- Where to go for entry level	283
COUNTRY- International and US regions	284
DIVERSITY- Gender, race and young at heart	291
JOBS- For free and for a "fee"	292
LINKS- How to get to all the rest	297
PUBLICATIONS- Classifieds online	298
RESUMES- For free and for a "fee"	301
SPECIALTY- Discipline and industry focus	306
A Final Note for Job Seekers about Networking	312
About the Authors	314

Introduction

Everyone needs a job. More than 100 million Americans work...or want to.

Your network of family, friends, classmates, acquaintances, career management specialists, job counselors, employee assistance professionals, colleagues and support groups are ready and willing to give you advice on how to manage the rest of your life, and maybe, just maybe, provide a little helpful advice on how to get another job...from their own personal experience.

Contract work and interim assignments are rapidly becoming a mainstream business option for the white collar, professional work force. Add to that the explosive growth of telecommuting and other flexible, alternative forms of work and it is easy to see why so many people begin searching for the next job the day they accept their current position.

In this new world, career management skills and strategies are more important than ever before. A new breed of professional networker is emerging. Focused and competent, unhappy about the lack of job security but unwilling to spend time whining about a reality that can't be changed, today's job seeker is quickly learning to "ramp-up" their job search, find leads faster and secure new employment in less time than their more traditional counterparts.

Today's job-seekers are learning to communicate with hiring managers, human resource professionals, recruiters and placement professionals instantly. The number of job seekers who have mastered "the hunt" is small but growing exponentially. They have incorporated emerging communication and information technologies into their mix of networking strategies.

As job seekers gain access to the net, more and more companies, publishers, organizations, associations and others are recognizing that they can connect... faster, at less cost and with more accuracy than ever before...to you.

• IBM announced, in the Wall Street Journal, their intention to place all 24,000 expected openings during 1997 on America's Job Bank, a free World Wide Web government job site designed for use by the nation's 2000+ employment offices.

• CareerPath, a company formed by the publishers of the nation's largest newspaper chains, grew from 6 original members to nearly 30 by the end of 1996. Posting more than 300,000 new jobs each month from their Sunday, classified help-wanted sections, job seekers quickly discovered that they get an edge by searching CareerPath's openings on Saturday, the day before the ads appear in print.

CAREERXROADS©
Job, Resume & Career Management Sites on the World Wide Web
• The 1997 Directory •

• Professional and trade associations are suddenly realizing they can offer an added service to their members (and generate additional income) by creating job banks accessible from the Internet. Instead of waiting for their monthly newsletter, members find out about open jobs in hours. Results from some of the more marketing savvy groups show increasing membership and solid examples or positions filled before the monthly mail reaches the door.

We are at a crossroads in a new job and career marketplace where "just-in-time hiring" and "just-in-time job searching" are connecting on the Internet.

Getting the edge in Cyberspace is fast becoming the worst kept secret in the job market. Faced with the need to reduce the time required to find, attract and acquire professional talent at lower cost, recruiters are flooding into the Internet armed with intelligent applicant tracking and resume database software products. They manage the flow of applicant information, review potential candidates and communicate their interest in a fraction of the time and at a lower cost than ever before. While most recruiters are still trying to skim an ocean of possibilities, a small vanguard are beginning to plumb the depths of this new technology.

Employers are rapidly incorporating new methods into their "kit bag" of recruiting tools along with their more traditional approaches.

There is a need for more information about what to do. Nearly 100 titles on Jobs and Careers crowd the shelves in every major book store, but only a handful even attempt to address the growing phenomenon of the World Wide Web and tell job seekers where the jobs are:
- where help wanted ads printed in Sunday's newspaper can be searched and read;
- where an opportunity can be identified remotely;
- where a resume can be mailed electronically and then received, scanned and acknowledged automatically...all in the space of a few minutes.

Most books cover the basics about how to get on the Internet, write a resume and tool around cyberspace. They all have useful information for the beginner.

CAREERXROADS is different.

This is not the place to learn how to connect to the internet, compare bulletin boards or how to telnet. This is a reference guide that will get you where you want to go once you know what you want to do.

CAREERXROADS©
Job, Resume & Career Management Sites on the World Wide Web
• The 1997 Directory •

There's a great passage from **Alice in Wonderland** where one of the characters in response to a question about "which road should be taken", asks instead "where do you want to go?" Upon hearing, the answer "I don't know", the character says, "If you don't know where you're going, then any old road will do"

This is the book for anyone who has scrolled down a screen of 800 job links and wondered how much time it would take to find the right one.

With so much to choose from, with new ideas, models and information streaming online, we focused exclusively on the Wold Wide Web. We excluded bulletin boards, gopher sites, most company sites, (there are now 50,000 with jobs), and the majority of search firm sites.

We've added a virtual twist to this real world directory. We know that for you to use CAREERXROADS effectively, you'll need an e-mail address. Register it with us and we'll send you updates of new job related sites as well as changes to existing sites. Let us know what you want and we'll incorporate it into our next edition.

CAREERXROADS is uniquely designed to be a part of your network.

Return this book

If you...

- are afraid to turn your computer on.
- don't need to look for a job.
- don't believe anyone is "out there".
- don't need an edge in your job search.
- have enough severance to look around for a VERY long time.
- have an (aunt/sister/cousin/friend/network) sending you all the (newspapers/magazines/job leads) from (Atlanta/ New York/LA/DC) every (week/2 weeks/month) and figure that's more than enough.
- are not responsible for staffing.
- are responsible for staffing but don't care how much ($$$) you spend or how long it takes.
- don't have an interest in the Internet or just haven't figured out how to get there.

...**CAREEERXROADS** isn't for you. Return this book and ask for a refund.

CAREERXROADS©
Job, Resume & Career Management Sites on the World Wide Web
• The 1997 Directory •

But, if you are...

...on the lookout for a new opportunity and want to...

- get an edge by adding technology to your job search strategy.
- learn where to find jobs on the "net".
- meet electronic "agents" that send you new leads without having to go back to a site again and again.
- post your resume where it has a better chance of being seen, scanned, searched and selected.
- reach your target companies in a fraction of the time it takes to send a letter.

...or, you are looking for candidates and want to....

- add technology to your sourcing strategy.
- target where job seekers are/will be looking.
- learn what makes one job site more effective than another.
- increase quality, reduce your cost per hire and time to fill positions.
- improve your company's WWW site to attract more quaifed candidates.

...then welcome to **CAREERXROADS**

- This is the most comprehensive, up-to-date directory to jobs and career information on the WWW (nearly 475 in-depth reviews of the "Best of the Best" and how to find all the rest)

- **And CAREERXROADS** won't go out-of-date. Register now to receive updates directly to your e-mail address...or stop by **http://www.careerxroads.com** and find out what is new. No e-mail yet? Don't worry, when you get it, we'll send everything you missed.

Good Hunting.

Tips and Tools for Job Seekers and Recruiters

CAREERXROADS©
Job, Resume & Career Management Sites on the World Wide Web
• The 1997 Directory •

The Strategic Career Manager:
Use the Internet to Your Competitive Advantage

by Gene D. Glatter
Sr. Career Management Consultant
geneglatter@worldnet.att.net
Right Associates
Princeton, NJ

Not long ago, I was introduced to a new client who had enjoyed a successful career in sales and marketing. In his most recent position, he served as Director of National Sales for a large healthcare/consumer products conglomerate. His specialization: opthalmic consumer products (or, as we say in plain English, "eye glasses").

During our first counseling session, my client expressed concern about the limited number of job opportunities there were in his field, largely as the result of corporate downsizing and consolidations. After validating his feelings, I recall asking, "But, isn't there any part of the opthalmics industry that's growing?" He paused momentarily to contemplate, and then his eyes widened knowingly as he explained, "You know, it's an interesting thing. My industry recently developed this new bifocal technology. Before it was introduced to the market, you could always tell when someone was wearing bifocals because you could see the line that separated the top from the bottom of the lens. Well, with this new technology, you can't see the line. Of course, the new bifocals cost a lot more than the old ones, but when the baby boomers started turning 40, they were ready to pay any price to avoid looking like their grandmothers. This really is a growth sector!"

As I had anticipated, here was yet another sales and marketing executive who understood the critical link between business strategy and market intelligence. I knew it wouldn't be long before he landed.

As a Career Management Consultant, I spend my days coaching corporate executives through two processes: the more pressing and immediate job transition and the longer term approach to continued career management. From CEOs to middle managers, many have had very impressive careers. There are times when I am awed by the achievements of my most successful clients. They have fine tuned the art of strategic business thinking. And you can bet that this ability didn't just develop overnight! Quite the contrary, highly successful executives are sure to eat market intelligence for breakfast! It wakes them up in the morning in the voice of a Bloomberg News Radio commentator and energizes them throughout their working day in the form of a Wall Street Journal column, a trusted associate's insightful comment or the contrary opinion of a competitor. Whatever the source, this "grist for the strategic thinking mill" is promptly digested and, once processed, applied to corporate business decisions that sometimes generate millions of dollars.

Yet, despite their many successes, it is unusual when a new client sees the similarly critical role that market intelligence plays in the career transition and ongoing career management processes. (Of course, this excludes the sales and marketing executives who - like my opthalmics client - are more inclined to take to the concept like a duck to water!) How, then, do I best facilitate that knowledge transfer? Herein lies my greatest challenge. To meet it, I propose that my clients conduct a SmartSearch.

Simply put, a SmartSearch is one that is equipped with enough market intelligence to steer a career in a direction that enhances one's immediate and long-term professional marketability. It uses a "funnel down" approach to the integration of market intelligence, growing more specific to the individual as the funnel narrows.

At the wide mouth of the SmartSearch funnel, "big picture" changes impacting the generic workforce and economy are considered. Three catalysts primarily responsible for driving this generic change are technology, globalization and/or demographics. By factoring their impact into the the career transition and ongoing career management processes, our decisions are infinitely more strategic.

As we step down through the narrowing parts of the SmartSearch funnel, our market intelligence is more industry or growth-sector specific. We target specific companies within the identified growth sector/s and learn about the ways in which our skills address their unique needs (or about the skills we're lacking and need to acquire). We learn about corporate cultures and reputations. As the funnel grows narrower, our knowledge of the targeted market enables strategic positioning and clarity of focus. We know the role we want to fill and where we want to fill it! Market intelligence plays a vital role in facilitating this strategic process.

The Internet is an invaluable resource for the strategic career manager. The remainder of this article spotlights a few of the more attractive career-related, market intelligence Web sites. While there are many others, all of the sites noted are excellent sources of information and absolutely free of charge.

Using the SmartSearch funnel as a model, I'll begin by taking a broad brush look at generic workforce and economic trends. If you'd like to learn more about these, I recommend the American Studies Web (http://www.georgetown.edu/crossroads/asw/pol.html#labor). Under the "Labor and Workplace Issues" sub-heading, you'll find a wealth of links to sites addressing labor relations; the impact of cultural, poliltical and technological changes in the workplace; trends in downsizing and outsourcing; labor relations and statistics - to name just a few. Another excellent site is the Bureau of Labor Statistics (http://stats.bls.gov/blshome.html) where you can access surveys, publications, programs, regional information and economic data pertinent to economic and workforce labor statistics. If it's the "people side" of workforce trends that interests you, go to HR Links (http://www.shrm.org/hrlinks/) and click on Work/Life. Here you can find information about such topics as the best companies for working mothers, eldercare resources and work family programs.

Taking a step down on the SmartSearch funnel, you'll want to take a look at industry-specific market intelligence. You'd be hard pressed to find a more comprehensive web site for industry-specific research than Fuld & Company's Competitive Intelligence Guide (http://www.fuld.com/i3/index.html). Select Industry Links and Data from the alphabetized Internet Intelligence Index, click on your industry of choice, then sit back and enjoy the ride! For example, by selecting environmental, I was presented with the "mother of all lists" with links to information of potential interest to environmental professionals, e.g. environmental companies, environmentally correct products, environmental trends, environmental recruiters, consultants and job sites, and the list goes on and on.

There are many other excellent web sites for locating industry or sector-specific market intelligence. One I recommend highly is Industry Link (http://www.industrylink.com/). Or, if you really want to dig into the heart and soul of an industry, go to the home page of a good industry-specific society or association. To find its Internet address, select Gateway to Associations from the American Society of Association Executives (http://www.asaenet.org/index.html). If it's not listed there, do a search from my favorite search engine, HotBot (http://www.hotbot.com/). Be sure to key in the full name of the targeted organization and specify "phrase" as a search parameter before executing your search. If none of the above points you at the targeted web site, it may not exist.

If you're curious about what a top notch, online association can do for you, check out the Society for Human Resource Management's Home Page (http://www.shrm.org/). Among its featured offerings, SHRM's site showcases great industry-specific articles, an impressive listing of current HR job openings and links to other web sites likely to interest the HR professional. SHRM members have privileged access to (among other things) an extraordinary collection of industry white papers. If they can't find information on the topic they're seeking, they can e-mail a request to the SHRM webmaster and expect a faxed report detailing the specified topic within 24 hours! SHRM gets my vote for the best online association. One hopes that other associations will follow suit.

Back to the SmartSearch funnel, one step further down brings us to company-specific information. For this purpose, you'd be hard pressed to find a better web site than Hoovers Online (http://www.hoovers.com/). At the top of the home page, type in the name of the targeted company or click on Select 10,000+ free Company Capsules and select it from a company listing. As a test run, I requested information about Bristol-Myers-Squibb. In response, Hoover's brought up some basic information about (e.g.) the company's home office and web site addresses, phone number, number of employees, ticker symbol, etc. But the real meat begins at the bottom of the screen. Here Hoover's links me to top-notch online market intelligence about BMS including (but not limited to) CNN news reports, full text news articles from major business journals and newspapers and recent company press releases. I can also link to any SEC document filed by BMS over the past two years (in this case there are no fewer than 35 10Ks, 10-Qs, S-8's, SC-13D, S-3's, 8-K's, etc.). If you're unsure about the type of market intelligence you'll find in these filings, see Disclosure's Guide to SEC Corporate Filings (http://www.disclosure.com/infobase/guide.cgi) and learn about such things as pending legal proceedings, corporate indebtedness and director/officer level compensation.

It's really hard to beat Hoover's for one-stop company-specific research, but there are other excellent sites. For unique competitive intelligence, select any one of the links at Pathfinder's Business Sites (http://pathfinder.com/@7Q5O4wUAMvuS4bZ/business/text.html). For example, by selecting Fortune: Special Reports, you can read Fortune's Corporate Reputations Survey 1996 which details the ways in which large, successful companies perceive their competition in terms of managerial effectiveness, quality of products or services, innovativeness and ability to attract and keep talented people. Last but certainly not least, don't miss The Riley Guide's excellent listing of links to company-specific research sites at Resources for Research to Improve Your Job Search (http://www.jobtrak.com/jobguide/research.html).

At the very bottom of the SmartSearch funnel, you'll want to learn about specific jobs. For example, where are they? What do they pay in New York? In Kansas City? What are the most frequently sought after skills? To answer these and other job-specific questions, link to some of the career megacenters from Yahoo's Business and Economy: Employment (http://www.yahoo.com/Business_and_Economy/Employment/). Here you'll be able to search through databases containing thousands of jobs representing every imaginable industry, function and level. For a function and/or industry-specific listing of jobs, go back to your association's web site. (For association links, try the Gateway to Associations mentioned above.) Any good professional association will post corporate job listings and/or link you to other sites that do the same. And if you're planning to relocate, find out about the cost of living at any one of 500 U.S. and Canadian cities by using the CMR Salary Calculator at CMR: The Center for Mobility Resources (http://www.homefair.com/homefair/cmr/cmr.html). You'll also be able to determine the income needed to maintain your current lifestyle at any one of the 500 cities. Interesting stuff!

You may be wondering about that opthalmics Sales Director mentioned at the top of this article. If you recall, his SmartSearch incorporated the impact of baby boomer demographics and new technology on the bifocal market. He soon went on to identify the issues and needs of strategically targeted companies. Not surprisingly, his search ended successfully with an opthalmics industry leader. The same search conducted without market intelligence would have lacked strategy and vision. With it, short-term goals were realized while long-term professional marketability was enhanced. Here's hoping the same for you!

Preparing Your Resume for E-Mail

by Will Matlack on behalf of Resumix, Inc.
Independent Public Relations Consultant
San Francisco, CA
wmatlack@msn.com

Because e-mail is immediate and requires no paper, copying or postage, it is the least expensive and fastest method of getting your resume into play. More companies are implementing technology that allows electronic submission of resumes, and many of these also include resume processing systems, like Resumix. These systems automatically process your resume to extract your skills, experience and other qualifications for immediate matching to the requirements of open positions. Companies with these capabilities usually make note of them in their ads or on their World Wide Web sites. Before you e-mail your resume, there are two key things to consider - file type and content.

File Type

If you have a data file of your current resume, submitting it is very easy. You have two basic options, Copy/Paste or Save As an RTF file. In the first option you need to have both your word processing document file open and your e-mail program open. Go to your resume document and perform a "select all" operation in the edit menu. You can also select the entire content of the document right clicking and dragging your mouse from the top of the document to the end.

After your selection is complete, move your mouse into your e-mail document and perform a paste operation. In Windows this can be done by either left clicking and selecting "paste" or holding down the 'Ctrl' key and pressing the 'v' key. All of the text of your resume will be pasted into the e-mail document ready for sending.

The important thing to remember about this method is that you will lose all of the document's formatting during transmission. This is not a major issue for companies using Resumix or other resume processing systems, but if you would like to retain some formatting, you need to save your resume in Rich Text Format (RTF) first. If you have a lot of formatting on your resume, RTF won't save all of it, but if you review the RTF file before sending it, you can fine tune it to get back a majority of your formatting.

Saving in RTF format is only slightly more complicated than the cut and paste process just described. The first step is to open your resume data file then select the "Save As" function in the "File" menu. A dialog box will open up giving you a wide variety of file types for the "Save As" process. Select the Rich

Text Format or RTF, change the file name to something like "ResumeRTF," then save the file. Changing the file name will ensure that your original file will remain intact. You can then perform the copy/past operation in the same manner as discussed above.

Another option is to send either the original word processed file or the RTF file as an attachment to your e-mail message, but this could add an unnecessary level of complication to the process. Resume processing systems may not be able to access the attachment directly.

Content

The rules for resume content are totally different for resumes that will be submitted to companies using resume processing systems, such as Resumix, versus those that process resumes manually. For example, the Resumix system extracts meaningful information on skills, experience and education directly from the e-mailed resume and places them in a comprehensive database. This data is then matched to the requirements of open positions to produce a list of the most qualified candidates. The system has no limitations on how much information can be extracted from a single resume.

This means that if your resume is being e-mailed to a company with a resume scanning system, you should put down every bit of information about yourself that you can think of. Since these systems are specifically used to match skill sets to position requirements, try to list every skill you can think of - the length of your resume simply won't matter. These systems allow you to represent your qualifications more fully than ever before.

Some companies that use Resumix offer an online program that will step you though the process of building an electronic resume that will be maximized for processing systems. Look for this program on company World Wide Web sites; it's called Resume Builder.

If your resume is going to a company that has not advertised a resume scanning system, you should prepare its content in the traditional manner for a paper resume. This means editing it for easy visual access to the information it contains and keeping its length to no more than two pages if possible. As explained above, you will have limited formatting available, so it is best to save the document as an RTF and make use of the formatting it provides you.

A general rule of thumb is to have two versions of your resume available - one for e-mailing to companies with processing capabilities and one for e-mailing to those who will visually process it. If in doubt, you can always send both versions.

CAREERXROADS©
Job, Resume & Career Management Sites on the World Wide Web
• The 1997 Directory •

Internet Technology Will Re-engineer the Hiring Process for Companies and Applicants

with permission from Greg Morse
Corporate Marketing Director
greg@restrac.com
Restrac, Inc.
http://www.restrac.com

In the corporate landscape of the 1990s, the ability to put the right skills in the right place at the right time translates to a distinct competitive advantage for any business. Increasingly, the Internet, in conjunction with highly-functional client server technologies, is fast emerging as a way to connect workers with employers, to their mutual benefit. The primary significance of the Internet for both businesses and job seekers is that it enables people to communicate easily and provides instantaneous access to information stored throughout the world. It is estimated that there are currently over 30,000 Internet sites containing career and job information (Authors' note: The National Association of Colleges and Employers estimates nearly 50,000 WWW sites with jobs alone at the beginning of 1997)

We are now witnessing an explosion in Internet functionality. It is no longer just a repository for various types of information, but rather a platform on which corporate applications can be deployed. Restrac, Inc. of Dedham, MA, a leading provider of client/server-based staffing solutions for human resources management, is one of many organizations harnessing the power of the Internet to improve candidate sourcing, provide line managers with recruiting tools and information, and reduce corporate time to hire and cost per hire. To-date, robust staffing tools have been available to only larger sized corporations, but in the future, companies like Restrac envision that virtually all businesses will be able to take advantage of these capabilities through the Internet.

Twenty years ago applicants were only exposed to the job opportunities that were listed in the local paper. Now people who are seeking jobs have access to a much larger view of the job market through the Internet. In fact, it is currently estimated that there are 35-40 million people on-line world-wide and that number is growing every day. As more and more people begin accessing the Internet as a job resource, the importance of the Internet in hiring will expand exponentially. Currently the Internet is being used as a meeting place where businesses and job applicants can communicate with each other with huge time and cost savings.

Creating A More Efficient Labor Market

The Internet, in conjunction with applicant tracking software, allows companies to eliminate many of the constraints associated with processing hard copy resumes. For example, a hiring manager can fill out an on-line requisition form in New York, and submit it to corporate staffing in San Francisco. Once approved, human resources can post it to an Internet job board with the click of a mouse, where it can be viewed by anyone with a web browser. Applicants can then apply for the position by e-mailing their resumes over the Internet where they are forwarded automatically to the company who posted the job. This is an area which has seen tremendous growth with many companies, particularly in technology industries, who have reported as much as a 40% increase of their resume volume being received in e-mail. Finally, the resumes enter the company's electronic resume pool, just as if they had been scanned from paper originals, completely by-passing the OCR (optical character recognition) process. Additionally, because these resumes are received electronically, they are available more quickly.

In addition to attracting candidates from postings on Internet job boards, companies can also receive resumes that have been forwarded to postings on an organization's own home page.

The Real Future of Internet Hiring: Applicant Pools

Imagine this: Your company is looking for a candidate with a particular set of job skills, say a software engineer who lives in Texas and speaks Spanish. You fill out an electronic job specification worksheet detailing these skills, click your mouse and voila! Only hours later a set of electronic resumes is downloaded to your hardrive. Resumes of individuals that meet your particular requirements. Farfetched? Not really.

Technology is being developed to allow businesses of any size to take full advantage of the pools of job applicants that currently reside on the Internet. These "job pools" will be created by the thousands of folks who respond to Internet job postings. The revolutionary aspect of this approach will be the ability of the technology to quickly scan, evaluate and prioritize each job candidate and deliver the information electronically to the HR department or hiring manager.

For qualified applicants, this type of technology increases their chances of being considered (in many cases for jobs they weren't even applying for), and increases the company's chances of finding the most highly qualified individuals. As these Internet models mature, the Internet will serve a central function in the formation of a more efficient labor market-one that will benefit both job applicants and companies of all sizes.

CAREERXROADS©
Job, Resume & Career Management Sites on the World Wide Web
• **The 1997 Directory** •

STRATEGIC STAFFING
Through Recruitment Automation

(Reprinted, with permission, from Employment Management Today, published quarterly by the Society for Human Resource Management, Spring, 1996)

by Ed Gagen   and   Ed Struzik
Flemington, NJ   Newtown, PA
gagened@aol.com   74003.3625@compuserve.com
Senior Consultant,   President,
The Hunter Group   B.E.K.S. Data Services

NOWADAYS, it's not so much a question of whether to automate, but of what to automate and to what extent. Any automation can help gain efficiencies with record keeping and the data management, and the argument to "automate everything" has strong appeal to paperwork-burdened employment managers. But before getting sucked into the glitzy promise of a "paperless recruitment office," we offer for your consideration the following guidelines on building an effective employment management system.

Determine Your Volume Requirements

First, establish your needs and capabilities by analyzing volume, structure, data management requirements, and technical environment. Volume is a key consideration of whether you need a spreadsheet, a self-developed database or a high-powered employment management system. Factors to consider are number of jobs to fill, variety of jobs, number of system users, number of resumes received, and the number of applicants to track. For example, if you fill 25 to 50 positions a year with relatively few applicants for each and only receive a few thousand resumes a year, a self-developed database application or small-scale employment management tool will suffice. However, if you fill hundreds of positions and receive tens of thousands of resumes each year, then you want to focus your efforts on a high end employment management system.

As a rule of thumb, if you are dealing with fewer than 100 openings to fill, or more if they are all similar positions, receive fewer than 5,000 resumes, and have two to three system users, you can get by with a good internally developed database program or a low-volume employment management system. These types of systems - whether stand alone or multi-user LAN applications - provide basic record keeping, correspondence generation, and reporting capabilities.

If you will be filling hundreds of positions, or fewer if the positions are varied, and receive 25,000+ resumes a year, and will have many users accessing the system over a local or wide-area network, then you will want to consider a high-end employment management system with a relational database, resume scanning and workflow capabilities.

Analyze the Structure of Your Recruiting Organization

Next, it's important to take a good look at the structure of your recruiting function; this analysis should influence the type of automation tool you'll need. Are you centralized or decentralized? A centralized recruiting function that supports many divisions or business units from one location will have different automation requirements from a decentralized structure. Some of these requirements will be driven by volume, some by culture.

Whether you centralize requisition and applicant information depends on your management approach and corporate culture. Centralized record maintenance makes it easier to manage headcount and measure performance and productivity. In any event, a centralized recruiting organization is likely to need a powerful, specialized employment management system, but an organization with distributed recruiting that doesn't need to centrally correlate data can manage its enterprise with a less expensive solution. Your current applicant tracking module built into your HRIS might even suffice.

Factor in Your Data Management Requirements

Data management is related to volume (the amount of data being tracked) and structure (the need for all data to be in one place). It also involves an organization's data needs and how data is used. Most organizations need to produce applicant flow reports to meet Affirmative Action requirements. Report capabilities beyond that are typically up to the organization. Tracking open and closed positions are other common data requirements from the recruiting department. Sources used to find candidates, cost per hire, time to fill, and customer (hiring manager) satisfaction reporting requirements are other performance and productivity measures for a recruiting staff to consider.

The bottom line is the more elaborate or complex an organization's data retrieval needs, the more sophisticated the application it will need to deliver the desired results. Sophisticated employment management systems are designed to capture and report on most or all of the areas listed above and more. If your organization's reporting needs are less involved, a less complex and costly system or an internal database tool may suffice.

Complement Your Technical Environment

Regardless of what automation approach you want to take the organization's Information Systems architecture needs to be able to support it. It is essential to involve your Information Technology group as early in the planning process as possible, especially in discussions about how to manage, retrieve and move data. Computer availability, software compatibility, desktop operating system (e.g., DOS, Windows), network availability (e.g., Novell), LAN/WAN needs and capability, IT support experience, reporting tools, and IT standards all need to be determined upfront. Even the best system is of no value if it performs poorly in your environment and is not easily supported.

Create Your Own Candidate Database

If you want an electronic, searchable skills/education summary of each job seeker, then you should definitely consider an employment management system. You can capture the searchable elements through data entry or scanning. Data entry could be the right approach if your volume is not very large, or mostly applications, as opposed to resumes. But if you receive thousands of resumes then we recommend that you take a look at systems that support resume scanning and full text search.

Using either approach, you will create a database of potential candidates for your own use, and that's what most employment managers consider luxury. Once you have them in your database, searching for the right one is a matter of technology (having a good, easy-to-use search engine) and technique (having recruiters develop good search skills). If you are able to get the right candidates into and out of your database, you should be able to reduce your recruiting costs and shorten your time to fill.

The Benefits of Automating

All this technobabble makes you wonder whether automating your employment office is worth the bother. But promises of increased efficiency, possible headcount savings, recruiting cost reductions, the luxury of your own database of qualified candidates, and streamlined selection processes are strong arguments to take the plunge.

If all you do is respond to resumes you receive, then a good typist with a word processing merge can handle it. However, if you need to refer to these individuals when they follow up or when the executive that nominated a candidate calls to check on the status, then you will need some type of applicant tracking mechanism such as a self-developed database application, a module in your HRIS, or an employment management system. This capability will enable you to record date received, source, correspondence, interviews, and any other activity that occurs for all job seekers.

Beyond the tracking, ability to get a variety of reports with the click of a mouse is also a tremendous time saver for any organization. Spending hours trying to verify an open requisition report, or preparing an "applicant flow" report becomes a thing of the past assuming the data in the system is current and accurate.

From Reactive to Strategic Recruitment

Companies that have already automated their recruiting function can now proactively search out candidates and include them in their database for future openings. They are able to find them quickly and cost effectively, thereby satisfying their customer, the hiring manager. And they are able to respond to requests quickly, exhibiting a professional response to management and job seekers. These tools go a long way to help an organization recruit people in a competitive marketplace. Essentially, a well-conceived recruitment automation system can help you tip the scale from reactive recruiting to a more strategic approach.

One caveat: Don't automate for the sake of automation. The key is, like most projects, build planning and analysis into the automation process to ensure that what you end up with fits your business needs, actually is cost effective, will be technically supportable in-house, and most importantly, easy to use. (Remember, the best system is the one people use.) The fact is that from the simple acknowledgment letters to complex candidate skills inventories, technology can improve efficiency, reduce costs, and improve the quality of the labor intensive employment process.

Notes on Designing Web Sites for Staffing
by Gerry Crispin & Mark Mehler

More than 50,000 sites (November 25,1996-Webcrawler) contain jobs. Several hundred of these are the third-party, government, private & commercial sites, publisher and association job databases reviewed in CAREERXROADS. The remainder are primarily companies listing their positions.

The most active sites claim at least 10,000 visitors each day. These numbers however are guesses at best. Ask them to provide independent audit information and, especially where search engines are used, ask how many times their job database is searched each day.)

The trend toward registering potential job seekers is growing. These agent-based sites will keep you informed via e-mail about current openings. Here, daily traffic measured by "hits", "searches" or whatever doesn't really matter. The total number of registered job seekers that can be contacted is all that matters. This web version of electronic direct mail could open up tremendous opportunity or equally noxious abuse if we get flooded with unwanted e-mail. If you are thinking of registering potential candidates at your site, we strongly encourage you to get their permission to forward (job) information to them in the future. Confirm their preferred e-mail address.

Before commercial web sites were available, internet staffing pioneers relied heavily on posting their company's open positions to newsgroups (specialized text based discussion forums) where job seekers lurked in the largest numbers. In 1994, as the World Wide Web developed, entrepreneurs, associations and publishers launched new sites to attract an increasing number of savvy job seekers. These sites began posting jobs to the newsgroups and extracting resumes from them for their own resume databases. Many sites still provide this service but check which newsgroups they work with. Today, there are literally tens of thousands of newsgroups. Only a small portion may be useful to your company. With a little research, you can link needed company skills to newsgroups with comparable interests and automate the posting internally.

In the past, long lists of links to employment sites were maintained on university servers. They were extremely helpful in directing the job seeker. Stanford, Texas A&M, Duke, William & Mary, U. of Michigan, WPI (when Margaret Riley kept her list there) and many others. Often, it was the college's career services office that provided the guidance. Many still do. Among them Purdue University has one of the best set of links. Unique individuals like Margaret Riley (The Riley Guide) and Harry Lemon (Harry Lemon's Bulletin Board List) were copied or linked everywhere until hundreds of additions (and deletions) began to create problems for the volunteers who maintained and organized the lists. As company's develop their site and begin looking for "partners" who can help send candidates their way, don't forget the career planning and placement offices. Most will be happy to add a link to your company's job page. You might even consider a small donation to help that "targeted" college maintain the link.

CAREERXROADS©
Job, Resume & Career Management Sites on the World Wide Web
• The 1997 Directory •

As commercial job sites and resume banks proliferated, they created "traffic" at their site with fresh openings. They also generated publicity and rapidly gained corporate support, especially from companies whose own sites were still "under construction" or where concerns regarding security and privacy suggested extreme caution. Technology has significantly reduced these concerns in the last year but it is critical that proper safety precautions be taken. If you don't have the internal expertise, it's better to work with a third party than do-it-yourself.

The first models on the web lacked internet "search" capability and their job databases were typically a folder containing job files in chronological order by the date received. Jobs were formatted using the same "rules" as many of the newsgroups.

As more and more ads were posted, scrolling and opening become time consuming and it was clear that some mechanism for searching the files was essential. The applicants couldn't (and wouldn't) spend hours scanning long lists of job titles. The obvious approach was to use an open "keyword" search engine where the "window" and all the positions that contained the word somewhere in the text would be available to be read. The downside to this approach was that the applicant often needed to be very creative to find all the jobs that fit their criteria without getting hundreds of jobs that didn't apply. Applicants immediately discovered that typing in "programmer" produced every kind of programming job and, of course, typing "human resources," would return every ad that contained "human resources" in the return address.

As search methodologies improved skill based approaches at web sites such as Intellimatch, CareerSite, Post-A-Job, and NationJob developed. These models required applicants check off their skills or interests from an online application form or checklist which then matched the applicants criteria against the jobs posted, or a comparable employer profile of the companies needs and requirements. The variations are endless.

The more choices an applicant has to search out fresh job leads, the better they like it i.e. to immediately see the "newest" positions posted; to be able to search on categories provided by the site; to search by keyword; to include or "click" on a specific region, title, discipline, industry or experience level; to leave a set of requirements, interests or skills, to be matched as opportunities arrive with the information about the match sent via email.

The search must be over almost before it begins. Speed is essential.

The applicant should have the option of downloading several openings simultaneously to print out later.

Yesterday, companies interested in electronic recruiting strategies, but with no Internet presence themselves, had little alternative but to pay to post each opening and absorb extra costs for company profiles and other services. Today, nearly every company with 1000+ employees either has a functioning web presence or plans to have a site up in the near future,

Associations with a web site are discovering opportunity for added service and income potential by offering posting jobs for their members. They make great partners.

Company human resource organizations and corporate recruiters are still struggling to create models that take advantage of the communication and speed of the net. Most of their problems have little to do with technology and a great deal to do with their internal processes. Getting a resume from a web posting via e-mail only to print it out and send it to the hiring manager through the interoffice mail is more common than many articles would have us believe.

A strategic staffing system that extracts needed core skills from an internal skill matrix, translates them to the corporate Intranet (accessible by all the company's employees), posts them to the company's Internet site while simutaneously informing selected third-party, university, association and other sites to drive fresh candidates quickly to their home page is a reality for very few. Those that do find significantly lower cost per hire and reduced "time-to-fill". Keeping company openings current, controlling the quality of communication, increasing the pool of applicants for future openings, tracking the flow of resumes through the hiring process and integrating internal and external hiring with other planned uses for websites, are just some of the many considerations. Few of today's solutions are seamless.

Web designs for staffing are not about meeting technical challenges. First and foremost, there is a need to step back and develop a strategic viewpoint. There is a critical need to partner with internal HRIS, external vendors, suppliers and others to create a vision before designing and implementing a model. There is also a requirement that the staffing processes designed to be managed for speed and communication to maximize the Internets strengths. Otherwise a more traditional solution may do just as well. Keep the picture in mind, recently published in USA Today, of the President of a small web design company standing by a telephone pole outside his offices in downtown San Francisco. He desperately needed a web designer but realized there were plenty within walking distance. Instead of some grand internet staffing strategy, he nailed a 3x5 card to the telephone pole with "Web Designer Wanted" written in magic marker. He had his hire in 1 hour.

When you get to the practical level of determining what to do on your company's staffing page, your goal should be to provide structured access to the job seekers who want to quickly get in, get what they want, and get out. The best designs will give the potential applicant and candidate the information they want, when they want it, with the least effort.

Here are a few additional suggestions:

• Place a prominent "jobs opportunity" link from your Company's Home Page to your "Job/Career Home Page."

• Provide separate links to "experienced" and "college"/"entry-level" openings.

• Provide a separate link to a corporate "culture" profile where you honestly describe the strengths and challenges you face as a company. What programs are in place to support growth? Stability? Service to others? Is there opportunity for shared profit and other rewards? Are there special mentoring, orientation or educational benefits that would appeal to entry level employees or others making the transition to your company or your industry?

• Give experienced job seekers the opportunity to quickly download and save all your current openings to their PC, or let them quickly search on several pre-defined titles, job skills, locations or other common-sense parameters.

• Allow the job seekers to register in a structured way by asking them to check the skills, experiences, and competencies your company needs. Ask them for permission to e-mail matching open positions over an extended period of time and get them to type in their preferred e-mail, fax or other address. The possibilities include searching and contacting large numbers of registered potential applicants as the openings are approved.

• For immediate critical needs offer an online application form or an e-mail link for the job seekers to post or attach their resume. (Hopefully into an automated scannable and searchable software package.)

• Emphasize that resumes be sent in formats you can read or scan. Offer suggestions. Show examples.

• Automate your system so that any resume received via e-mail automatically triggers a response to the sender acknowledging their interest and indicating when a response can be expected...or not.

• Send a letter to all community organizations, area libraries, and colleges with Internet access. Provide them with a copy of your logo, your internet address and a request that they make a link from any career resource material on their site to your jobs page. See if you can internally provide some contribution (e.g. $100) to the organizations as a non-profit donation to assist them in maintaining their services but especially their link to your site.

1997 will bring access to everyone. All current openings should be made available via the net. All planned openings should have registration capability. Watch for remote PC video applicant screening sites to become a hot topic during the year.

CAREERXROADS©
Job, Resume & Career Management Sites on the World Wide Web
• The 1997 Directory •

The 1997 Directory to Job, Resume and Career Management Sites on the World Wide Web

How to Use this Directory

There are no standards that dictate what a WWW job or resume site should look like, what information it should contain, how it should be organized, how the quality of that information might be measured, what means should be used to search it, deliver it or even what services might be provided.

Our organization of this Directory and our comments throughout CAREERXROADS are framed from the job seekers point of view:

[Sample site listing shown on left]

Rating
Web Site Name
Type of Site
Site Address (URL)
Contact Information

Site Information

Review

Sample Site

• What kind of site (**TYPE OF SITE**) is this? How can I reach this site via the WWW (**URL**)? How can I reach the owners (**CONTACT INFORMATION**)?

• Is this site committed to providing opportunity (**JOBS**), advice (**CAREER MANAGEMENT**), the means to communicate their skills and interests (**RESUME**) to others and/or does it provide connections (**LINKS**) to those who do?

• How expensive (**COST**) is it to see the openings that are posted here or to submit my resume? Do employers have any restrictions or expenses associated with posting their openings or searching for my resume?

• Are most of the jobs posted at this site organized with any critical emphasis such as the industry or economic sector of the economy (**INDUSTRY**), the geographic emphasis (**COUNTRY/...**), or the educational degree or skill requirements (**SPECIALTY**).

CAREERXROADS©
Job, Resume & Career Management Sites on the World Wide Web
• The 1997 Directory •

• **(COMMENTS)** Is the site easy to use? Is the information limited, extensive? Is the information fresh? How much does it cost? What else can job seekers, or employers, do to connect here?

The 1997 Directory is organized in two distinct sections:

The **Alpha Listing,** shown above, and the **Cross Reference Listings,** below, highlight each site's features, services or areas of emphasis

For example, a growing trend at the more sophisticated job sites is the development of "agent" like services. After registering your resume, skills or interests, some sites will perform a match of incoming positions and e-mail the job seeker a "lead." Conversely, some sites will match company openings as applicants submit their resumes/skills and periodically inform the employer of the match via e-mail. There are quite a few twists to this model as well as differences in cost and the type of information communicated (e.g. some sites will send the resume or job opening with all the information needed for direct contact between applicant and employer; others are coded to purposely prevent direct communication). However, they all attempt to automate a matching process online, and in most cases, offer a communication service that eliminates the applicant or the employer from having to surf (to) a site again and again. We believe this trend is positive and will continue to grow.

The Cross Reference Listings (See Table of Contents for page numbers) include:

• *Agents-* Sites which provide a matching service and e-mail information to the job seeker, the employer or both.

• *Career "Hubs"-* Commercial sites that attract the largest amount of applicant traffic by offering multiple services. The largest of these claim 10,000 or more visitors per day.

• *Career Management-* Sites which emphasize information about careers, job search and counseling.

• *College-* Sites that focus primarily or exclusively on the entry level job seeker. Some sites with multiple level services have a strong enough college presence that they have been included as well.

CAREERXROADS©
Job, Resume & Career Management Sites on the World Wide Web
• The 1997 Directory •

• **Country-** Sites that emphasize their regional focus. Larger sites where applicants can sort by region are noted in reviews but excluded from this index.

• **Diversity-** The focus of this index is to identify sites that will be especially helpful for women or a specific race or gender.

• **Jobs-** The majority of sites in this directory contain jobs. We have specifically indexed those that allow you to post your company openings for free.

• **Lists & Links-** The places to go to search on your own.

• **Publications-** The newspapers, trade publications and magazines that offer classified help wanted advertising online.

• **Resumes-** Sites that post for a "fee" and for "free".

• **Specialty -** Sites or specific pages on a site that only emphasize a single academic discipline, industry focus or some other special emphasis.

NEW this year! CAREERXROADS includes a Quick Review Rating for each site.

• Has jobs:

• Has resumes:

• Has career advice:

• One of the best in class:

You'll also see a reduced version of the home page for the sites, who in our opinion, offer the best value on the 'Net.

CAREERXROADS©
Job, Resume & Career Management Sites on the World Wide Web
• The 1997 Directory •

100 Careers in Cyberspace

Commercial Job Site
www.globalvillager.com/villager/CSC.html

Global Communications Services, Inc.
3130 Rt. 10 West, Denville, NJ 07834
Phone: 201-989-0501   Fax: 201-943-8137   e-mail: gv@globalvillager.com

Jobs? Yes
- Cost to post jobs: Fee
- Cost to see jobs: Free
- Specialty: All
- Industry: All
- Country/Region/State/City: US

Resumes? No
- Cost to post resumes: N/A
- Cost to see resumes: N/A

Links to Jobs? Yes

Career Advice? Yes

Information systems positions are posted for two months. Applicants can e-mail employer for direct information on open positions. Owners have multiple web sites, (see career China) charge $20 to post a job on line.

100 Careers in Wall Street

Commercial Job Site
www.globalvillager.com/villager/wsc

Global Communications Services, Inc.
3130 Rt. 10 West, Denville, NJ 07834
Phone: 201-989-0501   Fax: 201-943-8137   e-mail: gv@globalvillager.com

Jobs? Yes
- Cost to post jobs: Fee
- Cost to see jobs: Free
- Specialty: Finance/Business
- Industry: Finance
- Country/Region/State/City: US/EC/NY/NYC

Resumes? No
- Cost to post resumes: N/A
- Cost to see resumes: N/A

Links to Jobs? No

Career Advice? No

Employer is charged $20/position or $200/month for unlimited job posting. Mostly investment banking and finance positions.

4 Work

Commercial/Agent/College
www.4work.com

Jim Burkholder Access Influential Inc.
5650 Greenwood Plaza Blvd., Suite 250, Greenwood Village, CO 80111
Phone: 800-789-0145 Fax: 303-741-9702 e-mail: recuit@4work.com

Jobs? Yes
- Cost to post jobs: Fee
- Cost to see jobs: Free
- Specialty: All
- Industry: All
- Country/Region/State/City: US

Resumes? Yes
- Cost to post resumes: Free
- Cost to see resumes: Fee

Links to Jobs? Yes

Career Advice? Yes

Catalog of volunteer, high school student, internships, and full time positions. Jobs have direct contact information and are in many different fields. Good search engine. Typical fees to post jobs are in the $10-20 range depending on length of posting. Will also link to your site for free. 4Work has added an agent and allows employers access to post and manage their information directly. One of the most imporved sites this year. We like the focus on youngsters in high school and entry level

CAREERXROADS©
Job, Resume & Career Management Sites on the World Wide Web
• The 1997 Directory •

AAA Resume Service

Commercial Resume Site
www.infi.net/~resume

Dan Carmichael
2820 Lawndale Drive, Ste 112, Greensboro, NC 27408
Phone: 910-282-4343 Fax: 910-282-4343 e-mail: resume@nr.infi.net

Jobs? Yes
- Cost to post jobs: N/A
- Cost to see jobs: N/A
- Specialty: All
- Industry: N/A
- Country/Region/State/City: US

Resumes? Yes
- Cost to post resumes: Fee
- Cost to see resumes: Free

Links to Jobs? No

Career Advice? Yes

Advice & articles about interviewing, choosing a resume service, and a weekly "hints and tips" page. Typical service. Services cost $50-$100.

AAS Career Services

Association
www.aas.org

American Astronomical Society
2000 Florida Ave., Suite 400, Washington, DC 20009
Phone: 202-328-2010 Fax: 202-234-2560 e-mail:

Jobs? Yes
- Cost to post jobs: Fee
- Cost to see jobs: Free
- Specialty: Science/Astronomy
- Industry: All
- Country/Region/State/City: US

Resumes? No
- Cost to post resumes: N/A
- Cost to see resumes: N/A

Links to Jobs? Yes

Career Advice? Yes

American Astronomical Society has been around since 1899 for Astronomers and other scientists. Simple site but it gets the job done. Scroll on titles to open. $100 cost to employer. Nearly 100 jobs listed when we visited.

Abag Globe

Government
www.abag.ca.gov/bayarea/commerce/globe/globe.html

Brian Kirking Assoc. of Bay Area Governments
PO Box 2050, Oakland, CA 94604-2050
Phone: 510-464-7996 Fax: 510-464-7970 e-mail: briank@abag.ca.gov

Jobs? Yes
- Cost to post jobs: Free
- Cost to see jobs: Free
- Specialty: All
- Industry: Government
- Country/Region/State/City: US/West

Resumes? Yes
- Cost to post resumes: Free
- Cost to see resumes: Free

Links to Jobs? Yes

Career Advice? Yes

Bay area job database for local government open positions. Site gives direct contact information. Click on (other government job lists) and you will find good information about living in this area of the country.

About Work

Career Management
www.aboutwork.com

e-mail: walston@ivillage.com

Jobs? Yes
- Cost to post jobs: N/A
- Cost to see jobs: N/A
- Specialty: N/A
- Industry: N/A
- Country/Region/State/City: US

Resumes? No
- Cost to post resumes: N/A
- Cost to see resumes: N/A

Links to Jobs? Yes

Career Advice? Yes

Site has tons of career advice with a live chat room that you need to e-mail for free software so you can participate. Gives individuals information on being an entrepreneur, about working from home and our favorite- job survival. Good common sense info that most of us take for granted. Worth a visit and becoming a member (also free).

CAREERXROADS©
Job, Resume & Career Management Sites on the World Wide Web
• The 1997 Directory •

Academe This Week

Publisher/Trade Magazine
www.chronicle.com

Mike Snyder The Chronicle of Higher Education
1255 23rd Street NW, Suite 700, Washington, DC 20037
Phone: 202-246-2691 Fax: 202-466-1055 e-mail:

Jobs? Yes
- Cost to post jobs: Fee
- Cost to see jobs: Fee
- Specialty: Teaching
- Industry: Education/University
- Country/Region/State/City: US

Resumes? No
- Cost to post resumes: N/A
- Cost to see resumes: N/A

Links to Jobs? No

Career Advice? No

All current positions listed are those published weekly in the Chronicle of Higher Education. Broad range of faculty, research, administration and executive positions. (1000+). Openings are searchable by keyword and can be restricted by region. One of the pioneers. You must be a subscriber of the Chronicle ($75) to access their jobs info.

Academic Chemistry Employment Clearinghouse

College/University
hackberry.chem.niu.edu/ChemJobText.html

Steven Bachrach Northern Illinois University
e-mail: smb@smb.chem.niu.edu

Jobs? Yes
- Cost to post jobs: Free
- Cost to see jobs: Free
- Specialty: Science/Chemistry
- Industry: Education/University
- Country/Region/State/City: US

Resumes? No
- Cost to post resumes: N/A
- Cost to see resumes: N/A

Links to Jobs? No

Career Advice? No

Listings of Analytical, Bio-, Inorganic, Organic and Physical Chemistry positions. That's it. Limited but clearly focused.

CAREERXROADS©
Job, Resume & Career Management Sites on the World Wide Web
• The 1997 Directory •

Academic Employment Network

Commercial Job Site
www.academploy.com

400 Riverside Street, Portland, Maine 04103
Phone: 800-890-8283 Fax: 207-878-0913 e-mail: info@academploy.com

Jobs? Yes
- Cost to post jobs: Free
- Cost to see jobs: Free
- Specialty: Teaching
- Industry: Education
- Country/Region/State/City: US

Resumes? No
- Cost to post resumes: N/A
- Cost to see resumes: N/A

Links to Jobs? Yes

Career Advice? Yes

Teaching/academic, school administration and department head positions are posted. Job ads run for 30 days. Jobs are listed by state which makes for easy access. Direct contact info is listed. Also info on state teacher certification with 32 out of 50 states present when we visited. Nicely done site, easy to view.

ACM's Sigmod's Database Job Openings

Association
www.acm.org/sigmod/jobs

e-mail: sigmod@bunny.cs.uiuc.edu

Jobs? Yes
- Cost to post jobs: Free
- Cost to see jobs: Free
- Specialty: IT
- Industry: Education
- Country/Region/State/City: Int'l & US

Resumes? No
- Cost to post resumes: N/A
- Cost to see resumes: N/A

Links to Jobs? Yes

Career Advice? No

Association of Computer Machinery's Special Interest Group on Database Management. Contains University and company positions in engineering and computers (listings from 1995 through today). International as well as US opportunities. Public and private sector. Also plenty of grad assistant positions. Not heavily trafficked but several good links. You can print everything out directly.

CAREERXROADS©
Job, Resume & Career Management Sites on the World Wide Web
• The 1997 Directory •

Acorn Career Counseling

Commercial Resume Site
www1.mhv.net:80/~acorn/Acorn.html

Fred Nagle
8 Clay Court, Rhinebeck, NY 12572
Phone: 914-876-8617 Fax: e-mail: acorn@mhv.net

Jobs? No
- Cost to post jobs: N/A
- Cost to see jobs: N/A
- Specialty: N/A
- Industry: N/A
- Country/Region/State/City: US

Resumes? Yes
- Cost to post resumes: Fee
- Cost to see resumes: Free

Links to Jobs? Yes

Career Advice? Yes

The "Resume Doctor" shows you a defective resume and how to correct it. Also responds to e-mail inquiries. Provides phone counseling for $50/hour and $125-$150 range for resume writing etc. Job seekers should take a look at the doctor's advice, check out the suggestions and links to where it can be posted for free.

Ad One Classified Network

Publisher/Agent
www.adone.com

AdOne Classified Network, Inc.
Phone: 212-431-3309

Jobs? Yes
- Cost to post jobs: Fee
- Cost to see jobs: Free
- Specialty: All
- Industry: All
- Country/Region/State/City: US

Resumes? No
- Cost to post resumes: N/A
- Cost to see resumes: N/A

Links to Jobs? Yes

Career Advice? No

Interesting site for fans of CareerPath. AdOne serves as the classified Internet site for more than 200 small market newspapers primarily in the NJ, IL, FL, CO and CA marketplaces. Many are dailies and have help wanted advertising. Job seekers can use an agent (Ad Hound) to identify the job categories and regions to search. The agent will e-mail what it finds for 30 days. Applicants can also use links to specific papers and search each classified section online. This site is approaching a very nice size and model for secondary markets. Employers can place an ad directly at the site or through the newspapers although there is no information about whether the rates are included or are an added cost. Great site for jobseekers, awkward for recruiters.

CAREERXROADS©
Job, Resume & Career Management Sites on the World Wide Web
• The 1997 Directory •

Ad Search

Private site
www.adsearch.com

Miller Advertising Agency
Phone: 212-691-2929   e-mail: adinfo@adsearch.com

Jobs?: Yes
- Cost to post jobs: Fee
- Cost to see jobs: Free
- Specialty: All
- Industry: All
- Country/Region/State/City: US

Resumes?: No
- Cost to post resumes: N/A
- Cost to see resumes: N/A

Links to Jobs?: Yes

Career Advice?: No

Recruitment Advertising owner provides job database for their clients. Search engine for jobs and lists of newspaper websites are available.

Adia

Placement/Search/Temp
www.adia.com

Adia Personnel Services
Redwood Shores, CA 94065
Phone: 415-610-1096

Jobs? Yes
- Cost to post jobs: Fee
- Cost to see jobs: Free
- Specialty: All
- Industry: N/A
- Country/Region/State/City: US

Resumes? No
- Cost to post resumes: N/A
- Cost to see resumes: N/A

Links to Jobs? No

Career Advice? Yes

With more than 1100 offices in 32 countries, Adia's site is expected to support recruiters and provide open positons for job seekers.

CAREERXROADS©
Job, Resume & Career Management Sites on the World Wide Web
• The 1997 Directory •

Advance HTC

Publisher/Trade Magazine
www.advancehtc.com

Lynn McGarvey Montgomery Newspapers
290 Commerce Drive, Fort Washington, PA 19034
Phone: 215-542-0200 Fax: 215-542-7586

Jobs? Yes
- Cost to post jobs: Fee
- Cost to see jobs: Free
- Specialty: IT
- Industry: N/A
- Country/Region/State/City: US/E/PA

Resumes? No
- Cost to post resumes: N/A
- Cost to see resumes: N/A

Links to Jobs? Yes

Career Advice? Yes

Launched May, 1996, Advance HTC is a direct mail publication advertising high tech positions to 30,000+ professionals in the Delaware Valley, Philadelphia and NJ areas. Applicants can review openings and subscribe for free. Employers placing ads in this publication get this internet component for free.

Africa Online

Association/Diversity
www.AfricaOnline.com/AfricaOnline/jobs.html

Africa
Phone: 161-749-40215 e-mail: webmaster@AfricaOnline.com

Jobs? Yes
- Cost to post jobs: Free
- Cost to see jobs: Free
- Specialty: All
- Industry: All
- Country/Region/State/City: Int'l/Africa

Resumes? No
- Cost to post resumes: N/A
- Cost to see resumes: N/A

Links to Jobs? No

Career Advice? No

Community based site that encourages local involvement. They have jobs listed for free with direct contact information. Has a women's forum (chatroom) to discuss issues of the day. Nice attempt to get people interested in the internet.

CAREERXROADS©
Job, Resume & Career Management Sites on the World Wide Web
• The 1997 Directory •

Afro-Americ@: The Job Vault

Pub/Newspaper/Diversity
www.afoam.org/information/vault/vault.html

Afro-American Newspapers
2519 N. Charles Street, Baltimore, MD 21218
Phone: Fax: 410-554-8213 e-mail: afro-america@news

Jobs? Yes
- Cost to post jobs: Fee
- Cost to see jobs: Free
- Specialty: All
- Industry: All
- Country/Region/State/City: US

Resumes? No
- Cost to post resumes: N/A
- Cost to see resumes: N/A

Links to Jobs? Yes

Career Advice? No

Links to AT&T and job postings on the African-American Newspaper(only 1 posted when we visited). If you get bored from surfing for jobs this site has games on it that you can play.

Agricultural Job Listings

College/University
caticsuf.csufresno.edu:70/1/atinet/agjobs

Calif. State U. at Fresno

Jobs? Yes
- Cost to post jobs: Free
- Cost to see jobs: Free
- Specialty: Agriculture
- Industry: Agriculture
- Country/Region/State/City: US/W

Resumes? No
- Cost to post resumes: N/A
- Cost to see resumes: N/A

Links to Jobs? Yes

Career Advice? No

Jobs in several agriculture related categories. Limited information about how to post to this site but each position clearly posts all contct information.

AIP Physics Careers Bulletin Board

Association
aip.org:80/aip/careers/careers.html

American Institute of Physics

Jobs? Yes
- Cost to post jobs: Fee
- Cost to see jobs: Free
- Specialty: Physics
- Industry: N/A
- Country/Region/State/City: US

Resumes? No
- Cost to post resumes: N/A
- Cost to see resumes: N/A

Links to Jobs? No

Career Advice? No

The AIP Employment Database is updated weekly with position lisitings in 12 branches of physics, materials science and materials engineeering. Volunteers frm the Association provide career counsel on what you can do with a physics degree. To obtain jobs your browser must be configured to use telnet (telnet://aip.org/:23).

Airline Employment Ass't. Corps

Association
www.aeac.com/aeaac/scott.htm

T. Lahey II
Phone: 303-683-2322 Fax: 303-683-2322 e-mail: timlahey@msn.com

Jobs? Yes
- Cost to post jobs: Free
- Cost to see jobs: Fee
- Specialty: All
- Industry: Airline
- Country/Region/State/City: US

Resumes? Yes
- Cost to post resumes: Fee
- Cost to see resumes: Free

Links to Jobs? No

Career Advice? Yes

Site gives a lot of information on obtaining a career in the airline industry. Asks you to become a member for $10.00 a month to post your resume on the site. Easy to obtain information makes this a site to see if this is the industry for you.

AJR/ News Link

Association
www.ajr.com

Amy Krohn American Journalism Review
8701 Adelphi Road, Adelphi, MD 20783
Phone: 310-431-4771 Fax: 310-431-0097 e-mail: akrohn@ajr.umd.edu

Jobs? Yes
- Cost to post jobs: Fee
- Cost to see jobs: Free
- Specialty: Journalism
- Industry: N/A
- Country/Region/State/City: US

Resumes? No
- Cost to post resumes: N/A
- Cost to see resumes: N/A

Links to Jobs? No

Career Advice? No

Specialty site providing a simple job listing for professionals with journalism skills and career interests. Employers are charged $60-$100 to post single positions for 4 weeks.

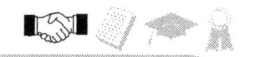

AK Jobnet - The Big Picture

Private site
www.ak.com.au/akjobnet.html

Bruce Handmen Austin Knight
Phone: 039-957-5533 e-mail: melbourne@ak.com.au

Jobs? Yes
- Cost to post jobs: Fee
- Cost to see jobs: Free
- Specialty: International
- Industry: All
- Country/Region/State/City: Int'l/AU

Resumes? No
- Cost to post resumes: N/A
- Cost to see resumes: N/A

Links to Jobs? Yes

Career Advice? No

International jobs listed by discipline for companies as well as blind listings for confidentiality. Links to usenet groups around the world. This is a site for the Austin Knight advertising agency who lists positions for their clients.

Alabama Jobs

Publisher/Newspaper
www.the-matrix.com/ph/ph.html

Birmingham Post Herald
P.O. Box 2553, Birmingham, AL 35202
Phone: 800-283-4255 Fax: 205-325-2410 e-mail: postherald@aol.com

Jobs? Yes
- Cost to post jobs: Fee
- Cost to see jobs: Free
- Specialty: All
- Industry: N/A
- Country/Region/State/City: US/S/AL/Birmingham

Resumes? No
- Cost to post resumes: N/A
- Cost to see resumes: N/A

Links to Jobs? No

Career Advice? No

Help-wanted classified ads published in this daily paper.

Allied Health Opportunities Directory

Publisher/Trade
www.gvpub.com

Great Valley Publishing Company
1288 Valley Forge Road, Valley Forge, PA 19482
Phone: 800-278-4400 Fax: 610-917-9040 e-mail: sales@gvpub.com

Jobs? Yes
- Cost to post jobs: Fee
- Cost to see jobs: Free
- Specialty: Health Care/Allied Health
- Industry: Health Care
- Country/Region/State/City: US

Resumes? No
- Cost to post resumes: N/A
- Cost to see resumes: N/A

Links to Jobs? No

Career Advice? No

Publisher of health care association and health care industry publications provides an internet component.

CAREERXROADS©
Job, Resume & Career Management Sites on the World Wide Web
• The 1997 Directory •

American Chemical Society Job Bank

Association
www.acs.org

American Chemical Society
Phone: 610-964-8061

Jobs? Yes
- Cost to post jobs: Fee
- Cost to see jobs: Free
- Specialty: Chemistry
- Industry: Chemical
- Country/Region/State/City: US

Resumes? No
- Cost to post resumes: N/A
- Cost to see resumes: N/A

Links to Jobs? No

Career Advice? No

The American Chemical Society has 151,000 members. You must be a member to access to their Internet based ACS Job Bank which includes ads from the "Chemical & Engineering News, a weekly publication to ACS members and the chemical industry. Employers must first pay for space in C&E News plus an added cost for the internet.

American Soc. of Agricultural Eng.

Association
asae.org/jobs

ASAE

Jobs? Yes
- Cost to post jobs: N/A
- Cost to see jobs: N/A
- Specialty: Engineering/Agricultural
- Industry: Agriculture
- Country/Region/State/City: US/MW

Resumes? No
- Cost to post resumes: N/A
- Cost to see resumes: N/A

Links to Jobs? Yes

Career Advice? No

Excellent links (nearly 150) to all the common sites and a ton of very unusual ones. Not to be missed if the MidWest is your focus regardless of your background.

America's Employers: The Job Seekers "Home"

Career Hub
www.americasemployers.com

Rose Emerson Career Relo Corp. of America
630 Third Avenue, New York, NY 10017
Phone: 212-681-6800 Fax: 212-681-6818 e-mail: profserv@americasemployers.com

Jobs? Yes
- Cost to post jobs: Fee
- Cost to see jobs: Free
- Specialty: All
- Industry: N/A
- Country/Region/State/City: US

Resumes? Yes
- Cost to post resumes: Fee
- Cost to see resumes: Fee

Links to Jobs? Yes

Career Advice? Yes

Top Design with FAQs and a "guided tour" for the uninitiated. Thousands of jobs, resumes and a conference room for members to conduct live meetings. Excellent directory of companies searchable by geography (50,000 companies listed by Industry), interactive career discussion forums, and Job Chat (live) career and job search assistance. Positions include e-mail links. Strong showing of Health Care, Legal, International, Academic and Government Jobs offset the usual technical. Easy to use. Employers cannot contact the candidate directly. Instead, they must use code. Lists of headhunters by function are downloadable. Employer fees range from $95 for a 4-week ad placement. Site claims that a majority of resumes in the database are executives and have been prescreened by their career counselors.

CAREERXROADS©
Job, Resume & Career Management Sites on the World Wide Web
• The 1997 Directory •

America's Job Bank

Government
www.ajb.dni.us:80/

US Government

Jobs? Yes
- Cost to post jobs: Free
- Cost to see jobs: Free
- Specialty: All
- Industry: All
- Country/Region/State/City: US

Resumes? No
- Cost to post resumes: N/A
- Cost to see resumes: N/A

Links to Jobs? Yes

Career Advice? No

Huge searchable database of job listings from across the country developed by the government's 2,000+ employment offices throughout the country. 250,000+ jobs. To post jobs, recruiters can post positions through the local unemployment office and eventually may get a password to post directly. Jobseekers will find a site that is slow and a little unwieldy to use. Very nice first try.

American Assoc. of Finance & Accounting

Placement/Links
www.aafa.com/

American Assoc. of Finance & Accounting
e-mail: mrklink@marketlink.com

Jobs? No
- Cost to post jobs: N/A
- Cost to see jobs: N/A
- Specialty: Finance/Accounting
- Industry: All
- Country/Region/State/City: US

Resumes? No
- Cost to post resumes: N/A
- Cost to see resumes: N/A

Links to Jobs? Yes

Career Advice? Yes

Network of 250 search firms specializing in accounting and placement. Long list of recruiting (retained and contingency) by location.

American Public Works Association

Association
www.fileshop.com:80/apwa/other.html

2345 Grand Blvd., Suite 500, Kansas City, MO 64108
Phone: 816-472-6100   e-mail: sysop@bbs.pubworks.org

Jobs? No
- Cost to post jobs: N/A
- Cost to see jobs: N/A
- Specialty: All
- Industry: Public/Government
- Country/Region/State/City: US

Resumes? No
- Cost to post resumes: N/A
- Cost to see resumes: N/A

Links to Jobs? Yes

Career Advice? Yes

Lots of links for information on positions in the public works industry. US government agencies, corporations, universities as well as international links are available at this site. Lots of information if this is your field of interest.

Anchorage Daily News

Publisher/Newspaper
www.adn.com

Anchorage News
1001 Northway Drive, Anchorage, AK 99508
Phone: 907-257-4293

Jobs? Yes
- Cost to post jobs: Fee
- Cost to see jobs: Free
- Specialty: All
- Industry: N/A
- Country/Region/State/City: US/NW/AL/Anchorage

Resumes? No
- Cost to post resumes: N/A
- Cost to see resumes: N/A

Links to Jobs? No

Career Advice? No

Newspaper Help Wanted Classifieds. Help Wanted Display Ads are not included. No extra charges as Employers must pay for ad in Newspaper.

Appointment Section

Commercial Job Site
taps.com

Internet App't. LTD.
United Kingdom
Phone: 441-712-219567   e-mail: frontdesk@taps.com

Jobs? Yes
- Cost to post jobs: Fee
- Cost to see jobs: Free
- Specialty: All
- Industry: All
- Country/Region/State/City: Int'l/United Kingdom

Resumes? Yes
- Cost to post resumes: Free
- Cost to see resumes: Fee

Links to Jobs? Yes

Career Advice? Yes

Site has over 40 companies listed where you can select what position you may be interested in and it will do a personal search for you by location, salary etc.. Several Fortune 500 companies are listed. Also has a listing for positions for consultants, contractors. Has several good career articles and a salary survey for numerous jobs in the United Kingdom.

CAREERXROADS©
Job, Resume & Career Management Sites on the World Wide Web
• **The 1997 Directory** •

APTA Home Page

Association
apta.edoc.com

American Physical Therapy Association

Jobs? No
- Cost to post jobs: N/A
- Cost to see jobs: N/A
- Specialty: Health Care/Physical Therapy
- Industry: Health Care
- Country/Region/State/City: US

Resumes? No
- Cost to post resumes: N/A
- Cost to see resumes: N/A

Links to Jobs? No

Career Advice? Yes

Physical Therapy Resource Center provides info on how to work with a recruiter and more. Links to opportunities weren't working. Lots of links about the profession.

Arizona Careers Online

Commercial Job/Diversity
amsquare.com/america/arizona.html

Diverse Data
287-2 North Meyer Ave., Tucson, AR 85701
Phone: 520-884-1320 Fax: 520-791-0955

Jobs? Yes
- Cost to post jobs: Fee
- Cost to see jobs: Free
- Specialty: All
- Industry: All
- Country/Region/State/City: US/SW/AR

Resumes? Yes
- Cost to post resumes: Fee
- Cost to see resumes: Free

Links to Jobs? Yes

Career Advice? Yes

Part of Help Wanted-USA Network. (See Help Wanted-USA). Employers can post jobs for $95/2 weeks. Good local links to community, government and church based job banks and support groups. Also has Arizona job hotlines and links to Arizona schools. Also has lots of links to diversity sites all over the country.

Arts Net Career Services Center

College/University
artsnet.heinz.cmu.edu/career/$career.html

Carnegie Mellon University
Pittsburgh, PA
Phone: 412-268-8436   e-mail: mamprog@andrew.anu.edu

Jobs? Yes
- Cost to post jobs: Free
- Cost to see jobs: Free
- Specialty: All
- Industry: Entertainment
- Country/Region/State/City: Int'l & US

Resumes? Yes
- Cost to post resumes: Free
- Cost to see resumes: Free

Links to Jobs? Yes

Career Advice? No

Top site for its class. Arts majors can find it all. Resumes/jobs posted for US and international as well. When you post your resume, your name shows up on the job page so that your friends will know which role in the cast you are applying for. Has a great list of links to plays, artists and other cultural events. Take a visit, it is well worth it. Everything is free.

Asian Career Net

Job Fair/Diversity
www.rici.com/acw

David Zing Recruit I.C.I
111 Pavonia Avenue, , Jersey City, NJ 07310
Phone: Fax: e-mail: dzing@rici.com

Jobs? Yes
- Cost to post jobs: Fee
- Cost to see jobs: Free
- Specialty: N/A
- Industry: N/A
- Country/Region/State/City: Int'l & US

Resumes? No
- Cost to post resumes: Free
- Cost to see resumes: Fee

Links to Jobs? No

Career Advice? Yes

The main purpose of Asian Career Net is to provide an online application form for Asians studying in the US to register for the company's major job fairs. Participants in the fairs include major Japanese firms seeking to hire graduating students planning to repatriate as well as other global companies seeking bi-lingual nationals for Pacific-rim subsidiaries. Employers can register for a booth at the Job Fair and are offered company profile, links to their web site and more. A "Resume-on-the-Net" employer fee based service is promised for 1997.

CAREERXROADS©
Job, Resume & Career Management Sites on the World Wide Web
• The 1997 Directory •

Asia-Net

Commercial Job/Agent
www.asia-net.com

Dale Bowen-President
603 Mission Street, Santa Cruz, CA 95060
Phone: 408-469-0781 Fax: 408-469-0782 e-mail: jobs@asia-net.com

Jobs? Yes
- Cost to post jobs: Fee
- Cost to see jobs: Free
- Specialty:
- Industry: All
- Country/Region/State/City: US & Int'l.

Resumes? Yes
- Cost to post resumes: Free
- Cost to see resumes: Fee

Links to Jobs? No

Career Advice? No

Providing Japanese, Chinese, and Korean Speaking Employment and Employees

Owner claims they can e-mail 20,000 bilingual professionals about your (employer's) opening. These professionals all speak English AND either Japanese, Chinese or Korean. Cost to employers is $795 for the first position and $395 for additional openings. Asia-net is a worthwhile model. Group e-mail has great potential for communication and these folks are among the first to recognize it and develop a specialty niche. It is also worth noting that Asia-net obtained permission from the professionals on their list to send them job communiques.

Association for Women in Computing

Association/Diversity
halcyon.com/monih/awc.html

Monica Hiatt Association for Women in Computing
41 Sutter Street, Ste. 1006, , San Francisco, CA 94104
Phone: 415-905-4663 e-mail: monih@upc.com

Jobs? Yes
- Cost to post jobs: Fee
- Cost to see jobs: Free
- Specialty: IT
- Industry: All
- Country/Region/State/City: US

Resumes? No
- Cost to post resumes: N/A
- Cost to see resumes: N/A

Links to Jobs? Yes

Career Advice? No

This site's focus is on the advancement of women in computing professions. Some links. E-mail allows members to interact with each other. Added a women's center for employment this past year.

Au Pair in Europe

Placement/Search/Temp
eidos.ca/aupair/

John/Corine Prince
PO Box 68056, Blakeley Postal Outlet, Hamilton, Ontario L8M3M7
Phone: 905-545-6305 Fax: 905-544-4121 e-mail: aupair@princeent.com

Jobs? Yes
- Cost to post jobs: N/A
- Cost to see jobs: N/A
- Specialty: Au Pair
- Industry: N/A
- Country/Region/State/City: Int'l

Resumes? Yes
- Cost to post resumes: Fee
- Cost to see resumes: N/A

Links to Jobs? No

Career Advice? No

If you are looking for a summer job or full time in Europe to be an Au Pair, this site may be the service for you. Charges $290 for applicants in the US and $295 outside the country. Site gives detailed information on what life as an Au Pair entails and what they are looking for. Does not post assignments so you must contact the site directly.

CAREERXROADS©
Job, Resume & Career Management Sites on the World Wide Web
• The 1997 Directory •

Auditions Online

Commercial Job Site
www.auditions.com

e-mail: stephen@auditions.com

Jobs? Yes
- Cost to post jobs: Free
- Cost to see jobs: Free
- Specialty: Entertainment
- Industry: Entertainment
- Country/Region/State/City: US/W/CA

Resumes? No
- Cost to post resumes: N/A
- Cost to see resumes: N/A

Links to Jobs? Yes

Career Advice? No

Site provides extensive lists of acting calls in Southern California.

Augusta (GA) Chronicle

Publisher/Newspaper
www.augustachronicle.com

725 Broad Street, P.O.Box 1928, Augusta, GA 30902
Phone: 706-724-0851 Fax: 704-724-0772

Jobs? Yes
- Cost to post jobs: Fee
- Cost to see jobs: Free
- Specialty: All
- Industry: N/A
- Country/Region/State/City: US/SE/GA/Augusta

Resumes? No
- Cost to post resumes: N/A
- Cost to see resumes: N/A

Links to Jobs? No

Career Advice? No

Positions posted in from the Sunday edition of this daily newspaper.

CAREERXROADS©
Job, Resume & Career Management Sites on the World Wide Web
• The 1997 Directory •

AWWA Job Listing

Association/Agent
www.awwa.org

Charles Berberich American Water Works Association
e-mail: cberberi@awwa.org

Jobs?: Yes
- Cost to post jobs: Free
- Cost to see jobs: Free
- Specialty: All
- Industry: Water
- Country/Region/State/City: US

Resumes?: No
- Cost to post resumes: N/A
- Cost to see resumes: N/A

Links to Jobs?: No

Career Advice?: No

Deceptively simple, but highly effective, job posting forum for the Drinking Water Industry. Employers are instructed how to electronically place, modify or delete a posting. Forum subscribers (no cost or requirement) automatically receive all postings to their e-mail address. Nearly 50 positions ranging from water treatment plant operator to Water Quality Superintendent were listed at the time of review.

A+ On-Line Resumes

Commercial Resume Site
www.hway.net/olresume

Merilee Goldberg
P.O. Box 811111, , Boca Raton, FL 33481
Phone: 305-475-1186 Fax: 305-475-0733 e-mail: webmaster@ol-resume.com

Jobs?: Yes
- Cost to post jobs: Fee
- Cost to see jobs: Free
- Specialty: All
- Industry: All
- Country/Region/State/City: US/SE/FL

Resumes?: Yes
- Cost to post resumes: Fee
- Cost to see resumes: Free

Links to Jobs?: Yes

Career Advice?: Yes

Employers can access resumes by state or function. Job seekers pay to have their resume posted. Site claims significant marketing is done on behalf of the job seekers. Standard site. Employers can post opportunities for $25.

CAREERXROADS©
Job, Resume & Career Management Sites on the World Wide Web
• The 1997 Directory •

A.E.P.S.

Commercial Job Site
www.aeps.com/aeps/aepshm.html

Aviation Employee Placement Service Sysops, Inc.
PO Box 550010, , Ft. Lauderdale, FL 33355
Phone: 954-472-6684 Fax: 954-472-8524 e-mail: aeps@sysops.com

Jobs?: Yes
- Cost to post jobs: Free
- Cost to see jobs: Fee
- Specialty: Pilot
- Industry: Aviation
- Country/Region/State/City: US

Resumes?: Yes
- Cost to post resumes: Fee
- Cost to see resumes: Free

Links to Jobs?: Yes

Career Advice?: Yes

You can post your resume for ten days for free and after that the charge depends upon your position (pilots $10/mth or $89 year, flight attendants $29 per year, all others $49 per year). Corporations can post their jobs for free. Members can see current jobs, others can see jobs older then 30 days for free. Awkward set up as you have to go back to the employer info page to get addresses of listed employers. Site also has an e-mail feature where members can share info. Good niche site that can only get better.

BAMTA

Commercial Job Site
mlds-www.arc.nasa.gov/BAMTA/

Dr. Susie W. Chu
e-mail: chu@mlds.arc.nasa.gov

Jobs? Yes
- Cost to post jobs: Free
- Cost to see jobs: Free
- Specialty: IT/Multimedia
- Industry: High Technology
- Country/Region/State/City: US

Resumes? No
- Cost to post resumes: N/A
- Cost to see resumes: N/A

Links to Jobs? Yes

Career Advice? No

Job Bank Directory provides openings for multimedia and web technology. Search or browse job categories. Employers fill out and post from a form format on-line. Ads automatically deleted after 4 weeks. Free for all.

Best Bets from the Net: Job Search

Links
www.lib.umich.edu:80/chdocs/employment/

U. of Michigan
e-mail: job-guide@unich.edu

Jobs? Yes
- Cost to post jobs: N/A
- Cost to see jobs: N/A
- Specialty: N/A
- Industry: N/A
- Country/Region/State/City: US

Resumes? No
- Cost to post resumes: N/A
- Cost to see resumes: N/A

Links to Jobs? Yes

Career Advice? Yes

Review of top job and employment related sites. Maintained by Career Planning office of U. of Mich. (Philip Ray and Bradley Taylor)

Best Jobs U.S.A.

Job Fair/Pub
www.bestjobsusa.com

Gisele Mattarese Recourse Communications, Inc.
1655 Palm Beach Lakes Blvd., West Palm Beach, FL 33401
Phone: 561-686-6800 Fax: 561-686-8043 e-mail: recoursel@aol.com

Jobs? Yes
- Cost to post jobs: Fee
- Cost to see jobs: Free
- Specialty: All
- Industry: N/A
- Country/Region/State/City: US

Resumes? No
- Cost to post resumes: N/A
- Cost to see resumes: N/A

Links to Jobs? Yes

Career Advice? Yes

Recourse Communications publishes Employment Review, promotes job fairs and has several other related businesses. Employers pay from $75 per posting for 8 weeks. Corporate profiles, links and banners are available and extra. Bookstore sells job hunting items.

Bio Online Career Center

Association
www.bio.com

John D. Turkel Vitadata Corporation
2855 Telegraph Ave., Suite 210, Berkeley, CA 94709
Phone: 510-548-1171 Fax: 510-548-1173

Jobs? Yes
- Cost to post jobs: Fee
- Cost to see jobs: Free
- Specialty: All
- Industry: Biotechnology/Pharmaceutical
- Country/Region/State/City: US

Resumes? No
- Cost to post resumes: N/A
- Cost to see resumes: N/A

Links to Jobs? Yes

Career Advice? No

Created by Vitadata Corporation for Biotechnology Industry Organization and supported by KPMG, Corning Pharm. and others, this site has a standard job search engine (titles and companies), career guides, a search firm list and resume bank with free posting. Significant "pages" of Biotech Industry information is constantly updated. Costs range from $115 to post a job up to the stratosphere for packages and sponsorship. Jobs are updated the 1st and 15th of each month.

Biomedical Positions

College/University
WWW.informatik.uni-rostock.de/hum-molgen/anno/position

Arthur A. B. Bergen The Netherlands Opthalmic Res. Inst.
P.O.Box 12141, 1100 AL, Amsterdam, The Netherlands
e-mail: bergen@amc.uva.n1

Jobs? Yes
- Cost to post jobs: Free
- Cost to see jobs: Free
- Specialty: Science/Biomedical/Genetics
- Industry: Higher Education/Research
- Country/Region/State/City: Int'l/US

Resumes? No
- Cost to post resumes: Free
- Cost to see resumes: Free

Links to Jobs? No

Career Advice? No

This communications forum in human genetics has several US and International openings in clinical area. Most post doc and research with major universities and corporation research labs. Jobs are periodically summarized and sent to all members.

CAREERXROADS©
Job, Resume & Career Management Sites on the World Wide Web
• The 1997 Directory •

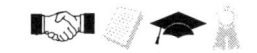

BioSpace Career Center

Commercial Job Site
www.biospace.com/sd/career

Timothy Fredel Synergistic Designs, Inc.
594 Howard Street, Ste. 400, San Francisco, CA 94105
Phone: 415-977-1600 Fax: 415-977-1606 e-mail: sdinfo.tlg.net

Jobs? Yes
- Cost to post jobs: Fee
- Cost to see jobs: Free
- Specialty: Science/Biotechnology
- Industry: Biotechnology/Pharmaceutical
- Country/Region/State/City: US

Resumes? No
- Cost to post resumes: N/A
- Cost to see resumes: N/A

Links to Jobs? No

Career Advice? Yes

All positions appear to be from four companies. Becton Dickinson, Bio-Rad Laboratories, Genelabs Technologies, Inc. and Roche Molecular Systems. Employer costs range upwards from $50 per ad per month. Nice feature are listings of schools with biotech related programs by region.

The Black Collegian Online

Pub./College/Diversity
www.black-collegian.com

Scott Edwards Black Collegiate Service, Inc.
140 Carodelet Street, , New Orleans, LA 70130
Phone: 504-523-0154 Fax: 504-523-0271 e-mail: scott@black-collegian.com

Jobs? Yes
- Cost to post jobs: Fee
- Cost to see jobs: Free
- Specialty: All
- Industry: All
- Country/Region/State/City: US

Resumes? No
- Cost to post resumes: N/A
- Cost to see resumes: N/A

Links to Jobs? Yes

Career Advice? Yes

This electronic version of The Black Collegian, a 26 year old, national career opportunities magazine, is replete with information, opportunities and connections. Employers can post a single job on their *Open Position* databasefor $55 over the cost of the ad in their publication or for as little as $75 for the online version alone. Excellent exposure to the minority community. Packages for employers wishing to sponsor the site and provide company profiles and links are also available. Highly recommended.

Black E.O.E Journal

Publisher/Trade/Diversity
www.usa-ca.com/blk_blkeoe_jrnl

R. Scott Hayward
4200 Wisconsin Ave., N.W., Suite 106-317, Washington, DC 20016
Phone: 800-487-5099 Fax: 714-974-3978

Jobs? Yes
- Cost to post jobs: Fee
- Cost to see jobs: Free
- Specialty: N/A
- Industry: N/A
- Country/Region/State/City: US

Resumes? No
- Cost to post resumes: N/A
- Cost to see resumes: N/A

Links to Jobs? No

Career Advice? Yes

Employment magazine with a college market focus, Black E.O.E includes extensive editorial coverage along with numerous ads from major corporations.

Boldface Jobs

Commercial Job Site
www.boldfacejobs.com

Fax: 410-418-4496 e-mail: jobs@boldfacejobs.com

Jobs? Yes
- Cost to post jobs: Fee
- Cost to see jobs: Free
- Specialty: All
- Industry: N/A
- Country/Region/State/City: US

Resumes? No
- Cost to post resumes: Fee
- Cost to see resumes: Free

Links to Jobs? Yes

Career Advice? No

BFJ provides a quick and easy to use search engine for both employers and job-seekers. Visitors can choose from among 10 "buttons" that include "Place (job) information online", and "Finding a candidate" to "Links to other Job Sites". Job-seekers can search lists of employers, universities and corporations by state. We checked the most recent (7 days) of openings and found 104 positions listed. The site is especially attractive as it allows both job seekers to post resumes and employers to post jobs FREE for 30 days. You can look at all the jobs that have been posted to the site for the last 7, 15 & 30 days or longer. Direct contact information to jobs.

CAREERXROADS©
Job, Resume & Career Management Sites on the World Wide Web
• The 1997 Directory •

Boston Globe

Publisher/Newspaper
www.boston.com

Kim Green Boston Globe
135 Morrissey Blvd., , Boston, MA 02107
Phone: 617-929-2167 e-mail: k_green@globe.com

Jobs? Yes
- Cost to post jobs: Fee
- Cost to see jobs: Free
- Specialty: All
- Industry: N/A
- Country/Region/State/City: US/NE/MA/Boston

Resumes? No
- Cost to post resumes: N/A
- Cost to see resumes: N/A

Links to Jobs? No

Career Advice? No

Newspaper help-wanted classified. This publisher also participates in CareerPath (See Career Path)

Boston Herald Job Find

Publisher/Newspaper
www.bostonherald.com/jobfind

Boston Herald
P.O. Box 289, , Boston, MA 02106
Phone: 617-426-4545 e-mail: jobfind@bostonherald.com

Jobs? Yes
- Cost to post jobs: Fee
- Cost to see jobs: Free
- Specialty: All
- Industry: All
- Country/Region/State/City: US/NE/MA

Resumes? No
- Cost to post resumes: N/A
- Cost to see resumes: N/A

Links to Jobs? Yes

Career Advice? Yes

Help-wanted classifieds printed in Sunday's newspaper are posted. Employers pay $75 to post their ad on the Internet but are NOT required to place the ad in the classified section of the Herald's print edition. A job finder allows jobseekers to search companies offering positions that meet your qualifications. You can also put a resume online to respond to advertisements.

Boston Job Bank

Commercial Job Site
www.bostonjobs.com

Charles Jukiewicz, Jr. C. Jukiewicz, Jr.
110 Church Street, Westwood, MA 02090
e-mail: charles@cybercom.net

Jobs? Yes
- Cost to post jobs: Free
- Cost to see jobs: Free
- Specialty: All
- Industry: All
- Country/Region/State/City: US/NE/Boston

Resumes? No
- Cost to post resumes: Free
- Cost to see resumes: Free

Links to Jobs? No

Career Advice? No

This is the shareware site of internet staffing. Employers post their own positions themselves. Easy to follow instructions. The promise is to send $20 to Charles within 2 weeks for a 4 week posting. Job seekers can post their resumes for free. Little activity but one of the simplest designs. Jobs listed for professionals in business, computers and sales.

Boulder Community Network

Government
www.bcn.boulder.co

Chamber of Commerce

Jobs? Yes
- Cost to post jobs: Free
- Cost to see jobs: Free
- Specialty: All
- Industry: All
- Country/Region/State/City: US/W/CO/Boulder

Resumes? No
- Cost to post resumes: N/A
- Cost to see resumes: N/A

Links to Jobs? Yes

Career Advice? No

Very local. Good example of "community" sites developing in cities throughout the country. Go to any search engine (Lycos, Yahoo, Alta Vista etc.). Type in the name of the city where you want to work and "jobs". Excellent results.

Brave New World

Publisher/Newspaper
www.newwork.com

e-mail: work@newwork.com

Jobs? No
- Cost to post jobs: N/A
- Cost to see jobs: N/A
- Specialty: Career Articles
- Industry: All
- Country/Region/State/City: US

Resumes? No
- Cost to post resumes: N/A
- Cost to see resumes: N/A

Links to Jobs? No

Career Advice? Yes

More then 2,000 articles from major publications on building your career and keeping it going. Lots of information that is updated daily.

Building Industry Exchange

Association
www.building.org

e-mail: webmaster@building.com

Jobs? Yes
- Cost to post jobs: Free
- Cost to see jobs: Free
- Specialty: All
- Industry: Construction
- Country/Region/State/City: US

Resumes? Yes
- Cost to post resumes: Free
- Cost to see resumes: Free

Links to Jobs? Yes

Career Advice? No

Industry based organization operating as a non-profit public service for the building/construction industry. Connections to companies, career, job resources and a resume database. Simple design. Easy to get in and out. Lots of jobs listed.

Bullseye Job Shop

Links/Newsgroups
interoz.com/usr/gcbristow

e-mail: gcbristow@interoz.com

Jobs? Yes
- Cost to post jobs: N/A
- Cost to see jobs: N/A
- Specialty: N/A
- Industry: N/A
- Country/Region/State/City: US

Resumes? No
- Cost to post resumes: N/A
- Cost to see resumes: N/A

Links to Jobs? Yes

Career Advice? Yes

Not the "One stop resource for job seekers" as the owner claims but several quality links- especially to newsgroups.

Business Job Finder Ohio State Univ.

University
www.cob.ohio-state,edu/dept/fin/osujobs.htm

Tim Opler Ohio State University
Fisher College of Business, Ohio
e-mail: opler.l@osu.edu

Jobs? Yes
- Cost to post jobs: Free
- Cost to see jobs: Free
- Specialty: Business
- Industry: N/A
- Country/Region/State/City: US

Resumes? No
- Cost to post resumes: N/A
- Cost to see resumes: N/A

Links to Jobs? Yes

Career Advice? Yes

Lots of links to company job pages and university career centers. Site provides direct contact for job information. Numerous links to major sites with jobs listed at all levels. Links for recent college grads and salary survey information for recent graduating classes. Worth a look.

Byron Employment Australia

Commercial Job Site
www.com.au/employment_australia/

David Bartnik Byron Media Pty Ltd.
e-mail: employment@byron.com.au

Jobs? Yes
- Cost to post jobs: Free
- Cost to see jobs: Free
- Specialty: All
- Industry: All
- Country/Region/State/City: Int'l/Australia

Resumes? No
- Cost to post resumes: N/A
- Cost to see resumes: N/A

Links to Jobs? Yes

Career Advice? No

International site with positions listed in Australia in numerous fields. Can e-mail your resume directly to the company that you are interested in. Has numerous links to other Australian job sites.

California Career and Employment Center

Commercial Job Site
www.webcom.com/~career/

Central Coast Employment Center
PO Box 2107, Monterey, CA 93942
Phone: Fax: 408-626-6156 e-mail: cces@netcom.com

Jobs? Yes
- Cost to post jobs: Fee
- Cost to see jobs: Free
- Specialty: All
- Industry: webcom.com/career/welcome.html
- Country/Region/State/City: US/W/CA

Resumes? No
- Cost to post resumes: Fee
- Cost to see resumes: Free

Links to Jobs? Yes

Career Advice? No

Under construction. Candidates can post resumes for $40/6months.

California Job Bank

Association
www.ccnet.com/CSNE/jobs/postings.html

Cal. Soc. of Newspaper Editors CSNE
3108 Adams Street, Alameda, CA 94501
Phone: 510-337-1832 e-mail: beckyday@csne.org

Jobs? Yes
- Cost to post jobs: Free
- Cost to see jobs: Free
- Specialty: Newspapers/Publishers
- Industry: Publications
- Country/Region/State/City: US

Resumes? No
- Cost to post resumes: N/A
- Cost to see resumes: N/A

Links to Jobs? Yes

Career Advice? No

Jobs posted free for members of CSNE, others charge $25 if in CA/NA, if outside $50. Links to editor/publisher classified and natiional diversity journalism job bank. There were 12 jobs posted on our last visit which will run for two weeks. If looking for a west coast journalism position this is the place to go.

Can Work Net

Commercial Job Site
hrdc.ingenia.com/canworknet/

e-mail: cwn-feedback@ingenia.com

Jobs? Yes
- Cost to post jobs: N/A
- Cost to see jobs: Free
- Specialty: All
- Industry: All
- Country/Region/State/City: Int'l/Canada

Resumes? No
- Cost to post resumes: N/A
- Cost to see resumes: N/A

Links to Jobs? Yes

Career Advice? Yes

Has links to Canadian companies and other major websites. Good information on career management and job finding clubs. Site also has places to obtain financial assistance if you are having trouble paying your bills. Nice search engine as site has numerous links to other places.

Canadian Job Source

Links to Jobs
www.irus.rri.uwo.ca/~jlaw/national.html

Jeff Lawrence

Jobs? No
- Cost to post jobs: N/A
- Cost to see jobs: N/A
- Specialty: All
- Industry: All
- Country/Region/State/City: Int'l/Canada

Resumes? No
- Cost to post resumes: N/A
- Cost to see resumes: N/A

Links to Jobs? Yes

Career Advice? No

Index listing of links to Canadian job information, recruiters, companies and job banks. Sponsors support this site. Can register and receive free e-mail regarding site updates. Site is in English/French.

Carbonate Your Brain

Company
www.7up.com

Dr. Pepper/Cadbury North America, Inc.
e-mail: 7up@drpepper.com

Jobs? Yes
- Cost to post jobs: Free
- Cost to see jobs: Free
- Specialty: Music
- Industry: Music
- Country/Region/State/City: US

Resumes? Yes
- Cost to post resumes: Free
- Cost to see resumes: Free

Links to Jobs? No

Career Advice? No

Unique site for summer positions in the music industry. Upbeat for the 7-up generation. Try to win free products, especially the t-shirts.

Career Action Center

Career Management
careeraction.org

Matha Reed Career Action Center
10420 Bubb Road. Ste 100, , Cupertino, CA 95014
Phone: 408-253-3200 Fax: 408-253-0505 e-mail: info-request@careeraction.org

Jobs? Yes
- Cost to post jobs: Free
- Cost to see jobs: Fee
- Specialty: All
- Industry: N/A
- Country/Region/State/City: US

Resumes? No
- Cost to post resumes: N/A
- Cost to see resumes: N/A

Links to Jobs? Yes

Career Advice? Yes

Emergence of a serious career counseling effort on the net is seen at this site. Information about career self-reliance, career fitness, books on career management and a listing of workshops and counseling programs can be found. Annual membership is in the $100 range. Privately funded, this non-profit organization claims 9000 members and is primarily California based. Originally a Resource Center for Women founded in 1973, employers can post opportunities for free. Searching the job database is restricted to members.

Career America

Career Hub/Agent
CareerAmerica.com

Cheryl Wayne
PO Box 4081, Mamouth Lakes, CA 93546
Phone: 619-934-3566 Fax: 619-934-1838 e-mail: technet@qnet.com

Jobs? Yes
- Cost to post jobs: Fee
- Cost to see jobs: Free
- Specialty: All
- Industry: All
- Country/Region/State/City: US

Resumes? Yes
- Cost to post resumes: Fee
- Cost to see resumes: Free

Links to Jobs? Yes

Career Advice? Yes

Site has "CJ Search", an agent who will search CA's job database for resumes based on your specifications as well as fpositions that match your skills. Site charges $75 to post a job for a month but you can post up to 10 jobs for $150 per month. To post your resume for one year costs $75. Check this site out, if it continues to do what it states, it can develop into a strong player.

Career Builder

Agent
www.careerbuilder.com

Stephen Abel NetStart, Inc.
516 Herndon Parkway, Herndon, VA 22070
Phone: 703-709-1001 Fax: 703-709-1004 e-mail: ifo@netstartinc.con

Jobs? Yes
- Cost to post jobs: Free
- Cost to see jobs: Free
- Specialty: All
- Industry: All
- Country/Region/State/City: US

Resumes? Yes
- Cost to post resumes: Free
- Cost to see resumes: N/A

Links to Jobs? No

Career Advice? Yes

Career Builder searches for posted positions by selecting applicant criteria that includes (specific) companies, locations or functions in addition to skill preferences. The site's Personal Agent checks the database 24 hours a day 7 days a week for job matches to your background and wakes you up with job lead info. Netstart is also selling its software (Teambuilder) for posting openings and managing replies to companies directly.

Career Center for Workforce Diversity

Pub/Trade/Diversity
www.eop.com

John Miller EOP, Inc.
150 Motor Pkwy, Hauppauge, NY 11788
Phone: 516-273-0066

Jobs? Yes
- Cost to post jobs: N/A
- Cost to see jobs: N/A
- Specialty: All
- Industry: N/A
- Country/Region/State/City: US

Resumes? No
- Cost to post resumes: N/A
- Cost to see resumes: N/A

Links to Jobs? Yes

Career Advice? Yes

Publishes "Equal Opportunity", "Women Engineer", "Minority Engineer", "Careers and the Disabled" and "Workforce Diversity" magazines. All help-wanted advertisers are supplied free links to their site. Excellent career related articles available for downloading. Primarily focused on the college market. (see EOP)

Career China

Commercial Job Site
www.globalvillager.com/villager/CC.html

Ya Li Global Communications Services Inc.
3130 Rt. 10 West, Denville, NJ 07834
Phone: 201-989-0501 Fax: 201-328-9216 e-mail: yli@glcs.com

Jobs? Yes
- Cost to post jobs: Fee
- Cost to see jobs: Free
- Specialty: All
- Industry: All
- Country/Region/State/City: Int'l/China

Resumes? Yes
- Cost to post resumes: Fee
- Cost to see resumes: Fee

Links to Jobs? Yes
Career Advice? Yes

Site offers job openings in mainland China, Taiwan, Hong Kong, Singapore and Japan. Site charges $20 per job to post or $200 per month for unlimited postings. "Jobs Wanted" costs $15.00 to post your resume. All jobs are coded yet you see the contact information/e-mail/phone. Resumes (268) were coded when we visited so there must be a charge to see and assume that passwords come with placing an advertisement. Site has potential and should be watched as the pacific rim is where the action is.

Career City

Career Hub
www.careercity.com

Paul Huekell Adams Media Corporation
260 Centre St., Holbrook, MA 02343
Phone: 617-767-8100 Fax: 617-767-2055 e-mail: webmaster@careercity.com

Jobs? Yes
- Cost to post jobs: Free
- Cost to see jobs: Free
- Specialty: All
- Industry: N/A
- Country/Region/State/City: US

Resumes? Yes
- Cost to post resumes: Free
- Cost to see resumes: Fee

Links to Jobs? Yes
Career Advice? Yes

This publisher of career literature is making a rapid move into the big leagues of job databases with a full service site that rivals anything on the web. Doesn't hurt that everything is free...almost. A "Job Express Form" is readily available for employers to post their openings one at a time or for high volume, employers can e-mail an entire file direct. The site cliams 125,000 jobs are posted. But only 8,000 are from their database. The rest are from newgroups and company databases that are linked or can be searched. Positions are kept open for 90 days. This site will attract large numbers of job seekers. It's easy to use, look for jobs, submit a resume, check out action-oriented articles, search for links to 20,000 companies or link to executive recruiters. Room on home page for "featured employers". Expect advertising rates to change in 1997.

CAREERXROADS©
Job, Resume & Career Management Sites on the World Wide Web
• The 1997 Directory •

Career Command Center

Commercial Job Site
www.CareerCommandCenter.com/ccc,html

Greg Franchina WorldBase, Inc.
4301 N. Fairfax Drive, Suite 1062, Arlington, VA 22203
Phone: 703-892-0717 Fax: 703-892-0705 e-mail: support@worldbaseinc.com

Jobs? Yes
- Cost to post jobs: Fee
- Cost to see jobs: Free
- Specialty: All
- Industry: IT/IS
- Country/Region/State/City: US

Resumes? Yes
- Cost to post resumes: Free
- Cost to see resumes: Fee

Links to Jobs? No

Career Advice? No

Site allows the employer to place their resumes on the database and they will scan them so all of your managers can have access. Cost depends on the package you select between $5,000 - $15,000. Site has great potential for those who want their managers to have resumes at their fingertips. Site concentrates on IT/IS applicants.

Career Connector

Commercial Job Site
www.wons.com/cc/

Wons K. Lee Career Connector Inc.
38-2608 Whiteley, North Vancouver, BC, Canada V7J2R6
Phone: 604-985-6746 Fax: 604-985-1623 e-mail: cc@wons.com

Jobs? Yes
- Cost to post jobs: Free
- Cost to see jobs: Free
- Specialty: All
- Industry: All
- Country/Region/State/City: US/Canada

Resumes? Yes
- Cost to post resumes: Fee
- Cost to see resumes: Fee

Links to Jobs? No

Career Advice? No

Free sight for posting jobs while charging $15 to post your resume for six months. Free to see resumes and the conCareer Counseling Lite

CAREERXROADS©
Job, Resume & Career Management Sites on the World Wide Web
• **The 1997 Directory** •

Career Counseling Lite

Career Management
www.execpc.com/~cclite/

Dr. Brent Evans
e-mail: cclite@execpc.com

Jobs? No
- Cost to post jobs: N/A
- Cost to see jobs: N/A
- Specialty: All
- Industry: All
- Country/Region/State/City: US

Resumes? No
- Cost to post resumes: N/A
- Cost to see resumes: N/A

Links to Jobs? Yes

Career Advice? Yes

Career counseling site where you can e-mail questions and the Dr. will respond in 48 hours/no charge. Site has links to other major career sites while also selling t-shirts with their CC-Lite logo. Nice idea.

Career Crafting

Career Management
www.well.com/user/careerc/

Howard Sambol Encompass
396 Durant Way, Mill Valley, CA 94941
Phone: 800-582-7337 Fax: 415-389-1868 e-mail: CareerCrft@aol.com

Jobs? No
- Cost to post jobs: N/A
- Cost to see jobs: N/A
- Specialty: All
- Industry: All
- Country/Region/State/City: US

Resumes? No
- Cost to post resumes: N/A
- Cost to see resumes: N/A

Links to Jobs? No

Career Advice? Yes

Site provides free career couseling information. You can also speak to a professionally trained career counselor for free by dialing their 800 number and if you get their answering machine they will even call you back. Site sells career crafting audiotape programs and also has a link to AOL where they provide online chat sessions from 4-6 PM on Tuesdays/Thursdays Pacific time. We like the call back feature for the free advice.

Career Doctor

Career Management
career-doctor.com

Barry Deutsch
e-mail: csareer-doctor@career-doctor.c

Jobs? Yes
- Cost to post jobs: N/A
- Cost to see jobs: N/A
- Specialty: All
- Industry: N/A
- Country/Region/State/City: US

Resumes? No
- Cost to post resumes: N/A
- Cost to see resumes: N/A

Links to Jobs? Yes

Career Advice? Yes

A Career Management site that has a little tongue-in-cheek. Excellent articles for the experienced career expert to chew on as well as a means to join an on going discussion group for career-related issues.

Career Exchange

Commercial Job Site
www.careerexchange.com/

Jason Moreau CorpNet InfoHub Ltd.
Unit E-7950 Huston Road, Delta, B.C., Canada V4G 1C2
Phone: 604-940-2754 Fax: 604-940-2840 e-mail: develop@corpinfohub.com

Jobs? Yes
- Cost to post jobs: Fee
- Cost to see jobs: Free
- Specialty: All
- Industry: All
- Country/Region/State/City: Int'l/US

Resumes? Yes
- Cost to post resumes: Free
- Cost to see resumes: N/A

Links to Jobs? No

Career Advice? Yes

Site has 115 jobs posted that are US and mostly Canadian based. Many IT positions but has all types of job at all levels with direct contact information available. You can also post your resume directly via e-mail. Cost to post jobs depends on the number you wish to post but is in the $17 to $35 range with an unlimited package for $450 per month. Jobs are posted for 30 days.

Career File's

Commercial Resume Site
www.careerfile.com

Cynthia Welch
PO Box 3331, Clock Tower Bus. Park, Pittsfield, MA 01202
Phone: 413-499-2498 Fax: 413-448-5673 e-mail: resume@careerfile.com

Jobs? Yes
- Cost to post jobs: Free
- Cost to see jobs: Free
- Specialty: All
- Industry: N/A
- Country/Region/State/City: US

Resumes? Yes
- Cost to post resumes: Free
- Cost to see resumes: Fee

Links to Jobs? No

Career Advice? No

Library of executive, managerial, and technical talent where employers can browse through resumes. If you want additional information on the candidates the charge is $6.95 per resume. For the job seeker they have a confidentiality feature that makes this site unique. Inexpensive way to obtain potential candidates. Also has links to find information about the New England area.

Career Finder

Publisher/Newspaper
www.chicago.tribune.com

Harry Phillips Chicago Tribune
401 N. Michigan Ave., Chicago, IL 60611
Phone: 312-222-4211 e-mail: hphillips@tribune.com

Jobs? Yes
- Cost to post jobs: Fee
- Cost to see jobs: Free
- Specialty: All
- Industry: N/A
- Country/Region/State/City: US/MW/IL/Chicago

Resumes? No
- Cost to post resumes: N/A
- Cost to see resumes: N/A

Links to Jobs? Yes

Career Advice? Yes

"Chicago Tribune" classifieds from previous 3 Sundays. All help-wanted categories and display ads are included at an extra cost of $1.50 per line for classifieds and $200 total for display ads. Openings will also appear on CareerPath.com. Links to company Web sites and other Tribune Company properties including Ft. Lauderdale Sun Sentinal.

Career Internet Working

Commercial Job Site
www.careerkey.com

5255 Younge Street, Suite 711, North York, Ontario, Canada M2N 6P4
Phone: 416-229-2666 Fax: 416-229-2943

Jobs? Yes
- Cost to post jobs: Fee
- Cost to see jobs: Free
- Specialty: All
- Industry: All
- Country/Region/State/City: Canada

Resumes? No
- Cost to post resumes: N/A
- Cost to see resumes: N/A

Links to Jobs? Yes

Career Advice? Yes

Positions are listed by category and direct contact information is available with e-mail access (lots of jobs in Canada posted). A long list of career information with a particularly good piece on negotiating on "the counter-offer quandary". Site has only been in operation since April, 1996 but has the potential to be a top site.

Career Lab

Career Management
www.careerlab.com/clab.htm

William Frank
304 Inverness Way South, STE 465, Englewood, Colorado 80112
Phone: 303-790-0505 Fax: 303-790-0606 e-mail: comments@careerlab.com

Jobs? Yes
- Cost to post jobs: N/A
- Cost to see jobs: N/A
- Specialty: All
- Industry: All
- Country/Region/State/City: US

Resumes? No
- Cost to post resumes: N/A
- Cost to see resumes: N/A

Links to Jobs? Yes

Career Advice? Yes

Site has a nice bookstore for career counseling info that you can purchase directly. Has some good Q&A regarding different career situations but site is really set up to sell the organization's consulting practice that charges $50 to $250 per hour for their advice.

Career Line

Association
www.careerline.com

ACM

Jobs? Yes
- Cost to post jobs: Free
- Cost to see jobs: Free
- Specialty: IT
- Industry: All
- Country/Region/State/City: US

Resumes? No
- Cost to post resumes: N/A
- Cost to see resumes: N/A

Links to Jobs? No

Career Advice? Yes

ACM's Career Counseling Service. Under construction

Have you found a site that isn't listed in CAREERXROADS?

Have you REGISTERED to receive FREE updates?

Keep us informed.

We'll keep you informed.

CAREERXROADS
Where Talent and Opportunity Connect on the Internet

Career Magazine

Career Hub
www.careermag.com

Cliff Daniels NCS Jobline, Inc.
2897 Mapleton Ave., Ste. 1A, Boulder, CO 80301

Jobs? Yes
- Cost to post jobs: Fee
- Cost to see jobs: Free
- Specialty: All
- Industry: All
- Country/Region/State/City: US

Resumes? Yes
- Cost to post resumes: Free
- Cost to see resumes: Free

Links to Jobs? Yes

Career Advice? Yes

National Career Magazine maintains a searchable index of 120 job related newsgroups as part of its service. Career articles, resume database and company positions searchable by location, skill and title as well as date posted are also available for the job applicant. Employer prices are $95 to post a position for 4 weeks. Unlimited subscription is available and prices vary depending upon whether you post directly or have NCS do it for you as with other services. This is one of the most flexible and successful sites on the internet. A directory of executive recruiters (15 categories) is also an excellent tool. Firms pay $100 for a 12 month listing ($200 with a link).

CAREERXROADS©
Job, Resume & Career Management Sites on the World Wide Web
• The 1997 Directory •

Career Mart

Commercial Job Site
www.careermart.com

BSA Advertising
Phone: 212-907-9300   e-mail: careermart@mcimail.com

Jobs? Yes
- Cost to post jobs: Fee
- Cost to see jobs: Free
- Specialty: N/A
- Industry: N/A
- Country/Region/State/City: US

Resumes? No
- Cost to post resumes: N/A
- Cost to see resumes: N/A

Links to Jobs? Yes

Career Advice? Yes

Links to 500 colleges, numerous publications and information helpful in researching companies. Employers pay in $100 range to post job opportunities.

Career Network

Placement Firm
phoenix.placement.oakland.edu/career/internet.ht

Jeffrey Mercure Huntington Group
Phone: 203-261-1166   e-mail: jeffm@hgllc.com

Jobs? Yes
- Cost to post jobs: Fee
- Cost to see jobs: Free
- Specialty: IT
- Industry: All
- Country/Region/State/City: US

Resumes? No
- Cost to post resumes: N/A
- Cost to see resumes: N/A

Links to Jobs? Yes

Career Advice? Yes

Search Firm Specializing in high tech openings is providing services on the back end of a university server's placement area. Applicants can create a resume and submit it online, search out job sites by location, company, or position as well as search newsgroups. Appears primarily for entry but not totally. Employers post jobs, links and other information from $50 and up. Other matching and search services are available, of course.

CAREERXROADS©
Job, Resume & Career Management Sites on the World Wide Web
• The 1997 Directory •

Career Mosaic

Career Hub
www.careermosaic.com

Jeffrey Hodes Bernard Hodes Advertising
555 Madison Avenue, NY, NY 10022
Phone: 800-624-7744 Fax: 212-486-4049 e-mail: sales@careermosaic.com

Jobs? Yes
- Cost to post jobs: Fee
- Cost to see jobs: Free
- Specialty: All
- Industry: All
- Country/Region/State/City: Int'l/US

Resumes? Yes
- Cost to post resumes: Free
- Cost to see resumes: Free

Links to Jobs? Yes

Career Advice? Yes

Career Mosaic is the on-line arm of Bernard Hodes Advertising and one of the first WWW job sites to mount a serious commercial venture. Multiple services include J.O.B.S. (Jobs Offered by Search) database of job listings, resume database, career management articles, employer profiles, web pages and links to company home pages. Employer cost to post a job is approximately $150 for 4 weeks although many packages are available. Link to your home page or have CM create, maintain or host your web site's job page. Resumes posted for free and searched by employers for free. Recent connections to Pacific rim expand the possibilities in the International arena. Among a handful of sites that attract the largest number of job seekers.

CAREERXROADS©
Job, Resume & Career Management Sites on the World Wide Web
• The 1997 Directory •

Career Network

Links
www.careers.org

Marc D. Snyder Career Resource Center
2508 Fifth Avenue, Ste. 147, , Seattle, WA 98121
Phone: 206-233-8672 Fax: 206-727-7970

Jobs? No
- Cost to post jobs: N/A
- Cost to see jobs: N/A
- Specialty: All
- Industry: All
- Country/Region/State/City: US

Resumes? No
- Cost to post resumes: N/A
- Cost to see resumes: N/A

Links to Jobs? Yes

Career Advice? Yes

Links to newsgroups. Career Articles. Links by field. Links by State (government jobs) and Region(other). Links to employers (free for employers). 100 best sites on the web for jobs. Simple and logical. This site has it all. Claims 11,000 links to jobs, employers, business, education and career service professionals.

Career Opportunities in Singapore

Commercial Job Site
www.singapore-careers.com

Singapore Econ. Dev. Board Int'l Manpower Programme
210 Twin Dolphin Drive, Redwood City, CA 94065
Fax: 415-591-1328 e-mail: joboffer@newsserver.technet.sg

Jobs? Yes
- Cost to post jobs: Fee
- Cost to see jobs: Free
- Specialty: All
- Industry: All
- Country/Region/State/City: Int'l

Resumes? Yes
- Cost to post resumes: Free
- Cost to see resumes: Fee

Links to Jobs? Yes

Career Advice? No

Direct contact information is located for positions. Jobs are coded so refer to the site for where you obtained the information. Has jobs in many different fields with additional information links on living in Singapore. Costs were not able to be verified.

Career Paradise/Emory University

College/University
www.emory.edu/career/index.html

John Youngblood Jr. Emory University Career Services
e-mail: iyoungb@emory.edu

Jobs? Yes
- Cost to post jobs: Free
- Cost to see jobs: Free
- Specialty: All/College
- Industry: All
- Country/Region/State/City: US

Resumes? No
- Cost to post resumes: N/A
- Cost to see resumes: N/A

Links to Jobs? Yes

Career Advice? Yes

EMORY
Colossal List of Career Links

(Hit stop on your browser to turn off animation)

Links + Explanations + Ratings = Colossally Cool!

Creative approach. Lots of tongue-in-cheek and lots of good links to job sites and companies with openings on the web. Creative artistry with graphics make this a unique site to view. Write ups on links give ratings for each site which we may not agree with but shows a lot of work went into this imaginative offering. Top site that should be viewed often for new concepts and ideas in cyberspace.

CAREERXROADS©
Job, Resume & Career Management Sites on the World Wide Web
• The 1997 Directory •

Career Path

Publisher/Newspaper
www.careerpath.com

Sue Stenberg New Century Network/CareerPath
Times Mirror Square, LA, CA 90053
Phone: 213-237-2233 Fax: 213-237-3119 e-mail: advertising@careerpath.com

Jobs? Yes
- Cost to post jobs: Fee
- Cost to see jobs: Free
- Specialty: All
- Industry: N/A
- Country/Region/State/City: US

Resumes? Yes
- Cost to post resumes: Free
- Cost to see resumes: Fee

Links to Jobs? Yes

Career Advice? Yes

Today You Can Search 128,117
Help Wanted Ads From Across the Country

23 major market newspapers had joined CareerPath by year end 1996. These publications include: The Atlanta Journal, Boston Globe, Chicago Tribune, Columbus Dispatch, Denver Post, Ft. Lauderdale Sun Sentinel, Hartford Courant, Los Angeles Times, Miami Herald, Minneapolis Star-Tribune, New York Times, Orlando Sentinel, Philadelphia Inquirer, Rocky Mountain News, San Jose Mercury News, and Washington Post. All have merged their Sunday help wanted ads into one central database (in addition to their own Web sites). Now with 75,000 to 100,000 "fresh" ads per week from the nation's largest newspapers, CareerPath is our pick for one of the country's top sites for job-seekers. Jobs are searched by first indicating "This Week's" or "Last Week's" ads and then choosing one or more newspapers. Note that on Saturday afternoon you are able to peruse Sunday ads that will be delivered the next day. Eventually, CareerPath may expand to 50 major market newspapers and provide many additional services for employers (Banners, Direct e-mail to registered Job-seekers, etc). Every job seeker on the Net needs to "Bookmark" this site. One flaw is the inconsistency of participating publications, some of which do not include all their ads because of technical difficulties or their insistence on added charges to the employer. Employers should ensure that ads placed in participating newspapers are automatically added to the Internet. Rumor has it that CareerPath is seriously considering placing ads direct to the Internet, bypassing the publications, for $250.

CAREERXROADS©
Job, Resume & Career Management Sites on the World Wide Web
• The 1997 Directory •

Career Planning Process

College/University
www.cba.bgsu.edu:80/class/webclass/nagye/career/

Bowling Green State University
Career Services, 360 Saddlemire St. Serv. Bldg., Bowling Green, OH 43420
Phone: 419-372-2356

Jobs? No
- Cost to post jobs: N/A
- Cost to see jobs: N/A
- Specialty: N/A
- Industry: N/A
- Country/Region/State/City: US

Resumes? No
- Cost to post resumes: N/A
- Cost to see resumes: N/A

Links to Jobs? No

Career Advice? Yes

Self assessment tools, Job assistance, Job links, Internet Job Search Info, Resume Help. Good model College site. Well designed. Knowledgeable about net resources.

Career Resumes

Commercial Resume Site
www.branch.com:80/cr/cr.html

Peter Newfield Branch Information Services
P.O. Box 509, Golden Bridge, NY 10526
Phone: 800-927-4611

Jobs? No
- Cost to post jobs: N/A
- Cost to see jobs: N/A
- Specialty: All
- Industry: All
- Country/Region/State/City: US

Resumes? Yes
- Cost to post resumes: Fee
- Cost to see resumes: N/A

Links to Jobs? No

Career Advice? Yes

Company provides resume preparation services for $150 - $300.

CAREERXROADS©
Job, Resume & Career Management Sites on the World Wide Web
• The 1997 Directory •

Career Shop

Commercial Job Site
www.tenkey.com

Tom Dike Tenkey Publishing Inc.
5422 Carrier Drive, Suite 201, Orlando, FL 32819
Phone: 800-639-2060 Fax: 407-351-3525 e-mail: cshopsales@tenkey.com

Jobs? Yes
- Cost to post jobs: Fee
- Cost to see jobs: Free
- Specialty: All
- Industry: All
- Country/Region/State/City: US

Resumes? Yes
- Cost to post resumes: Free
- Cost to see resumes: Fee

Links to Jobs? Yes

Career Advice? No

Primarily a resume database service with several customized services including "corporate recruiting websites" to help employers capture candidate information. Employers pay an annual fee to post unlimited positions and review resumes (1 option). Limited links to other sites. Applicants key in their resume on line. Employers can key word search. Owner offers money back guarantee if employer is not satisfied with resumes.

Career Site

Commercial Job Site/Agent
www.careersite.com

Seth Peets Virtual Resources Corporation
310 Miller Avenue, Ann Arbor, MI 48103
Phone: 313-213-9500 Fax: 313-213-9011 e-mail: seth@careersite.com

Jobs? Yes
- Cost to post jobs: Fee
- Cost to see jobs: Free
- Specialty: All
- Industry: All
- Country/Region/State/City: US

Resumes? Yes
- Cost to post resumes: Free
- Cost to see resumes: Free

Links to Jobs? Yes

Career Advice? Yes

Employers can post positions at a modest cost ($95) for 4 weeks. Employers can search the database and have newly posted resumes forwarded if they match established knowledge based criteria. Resumes are confidential. Employers can e-mail interest in an applicant through the site. Applicants who register at this site can have newly posted openings automatically searched by keywords and forwarded to an e-mail address (virtual agent's desktop). Confidentiality is maintained when employers search resume database. They see a "blinded" version. Well designed model.

CAREERXROADS©
Job, Resume & Career Management Sites on the World Wide Web
• The 1997 Directory •

Career Spot

Publisher/Newspaper
www.careerspot.com

Ft. Lauderdale Sun Sentinel
200 East Las Olas Blvd., Fort Lauderdale, FL 33301
Phone: 305-356-4000 Fax: 305-356-4093

Jobs? Yes
- Cost to post jobs: Fee
- Cost to see jobs: Free
- Specialty: All
- Industry: N/A
- Country/Region/State/City: US/SE/FL/Ft. Lauderdale

Resumes? No
- Cost to post resumes: N/A
- Cost to see resumes: N/A

Links to Jobs? No

Career Advice? No

Help wanted classifieds printed in Sunday's newspaper are posted. Employers will pay an additional $1/line to have their jobs posted on the web. This publisher participates in CareerPath (See CareerPath). Help wanted display ads are not included on the Internet site.

Career Surf

Commercial Job Site
careersurf.com

e-mail: sales@careersurf.com

Jobs? Yes
- Cost to post jobs: Fee
- Cost to see jobs: Free
- Specialty: All
- Industry: All
- Country/Region/State/City: US

Resumes? Yes
- Cost to post resumes: Fee
- Cost to see resumes: Free

Links to Jobs? Yes

Career Advice? Yes

Employers pay from $25 to post openings and can view resumes for free. Charge for posting resumes is in the $50 range and includes a live e-mail link. Links to career info are present to select.

Career Talk

Career Management
www.careertalk.com

Joe Stimac Seaton Corp.
P.O. Box 3096, Lawrence, KS 66047
e-mail: djs@careertalk.com

Jobs? No
- Cost to post jobs: N/A
- Cost to see jobs: N/A
- Specialty: All
- Industry: N/A
- Country/Region/State/City: N/A

Resumes? No
- Cost to post resumes: N/A
- Cost to see resumes: N/A

Links to Jobs? Yes

Career Advice? Yes

Weekly Internet Career Column featuring advice from authors, hiring managers and career advisors. Each week is archived and easily searched. Site also markets video based training programs called Winning Career Strategies, the Ultimate Job Search Kit and Mastering Jobs

Career Toolbox

Career Management
www.careertoolbox.com

Chivas Regal
Phone: 800-244-8271

Jobs? No
- Cost to post jobs: N/A
- Cost to see jobs: N/A
- Specialty: N/A
- Industry: N/A
- Country/Region/State/City: US

Resumes? No
- Cost to post resumes: N/A
- Cost to see resumes: N/A

Links to Jobs? No

Career Advice? Yes

No, we don't know why a liquor company decided to offer a sophisticated site chock full of career information, but the price is right. You can call for a free disk of all you find at the Web site...and more and all you have to pay is $.95 shipping.

Career Transitions

Career Management
www.bfservs.com:80/bfserv.html

Tony Davidson Best-BF Services, Inc.
P.O. Box 2698, Covington, GA 30210
Phone: 770-787-1141 e-mail: bfservs@mindspring.com

Jobs? Yes
• Cost to post jobs: Free
• Cost to see jobs: Free
• Specialty: N/A
• Industry: N/A
• Country/Region/State/City: US

Resumes? Yes
• Cost to post resumes: Fee
• Cost to see resumes: Free

Links to Jobs? Yes

Career Advice? Yes

Looking for a new career? Get help on how to place your resume on the internet. Links to several placement firms and a couple of job sites, particularly Help Wanted USA and OCC. This firm specializes in career transitions and provides generic career assistance. You can post your resume for $40 (annual) anf for $89.95 your resume will be posted to 25 Web sites.

Career WEB

Commercial Job Site
www.cweb.com

Sharon Carr Landmark Communications, Inc.
150 W. Brambleton Avenue, Norfolk, VA 23510
Phone: 800-871-0800 Fax: 757-623-5942 e-mail: info@cweb.com

Jobs? Yes
• Cost to post jobs: Fee
• Cost to see jobs: Free
• Specialty: N/A
• Industry: N/A
• Country/Region/State/City: US

Resumes? Yes
• Cost to post resumes: Free
• Cost to see resumes: Fee

Links to Jobs? Yes

Career Advice? Yes

Employers pay in the $65 range (4 weeks) to have their jobs matched against candidate information. The service offers applicants an online criterion-based form or "credential sets" to submit to openings. Begun originally as a Southeast based site, CareerWEB has expanded aggressively nationwide. Site is owned by a publisher who actively markets the site. A job match service, prescreening service, and bookstore are offered. Applications can be sent directly to employers or career fairs. Employers can add links, profiles, and candidate screening for additional costs. Applicants can post and store resumes for 6 months. Employers pay for the job match service.

CAREERXROADS©
Job, Resume & Career Management Sites on the World Wide Web
• The 1997 Directory •

CAREERXROADS

Career Management
www.careerxroads.com

Mark Mehler/Gerry Crispin MMC Group
P.O. Box 253, Kendall Park, NJ 08824
Phone: 908-821-6652 Fax: 908-821-1343 e-mail: mmc@careerxroads.com

Jobs? No
- Cost to post jobs: N/A
- Cost to see jobs: N/A
- Specialty: N/A
- Industry: N/A
- Country/Region/State/City: Int'l/US

Resumes? No
- Cost to post resumes: N/A
- Cost to see resumes: N/A

Links to Jobs? Yes

Career Advice? No

The 1996 Directory to Jobs, Resumes and Career Management on the World Wide Web

CAREERXROADS

Where Talent and Opportunity Connect on the Internet

The newest edition, "The 1997 Directory to Job, Resume and Career Management Sites on the World Wide Web", provides purchasers of CAREERXROADS with monthly e-mail updates. We don't really rate our site as one of the best on the net but, since this is our book, we can set it up any way we want. E-mail your comments, questions or suggestions to us and you'll find we will always respond to you. Where else can you have an ongoing discussion with the authors?

CAREERXROADS©
Job, Resume & Career Management Sites on the World Wide Web
• The 1997 Directory •

Career & Job Resources

Links to Jobs
www.goforit.com/tsunami/career.html

Market Works Corporation
e-mail: mktworks@goforit.com

Jobs? No
- Cost to post jobs: N/A
- Cost to see jobs: N/A
- Specialty: Links
- Industry: All
- Country/Region/State/City: US

Resumes? No
- Cost to post resumes: N/A
- Cost to see resumes: N/A

Links to Jobs? Yes

Career Advice? No

List of links to major career hubs and other sites. Great graphics and I love the movement of the envelope to reach their e-mail address but I do not understand the relationship of the Tsunami waves and the site. Maybe it's me?

Careers in Management Consulting

College/Job Site
www.cob.ohio-state.edu:80/dept/fin/jobs/consult.htm

Tim Opler Fisher College of Business
Ohio State University

Jobs? Yes
- Cost to post jobs: Free
- Cost to see jobs: Free
- Specialty: Finance/Business
- Industry: All
- Country/Region/State/City: US/MW

Resumes? No
- Cost to post resumes: N/A
- Cost to see resumes: N/A

Links to Jobs? Yes

Career Advice? Yes

Small list of openings. Extensive information, employers, types of consulting etc. are provided as a sample of what is available from the site's cd-rom product. Good research background and links to top consulting firms as well as other fields.

Careers On-Line

Government/Diversity
www.disserv.stu.umn.edu/tc/grants/col/

Donna Johnson U. of Minnesota, Disability Services
12 Johnston Hall, 101 Pleasant St., SE, Minneapolis, MN 55455
Phone: 612-626-8035 e-mail: careers@disserv.stu.umn.edu

Jobs? Yes
- Cost to post jobs: Free
- Cost to see jobs: Free
- Specialty: All
- Industry: All
- Country/Region/State/City: US/MW/MN

Resumes? No
- Cost to post resumes: N/A
- Cost to see resumes: N/A

Links to Jobs? Yes

Career Advice? Yes

Provides job search and employment information to people with disabilities. This is a cooperative effort of U. of Minnesota's Disability Services and US Dept. of Education funding. Job accommodation information, Adaptive technology products and resources and much more.

C. E. Weekly

Publisher/Trade
www.ceweekly.com

Jerry Erickson C.E.Publications
P.O.Box 97000, Kirkland, WA 98083
Phone: 206-823-2222 Fax: 206-821-0942 e-mail: publisher@ceweekly.com

Jobs? Yes
- Cost to post jobs: Fee
- Cost to see jobs: Fee
- Specialty: IT
- Industry: N/A
- Country/Region/State/City: US

Resumes? Yes
- Cost to post resumes: Free
- Cost to see resumes: Fee

Links to Jobs? No

Career Advice? Yes

Weekly publication for computer contract service firms. Positions can be viewed by the publications subscribers. Non-subscribers get a taste and see 15-20% of the posted openings. Employers pay print advertising costs plus $5 to place their opportunity on the web site.

Cell

Publisher/Trade
pacific.cell.com/cell/index.html

Cell Press
1050 Massachusetts Avenue, Cambridge, Mass 02138
Phone: 617-661-7057 Fax: 617-661-7061 e-mail: advertising@cell.com

Jobs? Yes
- Cost to post jobs: Fee
- Cost to see jobs: Free
- Specialty: All Sciences
- Industry: Science
- Country/Region/State/City: Int'l/US

Resumes? Yes
- Cost to post resumes: Free
- Cost to see resumes: Free

Links to Jobs? No

Career Advice? No

Cell and their publications post resumes and positions from their magazines on this web site. Good search engine allows you to easily find resumes for free and post jobs for a fee. Lots of open positions in the sciences with direct contact information. Can e-mail to candidates for additional information.

Chattanooga News Free Press

Publisher/Newspaper
www.chatpub.com

Chattanooga Free-Press
400 E. 11th Street, Chattanooga, TN 37401
Phone: 423-756-6900

Jobs? Yes
- Cost to post jobs: Fee
- Cost to see jobs: Free
- Specialty: All
- Industry: N/A
- Country/Region/State/City: US/S/TN/Chatanooga

Resumes? No
- Cost to post resumes: N/A
- Cost to see resumes: N/A

Links to Jobs? No

Career Advice? No

Newspaper help-wanted Classifieds. Help-wanted display ads are not included. No extra charges. Employers must pay for ad in Newspaper.

Chicago Software Newspaper

Publisher/Trade Magazine
www.chisoft.com

Jeffrey Hunt Chicago Software Newspaper
2N Riverside Plaza, Ste 2400, Chicago, IL 60606
Phone: 800-352-0931 Fax: 617-928-1919 e-mail: info@chisoft.com

Jobs? Yes
- Cost to post jobs: Fee
- Cost to see jobs: Free
- Specialty: IT
- Industry: N/A
- Country/Region/State/City: US/MW/IL/Chicago

Resumes? No
- Cost to post resumes: N/A
- Cost to see resumes: N/A

Links to Jobs? Yes

Career Advice? No

Monthly tabloid mailed directly to 10,000 software professionals. Ads placed in publication are posted at no additional cost. Direct placement is $150 for 90 days. Nearly 600 computer jobs in the IL area were posted when reviewed.

Chicago Sun Times

Publisher/Newspaper
www.suntimes.com

401 N. Wabash Ave., Chicago, IL 60611
Phone: 312-321-3000

Jobs? Yes
- Cost to post jobs: Fee
- Cost to see jobs: Free
- Specialty: All
- Industry: N/A
- Country/Region/State/City: US/MW/IL/Chicago

Resumes? No
- Cost to post resumes: N/A
- Cost to see resumes: N/A

Links to Jobs? No

Career Advice? No

Newspaper classified sections are on-line to view. Same old issue in that you can only see in column ads as displays are not yet available to be viewed on the web.

Chronicle of Higher Education

Publisher/Trade
www.chronicle.com

Mike Snyder 1255 23rd Street NW
Suite 700, Washington, DC 20037
Phone: 202-466-1080 e-mail: display@chronicle.com

Jobs? Yes
- Cost to post jobs: Fee
- Cost to see jobs: Free
- Specialty: Education
- Industry: Education
- Country/Region/State/City: US

Resumes? No
- Cost to post resumes: N/A
- Cost to see resumes: N/A

Links to Jobs? No

Career Advice? Yes

Site states it has 1,090 jobs listed but you must be a member of the Chronicle of Higher Education and have a password to see the positions. Interesting career management information.

Civil Eng. & Public Works Career Paths

Association
www.FileShop.COM:80/apwa/civil.html

American Public Works Association

Jobs? Yes
- Cost to post jobs: Free
- Cost to see jobs: Free
- Specialty: Engineering
- Industry: Government
- Country/Region/State/City: US

Resumes? No
- Cost to post resumes: N/A
- Cost to see resumes: N/A

Links to Jobs? Yes

Career Advice? Yes

Information from the American Public Works Association about Civil Engineering related careers. Has recently expanded this site to include a list of links to jobs and additional information about the industry.

Clearinghouse for T&D Resources

Commercial Job Site
proed.com

Stephen J. Olender ProEd Corporation
1730 Stickney Point Road, Sarasota, FL 34231
Phone: 941-921-5455 Fax: 941-923-2374 e-mail: proed@gate.net

Jobs? Yes
- Cost to post jobs: Free
- Cost to see jobs: Free
- Specialty: Human Resources/T&D
- Industry: Education
- Country/Region/State/City: US

Resumes? No
- Cost to post resumes: N/A
- Cost to see resumes: N/A

Links to Jobs? No

Career Advice? Yes

The clearinghouse is a tool to help people find continuing education opportunities including seminars, conferences and executive programs worldwide. This conference organizer offers free posting of human resource, training, management and executive development (higher education) positions.

CLNET

College/Diversity
latino.sscnet.ucla.edu/

Richard Chabran Chicano Studies Research Center
54 Haines Hall, University of Calif., Los Angeles 90024
e-mail: salinas@latino.sscnet.ucla.edu

Jobs? Yes
- Cost to post jobs: Free
- Cost to see jobs: Free
- Specialty: All
- Industry: All
- Country/Region/State/City: US/W/CA

Resumes? No
- Cost to post resumes: N/A
- Cost to see resumes: N/A

Links to Jobs? Yes

Career Advice? Yes

Site is well connected to the Southern California community. Jobs posted along with community information links etc. Good design. Diversity site. Also has a listing of gopher sites dealing with bi-lingual isses.

College Connection

Career Management
www.careermosaic.com/cm/cc/cc1.html

Jeffrey Hodes Bernard Hodes Advertising
555 Madison Avenue, New York, NY 10022
Phone: 212-758-2600

Jobs? Yes
- Cost to post jobs: Fee
- Cost to see jobs: Free
- Specialty: All/College
- Industry: All
- Country/Region/State/City: US

Resumes? Yes
- Cost to post resumes: Free
- Cost to see resumes: Free

Links to Jobs? Yes

Career Advice? Yes

(See Career Mosaic) Lots of good information for the recent graduate. How to write your resume, online job fairs as, as well as employer profiles on the clients of this help-wanted advertising firm.

College Grad Job Hunter

Career Management/College
www.collegegrad.com

Brian Kreuger Quantum Leap Publishing
6910 W. Brown Deer Road, Suite 201, Milwaukee, WI 53223
Phone: 414-377-8720 Fax: 414-377-8720 e-mail: webmaster@execpc.com

Jobs? Yes
- Cost to post jobs: Fee
- Cost to see jobs: Free
- Specialty: All
- Industry: N/A
- Country/Region/State/City: US

Resumes? No
- Cost to post resumes: N/A
- Cost to see resumes: N/A

Links to Jobs? Yes

Career Advice? Yes

Large database of jobs for college grads... and experienced professionals. Good job market info, employer links, help putting together and posting resumes to places where employers are "likely to look". Site is named after book of same name. Owner is selling their book and consulting services. Employers can add links to their site at no charge. Costs for employers $50 for 3 months. RealAudio job search information (four hours of audio). Well done and current. Easy to use.

CAREERXROADS©
Job, Resume & Career Management Sites on the World Wide Web
• The 1997 Directory •

Colorado Online Job Connection

Commercial Job Site
www.net1comm.com/~peak/

Steve Parker Peak Career Management, Inc.
1631 South Galena Street, Denver, CO 80231
Phone: 303-745-6433 Fax: 303-745-6425 e-mail: peak@neticomm.com

Jobs? Yes
- Cost to post jobs: Fee
- Cost to see jobs: Free
- Specialty: IT
- Industry: All
- Country/Region/State/City: US/W

Resumes? Yes
- Cost to post resumes: Fee
- Cost to see resumes: Free

Links to Jobs? Yes

Career Advice? Yes

Easy to get in and out of this placement agency site. Mostly positions in CO, WY, ID, CA. Applicants are charged $49 to post their resume. Employers can advertise jobs at a cost in the range of $100 per.

Columbus Dispatch

Publisher/Newspaper
www.dispatch.com

5300 Crosswind Drive, Columbus, OH 43228
Phone: 614-461-8803 Fax: 614-461-8525

Jobs? Yes
- Cost to post jobs: Fee
- Cost to see jobs: Free
- Specialty: All
- Industry: N/A
- Country/Region/State/City: US/E/OH

Resumes? No
- Cost to post resumes: N/A
- Cost to see resumes: N/A

Links to Jobs? No

Career Advice? No

Help wanted classifieds printed in Sunday's newspaper are posted. This publisher participates in CareerPath (See CareerPath). Help wanted display ads are not currently included on the internet site.

Comm Careers

Publisher/Trade Magazine
www.commweek.com

Trish Rising CMP Publications
600 Community Drive, Manhasset, NY 11030
Phone: 516-562-5218 Fax: 516-562-7830 e-mail: trising@cmp.com

Jobs? Yes
- Cost to post jobs: Fee
- Cost to see jobs: Free
- Specialty: IT
- Industry: N/A
- Country/Region/State/City: US

Resumes? No
- Cost to post resumes: N/A
- Cost to see resumes: N/A

Links to Jobs? No

Career Advice? No

Communications Week help wanted advertising is available along with company profiles, salary survey data, and links to other (CMP) publications.

Communication Week

Publisher/Trade Magazine
techweb.cmp.com/cw/cw.careers/index.html

CMP Media Group (See TechWeb)
600 Community Drive, Manhasset, NY 11030
Phone: 516-562-7688

Jobs? Yes
- Cost to post jobs: Fee
- Cost to see jobs: Free
- Specialty: IT
- Industry: All
- Country/Region/State/City: US

Resumes? No
- Cost to post resumes: N/A
- Cost to see resumes: N/A

Links to Jobs? No

Career Advice? No

Trade magazine. Employers placing ads in publication have internet option.

Computer Jobs Store (Atlanta)

Commercial Job Site
computerjobs.com

Michael K. Gilfillan The Computer Jobs Store, Inc.
2000 Powers Ferry Road, St 300, Atlanta, GA 30067
Phone: 770-850-0045 Fax: e-mail: info@computerjobs.com

Jobs? Yes
- Cost to post jobs: Fee
- Cost to see jobs: Free
- Specialty: IT
- Industry: N/A
- Country/Region/State/City: US/SE/GA/Atlanta

Resumes? Yes
- Cost to post resumes: Free
- Cost to see resumes: Fee

Links to Jobs? Yes

Career Advice? No

Employers join on an annual basis (37+ currently) to list (500) Atlanta and SE region computer positions posted daily. New feature does include a few nationwide openings. Employers also have company profile and links to their site. Costs are in the $25-$50 range to post. Job seekers can review an excellent selection of Industry and Career Information (e.g. this site includes contact information for the 100+ Computer Companies in the Atlanta Area. Link to Dallas ComputerJobs Store.

Computer Jobs Store (Dallas)

Commercial Job Site
computerjobs.com/dallas

Michael K. Gilfallan The Computer Jobs Store, Inc.
2000 Powers Ferry Road, St 300, Atlanta, GA 30067
Phone: 770-850-0045 e-mail: info@computerjobs.com

Jobs? Yes
- Cost to post jobs: Fee
- Cost to see jobs: Free
- Specialty: IT
- Industry: N/A
- Country/Region/State/City: US/SW/TX/Dallas

Resumes? Yes
- Cost to post resumes: Free
- Cost to see resumes: Fee

Links to Jobs? Yes

Career Advice? No

Sister site to Atlanta Computer Jobs Store (see Atlanta for more details) Has local information on jobs and the area that the site serves.

Computer Resellers Weekly

Publisher/Trade Magazine
techweb.cmp.com/crn/career/career.html

CMP Media Group
(See TechWeb), Manhasset, NY 11030

Jobs? Yes
- Cost to post jobs: Fee
- Cost to see jobs: Free
- Specialty: IT
- Industry: All
- Country/Region/State/City: US

Resumes? No
- Cost to post resumes: N/A
- Cost to see resumes: N/A

Links to Jobs? No

Career Advice? No

Employers placing ads in this publication have the option of adding the Internet.

Computer Retail Week

Publisher/Trade Magazine
techweb.cmp.com/crw/career/crw.career.html

CMP Media Group
(See TechWeb), 600 Community Drive, Manhasset, NY 11030

Jobs? Yes
- Cost to post jobs: Fee
- Cost to see jobs: Free
- Specialty: IT
- Industry: All
- Country/Region/State/City: US

Resumes? No
- Cost to post resumes: N/A
- Cost to see resumes: N/A

Links to Jobs? No

Career Advice? No

Employers placing ads in this publication have the option of adding the internet.

Computer Science Jobs in Academia

College/University
www.cs.brandeis.edu:80/~zippy/academic-cs-jobs.html

Patrick Tufts Brandeis University
e-mail: zippy@cs.brandeis.edu

Jobs? Yes
- Cost to post jobs: Free
- Cost to see jobs: Free
- Specialty: IT
- Industry: Higher Education
- Country/Region/State/City: US

Resumes? No
- Cost to post resumes: No
- Cost to see resumes: No

Links to Jobs? Yes

Career Advice? Yes

Numerous university faculty positions throughout the US are posted.

Computer World's IT Careers

Publisher/Trade/Agent
www.computerworld.com

Jay Savell Computerworld
500 Old Connecticut Path, Framingham, MA 01701
Phone: 800-343-6474 Fax: 508-620-7739 e-mail: jay_savell@cw.com

Jobs? Yes
- Cost to post jobs: Fee
- Cost to see jobs: Free
- Specialty: IT
- Industry: Computer
- Country/Region/State/City: US

Resumes? Yes
- Cost to post resumes: Free
- Cost to see resumes: N/A

Links to Jobs? Yes

Career Advice? Yes

Help Wanted ads published each week (listed for 90 days) are available with online search capabilities. Free resume posting (not searchable by employers) is combined with AGENT capability that informs jobseekers via e-mail about job matches. Extensive archive of Computerworld's career related articles that can be searched by keyword is also available. Other employer packages are available for corporate advertisers.

Connect

Links to Jobs
www.cabrillo.cc.ca.us/connect/docs/jobs.html

Lynn Hood Cabrillo College
Career Planning & Placement, 6500 Soquel Drive, Aptos, CA 95003
Phone: 408-479-6540 e-mail: lyhood@cabrillo.cc.ca.us

Jobs? No
- Cost to post jobs: N/A
- Cost to see jobs: N/A
- Specialty: All
- Industry: All
- Country/Region/State/City: US/CA

Resumes? No
- Cost to post resumes: N/A
- Cost to see resumes: N/A

Links to Jobs? Yes

Career Advice? No

Long list of links to all sorts of information that will help the job seeker. Well organized into specific categories with brief descriptions for some of the sites. Has a good list of links dedicated to California. Also list for college graduates which has extensive information.

Contract Employment Connection

Commercial Job Site
www.iquest.com/~ntes/index.html

NTES
309 Taylor Street, Scottsboro, AL 35768
Phone: 205-259-6837 e-mail: info@ntes.com

Jobs? Yes
- Cost to post jobs: Fee
- Cost to see jobs: Free
- Specialty: All
- Industry: IT
- Country/Region/State/City: US

Resumes? Yes
- Cost to post resumes: Free
- Cost to see resumes: Fee

Links to Jobs? Yes

Career Advice? Yes

E-mail your resume in ASCII text in the message body or mail it on a floppy so that the site will make it available to every technical service firm in the US. Positions listed from Hotflash magazine, mostly software, hardware, IS or engineering positions with contact or e-mail info present. Listing of contract recruiters by industry is also listed.

Contract Employment NACCB

Association
www.computerwork.com

NAACB
e-mail: webmaster@resourcecenter.com

Jobs? Yes
- Cost to post jobs: Fee
- Cost to see jobs: Free
- Specialty: IT
- Industry: IT
- Country/Region/State/City: US

Resumes? Yes
- Cost to post resumes: Free
- Cost to see resumes: Fee

Links to Jobs? Yes

Career Advice? No

The National Assoc. of Computer Consultant Businesses is a nationwide group of 280 companies. Site is for regular jobs and contract work. Direct contact info to member organizations. Lots of jobs available. Links to other chapters who also have job openings. You can post your resume on line to all of the chapters.

Contract Employment Weekly

Publisher/Specialty
www.ceweekly.wa.com

Jerry Erickson CE Publications
P.O.Box 97000, Kirkland, WA 98083
Phone: 206-823-2222 Fax: 206-821-0942 e-mail: webmaster@ceweekly.wa.com

Jobs? Yes
- Cost to post jobs: Fee
- Cost to see jobs: Free
- Specialty: IT
- Industry: All
- Country/Region/State/City: US

Resumes? Yes
- Cost to post resumes: Fee
- Cost to see resumes: N/A

Links to Jobs? Yes

Career Advice? No

Publisher provides a weekly updated list of contract technical employment positions from advertisers in its publications. Site states jobs are updated every half hour. Now that is service. Direct links to companies and a library of career information is also available.

Cool Works

Commercial Job Site
www.coolworks.com/showme/

Bill Berg Cool Works
P.O.Box 272, Gardiner, MN 59030
Phone: 800-806-2296 e-mail: coolworks@bigfoot.com

Jobs? Yes
- Cost to post jobs: Fee
- Cost to see jobs: Free
- Specialty: All
- Industry: Hospitality
- Country/Region/State/City: US

Resumes? No
- Cost to post resumes: N/A
- Cost to see resumes: N/A

Links to Jobs? Yes

Career Advice? No

When we last visited this site it had great information on jobs at ski resorts and national parks throughout the US. On our recent visit it seems Bill has decided to sell camping equipment while providing info on the greatest places to go camping/skiing. All that is great but the jobs disappeared from the site. Then we realized after our e-mail exchange that jobs are still there just a file away. Bill claims links to 20,000 jobs. Cost to post a job, is $75.

Coolware Electronic Job Finder

Commercial Job Site
none.coolware.com:80/jobs/location.html

Margaret Cooley
385 Forest Avenue, Palo Alto, CA 94301
Phone: 415-322-4722 Fax: 415-326-2479 e-mail: webmastr@coolware.com

Jobs? Yes
- Cost to post jobs: Fee
- Cost to see jobs: Free
- Specialty: All
- Industry: All
- Country/Region/State/City: US//W/CA/San Fran

Resumes? No
- Cost to post resumes: N/A
- Cost to see resumes: N/A

Links to Jobs? No

Career Advice? No

Employers are charged $49 for listing positions in the Bay Area. Map of local cities provided. Claim 1.2 million hits/month. Simple job format. Easy to use.

Corporate Aviation Resume Exchange

Commercial Job Site
scendtek.com/care

ScendTek Internet Corp.
Phone: 800-611-3565   e-mail: sti@scendtek.com

Jobs? Yes
- Cost to post jobs: Fee
- Cost to see jobs: Free
- Specialty: Aviation
- Industry: Aviation
- Country/Region/State/City: US

Resumes? Yes
- Cost to post resumes: Free
- Cost to see resumes: Free

Links to Jobs? Yes

Career Advice? No

Site caters to the aviation industry (flying talent) with resumes that can be posted and seen for free. Resumes are pre-formatted so it is easy to post. Niche site if you need a pilot or flight department personnel.

Corporate Offsite Resume Database

Commercial Resume Site
www.jobnet.com/CORD

Ward Christman Online Opportunities
422 W. Lincoln Highway, Suite 422, Exton, PA 19341
Phone: 610-873-6811   e-mail: Carol@jobnet.com

Jobs? No
- Cost to post jobs: N/A
- Cost to see jobs: N/A
- Specialty: All
- Industry: All
- Country/Region/State/City: USS

Resumes? No
- Cost to post resumes: N/A
- Cost to see resumes: N/A

Links to Jobs? N/A

Career Advice? Yes

New toy on the market that allows you access to your resumes via the web. Has e-mail capability of receiving and sending a reply. If you want your managers to have direct access to resumes this is one of the waves of the future. Check it out and see what they have to offer.

CAREERXROADS©
Job, Resume & Career Management Sites on the World Wide Web
• The 1997 Directory •

Crystallography Worldwide

www.unige.ch/crystal/w3vlc/crystal.index.html

Lachlan Cranswick University of Geneva
e-mail: lachlan@dmp.csiro.au

Jobs? Yes
- Cost to post jobs: Free
- Cost to see jobs: Free
- Specialty: Crystallography
- Industry: Crystallography
- Country/Region/State/City: Int'l/US

Resumes? No
- Cost to post resumes: N/A
- Cost to see resumes: N/A

Links to Jobs? Yes

Career Advice? No

Jobs posted all over the world on this site. Lots of post doc positions with direct links to the organization posting the position. Links to numerous countries/universities in the field of crystallography.

Cumbria Careers on the Net

Commercial Job Site
www.u-net.com/~c-career/

e-mail: ho@c-career.u-net.com

Jobs? Yes
- Cost to post jobs: Free
- Cost to see jobs: Free
- Specialty: All
- Industry: All
- Country/Region/State/City: Int'l/Cumbria

Resumes? No
- Cost to post resumes: N/A
- Cost to see resumes: N/A

Links to Jobs? Yes

Career Advice? Yes

Lists career centers that can help you find an opportunity. Also has links to major sites. Seems to be a starter site that is trying to provide career information and job information on Cumbria. Now the question is, "where is Cumbria"?

Cyber Hound

Links/Search Engine
www.thomson.com/cyberhound/default.html

Gale Research
835 Penobscot Bldg., 645 Griswold Street, Detroit, MI 48226-4094
Phone: 800-877-4253   e-mail: wolf@gale.com

Jobs? No
- Cost to post jobs: N/A
- Cost to see jobs: N/A
- Specialty: N/A
- Industry: N/A
- Country/Region/State/City: US

Resumes? No
- Cost to post resumes: N/A
- Cost to see resumes: N/A

Links to Jobs? Yes

Career Advice? N/A

Comprehensive reviews of sites by subject area professionals are promised. Cyber Hound offers 30 day free trial. As a search engine, Cyber Hound claims to take your criteria and return a list of sites that match your (job) interests. With such a broad range of solutions implied we decided to perform a complicated test and plugged in "jobs" as our subject term. We found zero response. This site will soon be up and running as the folks at cyber hound claim this glitch is temporary.

Cyberspace Jobs

Commercial Job Site
www.best.com:80/~lianne/

Lianne Thompson
465 Utah #3, San Francisco, CA 94110
Phone: 415-431-4076   e-mail: lianne@best.com

Jobs? No
- Cost to post jobs: N/A
- Cost to see jobs: N/A
- Specialty: All
- Industry: Cyberspace
- Country/Region/State/City: N/A

Resumes? No
- Cost to post resumes: N/A
- Cost to see resumes: N/A

Links to Jobs? Yes

Career Advice? Yes

Career information on 15 areas of jobs in cyberspace. Comments from people in the field with links to sites that will give you more information. Nice touch, in a small niche.

CAREERXROADS©
Job, Resume & Career Management Sites on the World Wide Web
• The 1997 Directory •

Dallas Morning News

Publisher/Newspaper
www.dallasnews.com/us.htm

Dallas Morning News
P.O. Box 655237, Dallas, TX 75265
Phone: 214-263-0456 e-mail: maxwell@cityview.com

Jobs? Yes
- Cost to post jobs: Fee
- Cost to see jobs: Free
- Specialty: All
- Industry: N/A
- Country/Region/State/City: US/SW/TX/Dallas

Resumes? No
- Cost to post resumes: N/A
- Cost to see resumes: N/A

Links to Jobs? No

Career Advice? No

Help Wanted advertising published in this paper's Sunday edition. Site is under construction so come back soon for a visit.

Decisive Quest

Career Management
www.decisivequest.com

Decisive Quest, Inc.
e-mail: rickd@decisivequest.com

Jobs? No
- Cost to post jobs: N/A
- Cost to see jobs: N/A
- Specialty: N/A
- Industry: N/A
- Country/Region/State/City: US

Resumes? No
- Cost to post resumes: N/A
- Cost to see resumes: N/A

Links to Jobs? No

Career Advice? Yes

Software company that claims it has a proprietary software product with templates to assist applicants in researching and applying for jobs online. Difficult to obtain confirmation, costs or examples.

The Definitive Internet Career Guide

Links
phoenix.placement.oakland.edu/career/internet.htm

Jobs? No
- Cost to post jobs: N/A
- Cost to see jobs: N/A
- Specialty: All
- Industry: All
- Country/Region/State/City: US

Resumes? No
- Cost to post resumes: N/A
- Cost to see resumes: N/A

Links to Jobs? Yes

Career Advice? No

Neat site allowing instant download of all its contents. Hundreds of links. Alpha order.

Denver Post

Publisher/Newspaper
www.denverpost.com

1560 Broadway, Denver, CO 80202
Phone: 303-821-1421

Jobs? Yes
- Cost to post jobs: Fee
- Cost to see jobs: Free
- Specialty: All
- Industry: N/A
- Country/Region/State/City: US/W/CO

Resumes? No
- Cost to post resumes: N/A
- Cost to see resumes: N/A

Links to Jobs? No

Career Advice? No

Help wanted classifieds printed in Sunday's newspaper are posted. Employers will pay an additional $1/line. This publisher participates in CareerPath (See CareerPath). Help wanted display ads are not included on the Internet site.

DesignSphere Online

Commercial Job Site
www.dsphere.net/jobs.html

Irene Woerner Cogent Software, Inc.
221 E. walnut St., Suite 215, Pasadena, CA 91101
Phone: 818-585-2788 Fax: 818-585-2785 e-mail: webmaster@dsphere.com

Jobs? Yes
- Cost to post jobs: Free
- Cost to see jobs: Free
- Specialty: Graphic Arts
- Industry: All
- Country/Region/State/City: US

Resumes? Yes
- Cost to post resumes: Free
- Cost to see resumes: Free

Links to Jobs? Yes

Career Advice? No

Advertise positions or post resumes free of charge. Niche site for graphic arts..

Have you found a site that isn't listed in CAREERXROADS?

Have you REGISTERED to receive FREE updates?

Keep us informed.

We'll keep you informed.

CAREERXROADS
Where Talent and Opportunity Connect on the Internet

DICE

Commercial Job Site
www.dice.com

J. Peterson Dice
P.O.Box 7070, Des Moines, IA 50309
Phone: 515-280-1144 Fax: 515-280-1452 e-mail: sysop@dice.com

Jobs? Yes
- Cost to post jobs: Fee
- Cost to see jobs: Free
- Specialty: IT
- Industry: All
- Country/Region/State/City: US

Resumes? Yes
- Cost to post resumes: Free
- Cost to see resumes: Fee

Links to Jobs? Yes

Career Advice? No

Data Processing Independent Consultants Exchange

A job search database for computer consultants and high-tech professionals.

A Bulletin Board accessible from the internet. Job search database for computer and high technology professionals. Thousands of listings. Candidate profiles are fee to post. Dice posts openings to various usenet groups and distributes candidate profiles (resumes) to subscribing companies each week. Site states has over 300 organizations as members. Unlimited posting for about $500/month.

CAREERXROADS©
Job, Resume & Career Management Sites on the World Wide Web
• The 1997 Directory •

Direct Marketing World Job Center

Commercial Job Site

Mainsafe Marketing Information
1113 Channing Way, Ste. 11, Berkeley, CA 94702

Jobs? Yes
- Cost to post jobs: Free
- Cost to see jobs: Free
- Specialty: Marketing
- Industry: All
- Country/Region/State/City: US

Resumes? No
- Cost to post resumes: N/A
- Cost to see resumes: N/A

Links to Jobs? Yes

Career Advice? Yes

Offers employers free job listings and resume search using an on-line form. Job seekers can e-mail to employers through the center. About 87, jobs mostly IS, sales and Eng. are listed. Post a resume as we saw over 85 posted on our visits. Some marketing information, links and databases maintained. Limited in scope but, for free, the price is right.

Disability Services at the Univ. of Minnesota

College/Diversity
www.disserv.stu.umn.edu/TC/Grants/COL/

University of Minnesota
MN
Phone: 612-626-0365   e-mail: careers@disserv.stu.umn.edu

Jobs? Yes
- Cost to post jobs: Free
- Cost to see jobs: Free
- Specialty: All
- Industry: All
- Country/Region/State/City: US/MN

Resumes? No
- Cost to post resumes: N/A
- Cost to see resumes: N/A

Links to Jobs? Yes

Career Advice? Yes

Site specificly lists job listing for disabled individuals and does a great job. Long lists of jobs, job hot lines and other programs in the Minnesota area. Direct contact information for jobs is on the site as well. Site has direct access form for posting a job.

CAREERXROADS©
Job, Resume & Career Management Sites on the World Wide Web
• The 1997 Directory •

Doctor Link

Private site
www.doctorlink.com

e-mail: drlink@doctorlink.comor

Jobs? Yes
- Cost to post jobs: Free
- Cost to see jobs: Free
- Specialty: Health Care/MD
- Industry: N/A
- Country/Region/State/City: US/NW/WA

Resumes? No
- Cost to post resumes: N/A
- Cost to see resumes: N/A

Links to Jobs? No

Career Advice? No

Employment section is under construction with some resumes but no jobs posted on our visit. Direct contact information is present and you can e-mail the job seeker directly. Nice niche, let's see what they do. Long list of medical links if you need information on a particular illness.

Drake Beam Morin

Career Management
www.dbm.com/candidate

Margaret Riley
100 Park Avenue, Third Floor, New York, NY 10017
Phone: 212-692-7700 e-mail: mfriley@ultranet.com

Jobs? No
- Cost to post jobs: N/A
- Cost to see jobs: N/A
- Specialty: All
- Industry: All
- Country/Region/State/City: US

Resumes? No
- Cost to post resumes: N/A
- Cost to see resumes: N/A

Links to Jobs? Yes

Career Advice? Yes

With Margaret Riley consulting for DBM this site has gained greatly with her input. Long list of links to places where you can post your resume for a fee or for free. Many interesting addresses to visit as this site is updated weekly with new information.

Eagleview

Commercial Job Site/Agent
www.eagleview.com

Amy Shea
1601 Trapelo Road, Waltham, MA 02154-7300
Phone: 617-672-6010 Fax: 617-672-6010 e-mail: evi@eagleview.com

Jobs? Yes
- Cost to post jobs: Free
- Cost to see jobs: Free
- Specialty: Agent
- Industry: N/A
- Country/Region/State/City: US

Resumes? Yes
- Cost to post resumes: Fee
- Cost to see resumes: Fee

Links to Jobs? Yes

Career Advice? Yes

WHERE THE BEST JOBS FIND YOU!

EAGLEVIEW.

Site provides an AGENT that matches your background to their clients needs. This service allows candidates to mail or down load their profile which will be available to companies looking for specific individuals. Standard cost is $5,000 per year for corporations to search their database. Candidate has a multimedia component where job seekers can record digitalized audio/video interview that employers will review when looking at their resume/profile (presently only available in the New England area as you must go to one of their locations to do this). For $100 the applicant pays for confidentiality of their data if they require this aspect of the service. You need to become part of their career network and download their software to see jobs posted which could be seen as a drawback to some. A top site with an interesting future ahead

Ed Physician

Commercial Job Site
www.edphysician.com/

Ralph Single
PO Box 1361, Derry, New Hampshire 03038
Phone: 603-437-2989 Fax: 603-437-2989 e-mail: info@edphysician.com

Jobs? Yes
- Cost to post jobs: Free
- Cost to see jobs: Free
- Specialty: Health Care/MD
- Industry: Health Care
- Country/Region/State/City: US

Resumes? No
- Cost to post resumes: N/A
- Cost to see resumes: N/A

Links to Jobs? Yes

Career Advice? In future

Job opportunities for Emergency Room Doctors. Search engine by state makes it easy to find direct contact info. Site is new as career information section/articles of interest are still under construction. Job postings at present are free and nicely done.

Educator's Network EDNET

Commercial Job Site
pages.prodigy.com/CA/luca52a/bagley.html

Karla Freedman Educator's Network-EDNET
5426 Woodlake Avenue, Woodland Hills, CA 91367
Phone: 818-999-9432 Fax: 818-999-5134 e-mail: luca52a@prodigy.com

Jobs? Yes
- Cost to post jobs: Fee
- Cost to see jobs: Free
- Specialty: Teaching
- Industry: Education
- Country/Region/State/City: US/Southern CA

Resumes? No
- Cost to post resumes: N/A
- Cost to see resumes: N/A

Links to Jobs? Yes

Career Advice? No

Teacher postings for Southern CA that gives you the basics and then refers you back to the district to get the real scoop. Jobs are posted within 48 hours and you can post your first initial openings for 3 months for free. After the free period the cost is $300 for the next 12 months for unlimited openings. Site is new and one to watch.

Electric Power NewsLink

Publisher/Trade Magazine
www.powermag.com

McGraw-Hill/Power
1221 Ave. of the Americas, New York, NY 10020

Jobs? Yes
- Cost to post jobs: Fee
- Cost to see jobs: Free
- Specialty: Power Engineering
- Industry: Power Generation
- Country/Region/State/City: US

Resumes? No
- Cost to post resumes: N/A
- Cost to see resumes: N/A

Links to Jobs? Yes

Career Advice? No

Positions listed through this publication. Articles on the industry gives you an insight into which corporations will be your next employer.

Electronic Engineering Times

Publisher/Trade Magazine
www.techweb.cmp.com/eet/823/

Lynette McGill Hodge CMP Media Group
(See TechWeb)
Phone: 800-598-7689 e-mail: 1hodge@cmp.com

Jobs? Yes
- Cost to post jobs: Fee
- Cost to see jobs: Free
- Specialty: IT
- Industry: High Technology
- Country/Region/State/City: US

Resumes? No
- Cost to post resumes: N/A
- Cost to see resumes: N/A

Links to Jobs? No

Career Advice? Yes

Companies can post ads to the EETimes web site for $150 if an ad is running in the publication. (ads accepted by e-mail). The cost rises to $1000 if no ad is running in EETimes. Additional $400/month buys a hyperlink to the company's home page.

Emergency Medicine Practice Opportunity

Commercial Job Site
www.njnet.com/~embbs/jobjob-stat.html

Triple Star Systems
7 Hickory Court, , Middlesex, NJ 08806
Phone: Fax: e-mail: ashrafn@aol.com

Jobs? Yes
- Cost to post jobs: Fee
- Cost to see jobs: Free
- Specialty: Health Care/MD
- Industry: Health Care
- Country/Region/State/City: US

Resumes? Yes
- Cost to post resumes: Fee
- Cost to see resumes: Free

Links to Jobs? Yes

Career Advice? Yes

Site includes information on treatments/ailments as well as "jobs posted". A database called "the national physician job listings directory" is searchable by alpha or function. Contact information is listed. Cost is $20 per month per position with a 2 month minimum. You can post your resume in the help wanted section for $30 for 3 months. Of all the physician sites that we have seen, this one gives the most back to the community. Good articles in a broad range of topics. Nice job.

Quick Review Rating for each site.

- Has jobs:

- Has resumes:

- Has career advice:

- One of the best in class:

The sites that offer the best value on the 'Net are highlighted by showing a reduced version of their Home Page.

CAREERXROADS©
Job, Resume & Career Management Sites on the World Wide Web
• The 1997 Directory •

Employment Channel

Publisher/Cable
www.employ.com

NYC Cable Companies (Channel 72&74)

Jobs? Yes
- Cost to post jobs: Fee
- Cost to see jobs: Free
- Specialty: All
- Industry: N/A
- Country/Region/State/City: US/NE/NY/NYC

Resumes? No
- Cost to post resumes: N/A
- Cost to see resumes: N/A

Links to Jobs? No

Career Advice? No

Overhyped home page, "the only interactive www-based employment service," but does have nice feature for employers to post jobs to a www based site that are also shown on cable in a million plus homes in NY City's five boroughs. Job seekers can check out the jobs without having to go find the cable station...and wait for it to show up.

Employment Edge

Placement/Search Firm
www.employmentedge.com:80/employment.edge/

P.O. Box 11602, Shawnee Mission, KS 66207
Phone: Fax: 913-341-9716   e-mail: jobs@employmentedge.com

Jobs? Yes
- Cost to post jobs: Free
- Cost to see jobs: Free
- Specialty: All
- Industry: All
- Country/Region/State/City: US

Resumes? No
- Cost to post resumes: N/A
- Cost to see resumes: N/A

Links to Jobs? No

Career Advice? No

Placement firm that lists their own jobs and those posted by other companies on the internet. Positions listed under " Accounting, Auditing, Eng., Mgmt., Programming, MIS/SW Eng. and Everything Else".

CAREERXROADS©
Job, Resume & Career Management Sites on the World Wide Web
• The 1997 Directory •

Employment Online

Publisher/Newspaper
152.52.2.152/classads/employment/careers.html

The News & Observer Publishing Co.
PO Box 191, Raleigh, NC 27602
Phone: 919-829-4800 Fax: 919-829-4824 e-mail: mchoate@nando.net

Jobs? Yes
- Cost to post jobs: Fee
- Cost to see jobs: Free
- Specialty: Classifieds
- Industry: All
- Country/Region/State/City: US/NC/WA/CA/AL

Resumes? No
- Cost to post resumes: N/A
- Cost to see resumes: N/A

Links to Jobs? Yes

Career Advice? No

Classified advertising online for the Raleigh News & Observer, The News Tribune, Tacoma W:; The Sacramento Bee, Sacramento CA; The Modesto Bee, Modesto CA; Anchorage Daily News, Anchorage AL; Tri-City Herald, Richland WA.

Employment Opportunities in Water Resources

College/University
www.uwin.siu.edu/announce/jobs/

e-mail: admin@uwin.siu.edu

Jobs? Yes
- Cost to post jobs: Free
- Cost to see jobs: Free
- Specialty: Environmental
- Industry: Water
- Country/Region/State/City: US

Resumes? Yes
- Cost to post resumes: Free
- Cost to see resumes: Free

Links to Jobs? Yes

Career Advice? Yes

Academic and non-academic positions in water resources. Visitors can register with a directory for "experts" from acid rain to water monitoring. Nice touch.

Employment Resources

Career Management
www.nova.edu/Inter-Links/employment.html

Rob Kabacoff, Ph.D.
Nova Southeastern University, Ft. Lauderdale, Fl 3314
Phone: 305-475-7581 e-mail: kabacoff@cps.nova.edu

Jobs? No
- Cost to post jobs: N/A
- Cost to see jobs: N/A
- Specialty: All
- Industry: All
- Country/Region/State/City: US

Resumes? No
- Cost to post resumes: N/A
- Cost to see resumes: N/A

Links to Jobs? Yes

Career Advice? Yes

Provides links to major sites for jobs and career information Lots of general data, not necessarily related to a job search but when I get tired I like to play the games on this site or read the latest jokes.

Employnet

Resume Service
employnetinc.ksi.com

Jim Chrisholm 111 Broadway
Floor 8, New York, NY 10006
Phone: 212-634-0604 Fax: 212-634-0611 e-mail: resume@employnet-inc.com

Jobs? No
- Cost to post jobs: N/A
- Cost to see jobs: N/A
- Specialty: All
- Industry: N/A
- Country/Region/State/City: US

Resumes? Yes
- Cost to post resumes: Fee
- Cost to see resumes: Free

Links to Jobs? No

Career Advice? Yes

Typical resume retrieval site that charges $49.00 per year to post your resume. Employment agencies can search the database for candidates for free. Why this site excludes corporations is beyond our scope. Nice article on preparing an electronic resume.

ENews

Publisher/Trade Magazine
www.sumnet.com/enews

Diana Basso Electronic News
2 5th Avenue, 4th Floor, New york, NY 10001
Phone: 212-736-5122 e-mail: jobs@employmentedge.com

Jobs? Yes
- Cost to post jobs: Fee
- Cost to see jobs: Free
- Specialty: Engineering/Elect.
- Industry: Electronics
- Country/Region/State/City: US

Resumes? No
- Cost to post resumes: N/A
- Cost to see resumes: N/A

Links to Jobs? Yes

Career Advice? No

Ads placed in Electronic News ($125/inch) are put on their web site at no charge.

Engine Room

Commercial Job Site
www.iweb.co.uk/iwsearch.html#map

i web
United Kingdom
e-mail: jobs@iweb.co.uk

Jobs? Yes
- Cost to post jobs: Fee
- Cost to see jobs: Free
- Specialty: All
- Industry: All
- Country/Region/State/City: Int'l/United Kingdom

Resumes? Yes
- Cost to post resumes: Free
- Cost to see resumes: N/A

Links to Jobs? No

Career Advice? No

Easy to use search engine for jobs in the United Kingdom. Direct contact information for jobs at all levels and for all professions. Nice job. Site seems to be owned by a recruiting agency but jobs are posted by many different firms.

CAREERXROADS©
Job, Resume & Career Management Sites on the World Wide Web
• The 1997 Directory •

Engineering Job Source

Publisher/Newspaper
www.wwnet.com/~engineer/

Jean Eggertsen
2016 Manchester #24, Ann Arbor, MI 48104
Phone: 313-971-6995 Fax: 313-677-4386 e-mail: enginer@wwnet.com

Jobs? Yes
- Cost to post jobs: Fee
- Cost to see jobs: Free
- Specialty: Engineering
- Industry: All
- Country/Region/State/City: US/Michigan/Illinois

Resumes? No
- Cost to post resumes: N/A
- Cost to see resumes: N/A

Links to Jobs? Yes

Career Advice? No

Engineering Job Source publishes two weekly e-mail listings of classified jobs sent to subscribed engineers and related fields via e-mail for free. Cost to employers is $50 per week for each ad. Site is primarily for Michigan & Illinois. They understand the power of e-mail. One of the few who does.

Engineering Jobs

Commercial Job Site
www.engineeringjobs.com

Wayne Black
Phone: 510-237-3323 Fax: 510-237-3324 e-mail: engineeringjobs.com

Jobs? Yes
- Cost to post jobs: Free
- Cost to see jobs: Free
- Specialty: Engineering
- Industry: All
- Country/Region/State/City: US

Resumes? Yes
- Cost to post resumes: Free
- Cost to see resumes: Free

Links to Jobs? Yes

Career Advice? No

Nice list of links for engineering positions listed by large and small companies. Employers can link their positions open for free while seeing brief resume profiles of potential candidates. You can post your resume via linking to this site also for free. Good job on a sight that gets it.

Engineering News Record

Publisher/Trade
www.enr.com

Gabrielle Boguslawski McGraw-Hill
1221 Avenue of the Americas, New York, NY 10020
Phone: 800-458-3842 Fax: 212-512-4039 e-mail: gbogusla@mcgraw-hill.com

Jobs? Yes
- Cost to post jobs: Fee
- Cost to see jobs: Free
- Specialty: Construction/Engineering Design
- Industry: Construction
- Country/Region/State/City: Int'l & US

Resumes? No
- Cost to post resumes: N/A
- Cost to see resumes: N/A

Links to Jobs? Yes

Career Advice? Yes

Ads placed in this weekly publication are posted at their internet site. Positions are listed by the week they appear, (approximately 100/week). Architectural, engineering & construction are prominently featured. Environmental engineering positions are also posted. Nice feature at the site includes an easy to use search engine to find A/E/C companies by region and specialty. Also listed are the publication's annual Top 400/500 firms in the field.

Entry Level Job Seeker Assistant

Career Management/College
members.aol.com/Dylander/jobhome.html

Joseph E. Schmalhofer
e-mail: Dylander@aol.com

Jobs? Yes
- Cost to post jobs: N/A
- Cost to see jobs: N/A
- Specialty: All
- Industry: N/A
- Country/Region/State/City: US

Resumes? Yes
- Cost to post resumes: Free
- Cost to see resumes: Free

Links to Jobs? Yes

Career Advice? Yes

Advice and links for the new graduate. Owner makes strong effort to include and maintain active links to companies that have at least 1 entry level job posted. New grads can link to their resumes. Straightforward site.

The Environmental Careers Organization

Association
www.eco.org

Celine Pering Environmental Careers Organization, Inc.; The
e-mail: cpering@eco.org

Jobs? Yes
- Cost to post jobs: Free
- Cost to see jobs: Free
- Specialty: Environmental
- Industry: All
- Country/Region/State/City: US

Resumes? Yes
- Cost to post resumes: Free
- Cost to see resumes: Free

Links to Jobs? Yes

Career Advice? Yes

This site promotes environmental careers and provides info on paid internships. Site maintains employment resources, conference schedules and job listings for its national non-profit owner. Several specialized links to other environmental resources are also maintained.

EOP

Publisher/Diversity
www.eop.com

John Miller EOP, Inc.
1160 East Jerhico Turnpike, Ste 200, Huntington, NY 11743
Phone: 516-421-9421

Jobs? Yes
- Cost to post jobs: Fee
- Cost to see jobs: Free
- Specialty: All
- Industry: All
- Country/Region/State/City: US

Resumes? No
- Cost to post resumes: N/A
- Cost to see resumes: N/A

Links to Jobs? Yes

Career Advice? Yes

Outstanding effort by a publisher to bring together diversity resources for the disabled, women, hispanics and african americans. Job advertisers are listed with contact information by publication. Site has several excellent downloadable articles. Conferences and job fairs are also maintained.

EPage Greater NYC Classifieds

Commercial Job Site
ep.com

Brad Waller
PO Box 2356, Redondo Beach, CA 90278
Phone: 310-792-0128 Fax: 310-792-0128 e-mail: epage@ep.com

Jobs? Yes
- Cost to post jobs: Fee
- Cost to see jobs: Free
- Specialty: All
- Industry: All
- Country/Region/State/City: US

Resumes? No
- Cost to post resumes: N/A
- Cost to see resumes: N/A

Links to Jobs? No

Career Advice? No

"Let Your Mouse Do The Walking", is their slogan and it fits. All kinds of classifieds jobs are here, really. Employers post and delete from the site for FREE. Headhunters pay $8 per month per region, $28/month for all regions (4). Ads are listed by region and area code. They can be browsed by type of ad (Full Time, P/T, Summer etc) or by area code or region. This has the look and feel of a local classified...a very local classified.

Equipment Leasing Association

Association
www.elaonline.com

Charles Britt
1300 N. 17th Street, Suite 1010, Arlington, VA 22209
Phone: 703-527-8655 Fax: 703-527-2649 e-mail: ela@elamail.com

Jobs? Yes
- Cost to post jobs: Fee
- Cost to see jobs: Free
- Specialty: Leasing
- Industry: Equipment Leasing
- Country/Region/State/City: US

Resumes? No
- Cost to post resumes: N/A
- Cost to see resumes: N/A

Links to Jobs? Yes

Career Advice? No

To post a job costs $295 for six weeks for an ELA member or $495 for non-members. They will not post your job until they get your check. They do take credit cards. Lots of info about the industry. Lists of links to minority sites.

Euro Jobs on Line

Commercial Job Site
www.belganet.be/~belganet/jobs/jobs.htm

e-mail: pub01103@innet.be

Jobs? Yes
- Cost to post jobs: Free
- Cost to see jobs: Free
- Specialty: All
- Industry: All
- Country/Region/State/City: Int'l

Resumes? No
- Cost to post resumes: N/A
- Cost to see resumes: N/A

Links to Jobs? Yes

Career Advice? No

Site has 108 registered companies that have posted jobs on this European web site. Has positions in countries such as Denmark, France, Germany, Ireland, Italy, Spain, United Kingdom and the US. Large listing also of European headhunters make this site one to watch in the future.

Execubank

Commercial Resume Site
www.realbank.com

RealBank
429 East 52nd Street, Suite 6-D, New York, NY 10022
Phone: 212-355-6159 Fax: 212-751-3797 e-mail: rebank@soho.ios.com

Jobs? Yes
- Cost to post jobs: Free
- Cost to see jobs: Free
- Specialty: Finance/Banking
- Industry: Finance/Banking
- Country/Region/State/City: US/E/NY/NYC

Resumes? Yes
- Cost to post resumes: Free
- Cost to see resumes: Free

Links to Jobs? No

Career Advice? No

Execubank bills itself as the resume bank of banking, finance, legal, marketing & sales executives. Not a large site but free to employers who want to post positions. Fee based for applicants who pay $99. Execubank will create confidential profiles and forward contact information and leads of interested companies.

Exec-U-Net

Commercial Job Site
www.execunet.com

Dave Opton Exec-U-Net, Inc.
25 Van Zant Street, Norwalk, CT 06855
Phone: 203-851-5180 Fax: 203-851-5177 e-mail: execunet@execunet.com

Jobs? No
- Cost to post jobs: N/A
- Cost to see jobs: N/A
- Specialty: All
- Industry: N/A
- Country/Region/State/City: ALL

Resumes? No
- Cost to post resumes: N/A
- Cost to see resumes: N/A

Links to Jobs? Yes

Career Advice? Yes

Applicants pay $110 (3 months) to $290 ($12 months) to receive job leads. Exec-U-Net is one of the strongest job search and career management networking organizations. Positions listed with Exec-U-Net are in all disciplines ($75k salary and up). Only fee paid subscribers can obtain listings. Employers or Search firms can list jobs at no charge. Ability to access job information from this site is still under construction. Organization has meetings through out the country so members/non-members can share job leads. Worth a look.

Extreme Resume Drop

College/University
www.mainquad.com/resumedrop.html

Mary Fitzgibbons Main Quad Global Comm for Coll Stud
1770 Union Street, San Francisco, CA 94123
Phone: 415-353-0686 Fax: 415-353-0685 e-mail: maryh@mainquad.com

Jobs? No
- Cost to post jobs: N/A
- Cost to see jobs: N/A
- Specialty: College Students
- Industry: All
- Country/Region/State/City: US

Resumes? Yes
- Cost to post resumes: Free
- Cost to see resumes: Free

Links to Jobs? Yes

Career Advice? No

Site will link you to over 200 corporations and college/job opening. Will take your resume and, only with your permission, send it to those recruiters who you select for free. Site is for recent college graduates or those looking for internships. Cost to employer ?

E-Span

Career Hub/Agent
www.espan.com

E-Span (Interactive Employment Network)
8440 Woodfield Crossing, Ste 170, Indianapolis, IN 46240
Phone: 800-682-2901 e-mail: info@e-span.com

Jobs? Yes
- Cost to post jobs: Fee
- Cost to see jobs: Free
- Specialty: All
- Industry: All
- Country/Region/State/City: US

Resumes? Yes
- Cost to post resumes: Free
- Cost to see resumes: Fee

Links to Jobs? Yes

Career Advice? Yes

Your Online Employment Connection

Job Search Choose from two powerful avenues to a new position. Search by keyword, or customize your search to fit your criteria and capabilities.

Career Companion(sm) Take advantage of more than 4,000 resources for professionals whose focus is on more than browsing.

HR Professional Tap into E-Span's rich HR resources to enhance your performance and productivity.

E-Span's New Career Mail Service

A major commercial venture that began with the Bulletin Boards, E-Span's job listings can be found on GEnie, AOL, and e-World at "e-span"; on Prodigy (PPNS90A), on Exec-PC and ChannelOne at (info@e-span.com), Delphi (cathygavin), IndustryNET (davidm.james), ComuServe (76702.1711) as well as the WWW. Employer job posting packages are available beginning at about $600 for 10 jobs (recently offered 1 posting for $99). A Career Forum on CompuServe and many other services are available. Employers posting positions on a three month contract ($1900) or longer can access resume database for searches.

Federal Jobs Digest

Publisher/Trade
www.jobsfed.com

Breakthrough Publications, Inc.
Phone: 800-824-5000 Fax: 914-762-5695 e-mail: webmaster@jobsfed.com

Jobs? Yes
- Cost to post jobs: N/A
- Cost to see jobs: Free
- Specialty: Government Jobs
- Industry: US Government
- Country/Region/State/City: US

Resumes? Yes
- Cost to post resumes: Fee
- Cost to see resumes: N/A

Links to Jobs? Yes

Career Advice? No

Site has direct contact information on Federal jobs around the country. Site charges $40 to advise you which jobs will match your qualifications. You send them your resume and they must do a search of the federal job database to match your skills with current openings. May save you some time but they take 3-4 weeks to get you back the info and the jobs could be filled by then.

F-o-r-t-u-n-e Personnel Consultants

Placement/Search/Temp
www.fpcweb.com

Ed Brochin F-o-r-t-u-n-e Franchise Corporation
1155 Avenue of the Americas, 15th Floor, NY, NY 10036

Jobs? Yes
- Cost to post jobs: Fee
- Cost to see jobs: Free
- Specialty: All
- Industry: All
- Country/Region/State/City: US

Resumes? No
- Cost to post resumes: N/A
- Cost to see resumes: N/A

Links to Jobs? Yes

Career Advice? Yes

Job seekers can connect to more than 60+ independently owned offices of this permanent and interim placement firm. Excellent feature is the ability to search from 30+ specialty and industry categories to target in on the offices that specialize in your areas of interest. Connect directly to those offices that have home pages or send them an e-mail resume.

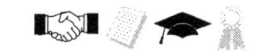

FedWorld Information Network

Government
www.fedworld.gov/jobs/jobsearch.html

US Government
Phone: 703-487-4850 e-mail: webmaster@fedworld.gov

Jobs? Yes
- Cost to post jobs: Free
- Cost to see jobs: Free
- Specialty: All
- Industry: Government
- Country/Region/State/City: US

Resumes? No
- Cost to post resumes: N/A
- Cost to see resumes: N/A

Links to Jobs? No

Career Advice? Yes

Major port of entry to the government's www presence and their jobs. Unfortunately the easiest jobs to track down are those for the Dept. of Interior. Applicants can also search a database of 1500 U.S. Government job announcements updated daily.

Finding A Job

Company
www.dbisna.com/dbis/jobs/vjobhunt.htm

Dun and Bradstreet Information Services
Phone: 800-738-4638 e-mail: employers@dbisna.com

Jobs? No
- Cost to post jobs: N/A
- Cost to see jobs: N/A
- Specialty: N/A
- Industry: N/A
- Country/Region/State/City: Int'l & US

Resumes? No
- Cost to post resumes: N/A
- Cost to see resumes: N/A

Links to Jobs? No

Career Advice? Yes

Information provider is selling its business directory disk for linking to thousands of companies as well as reports on individual companies at $20 a pop. This site is misleading unless research is your game.

Finding and Getting a Job

Career Management
edie.cprost.sfu.ca/~gophers/find.html

Quinn Merio
e-mail: memo@sfu.co

Jobs? No
- Cost to post jobs: N/A
- Cost to see jobs: N/A
- Specialty: N/A
- Industry: N/A
- Country/Region/State/City: N/A

Resumes? No
- Cost to post resumes: N/A
- Cost to see resumes: N/A

Links to Jobs? No

Career Advice? Yes

Nicely organized, quickly downloadable career management advice in bits and pieces just short enough to make the point and long enough to be useful. Has added a strong list of Canadian links to help you in your job search.

Finishing.com

Commercial Job Site
www.finishing.com/Directory/wanted.html

Ted Mooney
14 Fiddlers Elbow, Kinnellon, NJ 07405
Phone: 201-838-1346 Fax: 201-283-0766 e-mail: tmooney@intac.com

Jobs? Yes
- Cost to post jobs: Free
- Cost to see jobs: Free
- Specialty: All
- Industry: Finishing
- Country/Region/State/City: US

Resumes? No
- Cost to post resumes: N/A
- Cost to see resumes: N/A

Links to Jobs? No

Career Advice? No

The "Home Page of the Finishing Industry" contains a jobs page with positions related to anodizing, buffing, conversion coating, metal finishing, painting, polishing and more. Simple and scrollable. Free posting for employers.

Food and Drug Packaging

Publisher/Trade Magazine
www.fdp.com

Carole Orlando
210 South 5th Street, Ste. 202, St. Charles, IL 60174
Phone: 708-377-0100 Fax: 708-377-1678

Jobs? Yes
- Cost to post jobs: Fee
- Cost to see jobs: Free
- Specialty: Engineering/Packaging
- Industry: Packaging
- Country/Region/State/City: US

Resumes? No
- Cost to post resumes: N/A
- Cost to see resumes: N/A

Links to Jobs? No

Career Advice? No

Employers advertise in this nicihe publication but the positions are not posted at their website until the magazine is published.

For The Record

Publisher/Trade
www.gvpub.com

Great Valley Publishing Company
1288 Valley Forge Road, Valley Forge, PA 19482
Phone: 800-278-4400 Fax: 610-917-9040 e-mail: sales@gvpub.com

Jobs? Yes
- Cost to post jobs: Fee
- Cost to see jobs: Free
- Specialty: Health Care/Health Information
- Industry: Health Care
- Country/Region/State/City: US

Resumes? No
- Cost to post resumes: N/A
- Cost to see resumes: N/A

Links to Jobs? Yes

Career Advice? No

Health Information Management opportunities are available from this monthly publication.

Forty Plus of Northern California

Association/Diversity
web.sirius.com/~40plus

Forty Plus
740 Lockheed Street, Oakland, CA 94603
Phone: 510-430-2400 Fax: 510-430-1750 e-mail: 40plus@sirius.com

Jobs? No
- Cost to post jobs: N/A
- Cost to see jobs: N/A
- Specialty: All
- Industry: N/A
- Country/Region/State/City: US

Resumes? Yes
- Cost to post resumes: Fee
- Cost to see resumes: Free

Links to Jobs? US

Career Advice? No

Awkward setup for employers to respond to candidate info: Candidates first post a resume (synopsis) in 10 easy to search categories. Employers must fax interest with candidate code to 40+. No cost to the employer. Candidates must be members of 40 plus and make $40k. This site has links to several other Forty Plus Web sites and lists contact information to at least 20 more around the US.

Franklin Search Group

Placement/Search Firm
www.medmarket.com/tenants/fsg/postjobs.htm#

Dr. Frank Heasley Franklin Search Group
5632 SW 88 Terace, Cooper City, FL 33328
Phone: 954-434-5332 Fax: 305-434-4840 e-mail: fheasley@chemistry.com

Jobs? Yes
- Cost to post jobs: Free
- Cost to see jobs: Fee
- Specialty: Science/Health Care
- Industry: Biotechnology/Pharmaceutical
- Country/Region/State/City: US

Resumes? No
- Cost to post resumes: Free
- Cost to see resumes: Fee

Links to Jobs? No

Career Advice? No

Check out http://www.chemistry.com Site serves the pharmaceutical, biotech and medical industries with job listings and a resume database. Employers pay several hundred dollars per quarter to search the resume database. Over 100 jobs listed which employers can do for free but candidates must submit their resume to site database to obtain contact information.

Frasernet

Association/Diversity
www.frasernet.com

George Fraser Success Guide
e-mail: fraser@frasernet

Jobs? Yes
- Cost to post jobs: Fee
- Cost to see jobs: Free
- Specialty: All
- Industry: N/A
- Country/Region/State/City: US

Resumes? Yes
- Cost to post resumes: Fee
- Cost to see resumes: Free

Links to Jobs? No

Career Advice? Yes

"Success Guide" is a popular business-networking guide for African Americans and this web site extends George Fraser's reach and networking skills into cyberspace. The site is fully operational with jobs, contacts and opportunities. Members have the option of going public with their resumes. Employers can find vendors, see resumes for free or post opportunities for 6 months for $59.00 (all done on-line).

Future Access Employment Guide

Commercial Job Site
futureaccess.com:80/employ.html

PO Box 584, Saratoga, CA 95071-0584
Phone: 408-867-3719 e-mail: webmaster@futureaccess.com

Jobs? Yes
- Cost to post jobs: Fee
- Cost to see jobs: Free
- Specialty: All
- Industry: All
- Country/Region/State/City: US

Resumes? Yes
- Cost to post resumes: Free
- Cost to see resumes: Free

Links to Jobs? No

Career Advice? No

Site where you can post your resume for free and it can be seen the same way. For employers the cost is $10 per month to post a job. Updates resume database daily while being easy to use.

Future Business Centre On-Line

Commercial
www.webb.com/future

503 Plainsboro Road, P.O.Box 3206, Princeton, NJ 08543
Phone: 609-734-9100 Fax: 609-734-8490 e-mail: futurejob@webb.com

Jobs? Yes
- Cost to post jobs: Fee
- Cost to see jobs: Free
- Specialty: All
- Industry: All
- Country/Region/State/City: Int'l/US

Resumes? Yes
- Cost to post resumes: Free
- Cost to see resumes: Fee

Links to Jobs? Yes

Career Advice? Yes

Employers can search this new site's database for $100 per search, post an open position for $100/4 wks or post confidentially for $250. And finally, by paying 15% you (the employer) can have a live person do an "Express SEARCH" to fill your position. Seems to us that these owners missed out on their pricing when the most successful sites are providing significantly more for less cost.

Future Med

Search Engine
ourworld.compuserve.com/homepages/futuremed

Suite 94, #305-4625 Varsity Drive N.W., Calgary, Alberta, Canada T3A OZ9
e-mail: 102562.632@compuserve.com

Jobs? Yes
- Cost to post jobs: N/A
- Cost to see jobs: N/A
- Specialty: Health Care
- Industry: Health Care
- Country/Region/State/City: Int'l./US

Resumes? No
- Cost to post resumes: N/A
- Cost to see resumes: N/A

Links to Jobs? Yes

Career Advice? No

Specialized job "Search Engine" under construction. Owner claims that you can input up to three keywords and the search engine will produce medical related links in 28 diferent categories. Not working at time of review. Section on external links listed several emergency medical sites. Int'l. section was simply selling a directory. Worth a look if the search engine becomes functional. May have openings posted at the site in the future but only 1 was listed.

CAREERXROADS©
Job, Resume & Career Management Sites on the World Wide Web
• The 1997 Directory •

The Gate

Publisher/Newspaper
www.sfgate.com/classified/index.html

Jobs? Yes
- Cost to post jobs: Fee
- Cost to see jobs: Free
- Specialty: All
- Industry: N/A
- Country/Region/State/City: US/W/CA/ San Francisco

Resumes? No
- Cost to post resumes: N/A
- Cost to see resumes: N/A

Links to Jobs? No

Career Advice? No

San Francisco Chronicle and Examiner Classifieds. Can search ads by the day of the week while showing 100% in column only. Display advertisements are not shown. Limited articles to gain information on the area are shown on this site.

Georgia Job Bank

Commercial Resume Site
www.mindsprin.com/~exchange/jobbank/ga/jobs.html

JobBank
3232 Cobb Parkway, Ste. 611, Atlanta, GA 30339
Phone: 404-815-0770 e-mail: resume@jobbankusa.com

Jobs? No
- Cost to post jobs: N/A
- Cost to see jobs: N/A
- Specialty: All
- Industry: N/A
- Country/Region/State/City: US/SE/GA

Resumes? Yes
- Cost to post resumes: Fee
- Cost to see resumes: Free

Links to Jobs? Yes

Career Advice? No

JobBank is a resume distribution service and subset of JobBank USA (See listing). Resume posting costs $24.95. Make sure you know where your resume is going.

GeoWeb for GIS/GPS/RS

Industry Vendor
www.ggrweb.com

Henry Hoffman GeoWeb
1271 Country Place Circle, Houston, TX 77079
Phone: 713-994-9903 Fax: 713-988-0071 e-mail: geoweb@ggrweb.com

Jobs? Yes
- Cost to post jobs: Free
- Cost to see jobs: Free
- Specialty: Geographic Systems
- Industry: N/A
- Country/Region/State/City: US

Resumes? Yes
- Cost to post resumes: Fee
- Cost to see resumes: Free

Links to Jobs? Yes

Career Advice? Yes

Positions available for professionals with geographic information systems, global positioning systems and remote sensing companies. Applicants pay $19 to post resumes for 3 months. Employers search for free.

Get a Job!

Commercial Job Site
www.getajob.com

Phone: 503-653-9912 Fax: 503-725-0834

Jobs? Yes
- Cost to post jobs: Fee
- Cost to see jobs: Free
- Specialty: All
- Industry: N/A
- Country/Region/State/City: US

Resumes? No
- Cost to post resumes: N/A
- Cost to see resumes: N/A

Links to Jobs? Yes

Career Advice? Yes

Links to employers with technical positions. Claims database has several hundred opportunities and claims "dozens" added each week. Search engine is limited. Career information and bookstore.

Getting A Job

Company/College
www.americanexpress.com/student/moneypit/getjob/getajob.html

American Express University

Jobs? Yes
- Cost to post jobs: N/A
- Cost to see jobs: Free
- Specialty: N/A
- Industry: N/A
- Country/Region/State/City: US

Resumes? No
- Cost to post resumes: N/A
- Cost to see resumes: N/A

Links to Jobs? Yes

Career Advice? Yes

Nice college site with tips on self assessment, resume design and Princeton Reviews, "How to Survive Without Your Parent's Money". Internships listed from among the top companies in the country.

Have you found a site that isn't listed in CAREERXROADS?
Have you REGISTERED to receive FREE updates?
Keep us informed.
We'll keep you informed.

CAREERXROADS
Where Talent and Opportunity Connect on the Internet

CAREERXROADS©
Job, Resume & Career Management Sites on the World Wide Web
• The 1997 Directory •

Getting Past Go: A Survival Guide for College

Career Management/College

www.lattanze.loyola.edu:80/mongen/home.html

Chris Webb Monumental General Insurance Group
1111 N. Charles St., Baltimore, MD 21201
Phone: 410-685-5500 Fax: 410-347-8693

Jobs? No
- Cost to post jobs: N/A
- Cost to see jobs: N/A
- Specialty: All
- Industry: N/A
- Country/Region/State/City: ALL

Resumes? No
- Cost to post resumes: N/A
- Cost to see resumes: N/A

Links to Jobs? Yes

Career Advice? Yes

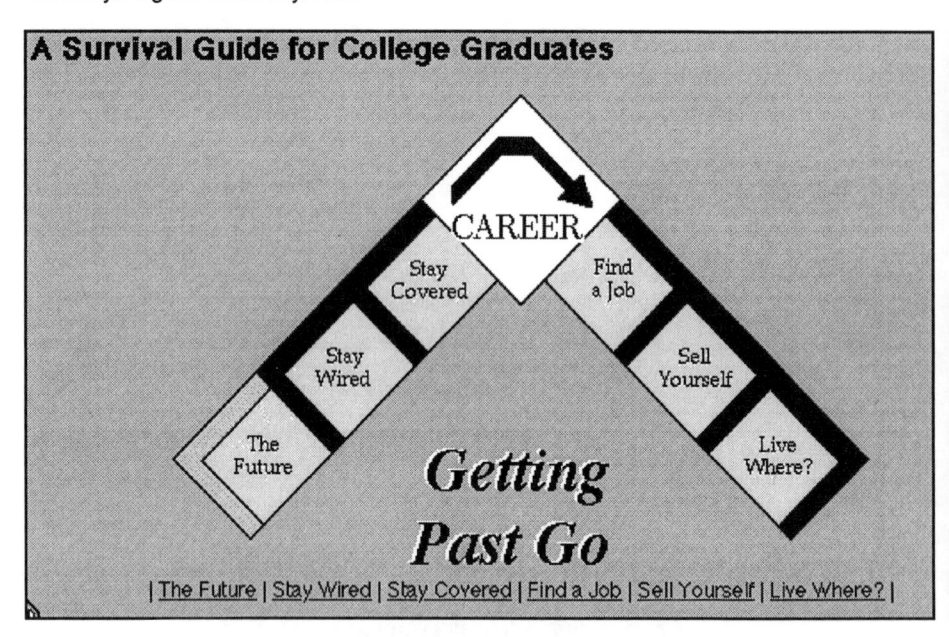

A broad range of advice for the college grad is offered covering all the right bases. From marketing yourself to health insurance, Getting Past Go also includes information on writing a resume, finding a job or insurance, moving to a new area and much more. Creative well written articles on career management for the entry level professional make this one of our top picks.

CAREERXROADS©
Job, Resume & Career Management Sites on the World Wide Web
• The 1997 Directory •

Global Job Net

Links to Jobs
riceinfo.rice.edu/projects/careersChannelsix.html

Michael Breu Rice University
9 Sunset Blvd, Houston, TX 7705-1898
Phone: 713-630-8191 e-mail: breu@rice.edu

Jobs? No
- Cost to post jobs: N/A
- Cost to see jobs: N/A
- Specialty: Links
- Industry: N/A
- Country/Region/State/City: Int'l

Resumes? No
- Cost to post resumes: N/A
- Cost to see resumes: N/A

Links to Jobs? Yes

Career Advice? No

Links to international job sites in Africa, Asia, Australia, Europe & India. Links also to several major sites but that is all there is.

Global Job Services

Commercial Job Site/Agent
www.indirect,com/www/dtomczyk/

Dee Tomczyk Global Job Services
1001 N. Pasadena #25, Mesa, AZ 85201
Phone: 602-655-1790 Fax: 602-655-1722

Jobs? Yes
- Cost to post jobs: N/A
- Cost to see jobs: N/A
- Specialty: N/A
- Industry: N/A
- Country/Region/State/City: Int'l./US

Resumes? Yes
- Cost to post resumes: Fee
- Cost to see resumes: N/A

Links to Jobs? No

Career Advice? No

Job seekers pay $25 for customized help from owner who conducts three searches of the internet based on your (resume) skill criteria. Refund guarantee if owner doesn't come up with at least one legitimate match.

Good Works (Social Service)

Association
www.essential.org/goodworks/

Good Works
PO Box 19405, Washington, DC 20036
e-mail: ei@essential.org

Jobs? Yes
- Cost to post jobs: Free
- Cost to see jobs: Free
- Specialty: N/A
- Industry: Non-Profit
- Country/Region/State/City: ALL

Resumes? No
- Cost to post resumes: N/A
- Cost to see resumes: N/A

Links to Jobs? US

Career Advice? Yes

National directory of social change organizations, public interest careers, companies and typical jobs for each. Site has a map of the USA. Click on a state to find specifics about organizations and jobs in that area. Site has direct contact information about volunteer positions and projects around the country.

Gordon Group Home Page

Links to Jobs
www.owt.com/jobsinfo/jobsinfo.htm

Bob Gordon Partenariat CanWorkNet Partnership
4th Floor, Place du Portage, Ottawa, Ontario, Canada K1A0J9
Phone: 819-994-3556 e-mail: gordons@oneworld.owt.com

Jobs? No
- Cost to post jobs: N/A
- Cost to see jobs: N/A
- Specialty: Links
- Industry: N/A
- Country/Region/State/City: Int'l/Canada

Resumes? No
- Cost to post resumes: N/A
- Cost to see resumes: N/A

Links to Jobs? Yes

Career Advice? Yes

Lots of links to numerous sites with job and career management information that can be seen in easy to read alphabetical order. Also has included "Tools of the Trade" to help you in your job search. Also has recently placed a link for positions in the Mid-Columbia area of Canada.

CAREERXROADS©
Job, Resume & Career Management Sites on the World Wide Web
• The 1997 Directory •

GrapeVine

Career Management
jobs.index.com/gv.htm

Ray Osborne
1656 Espanola Avenue, Ste 7, Holly Hill, FL 32117

Jobs? No
- Cost to post jobs: N/A
- Cost to see jobs: N/A
- Specialty: All
- Industry: All
- Country/Region/State/City: US

Resumes? No
- Cost to post resumes: N/A
- Cost to see resumes: N/A

Links to Jobs? Yes

Career Advice? Yes

A forum for job networking managed by an individual with a strong commitment to offer help. Interesting tools and ideas. We could all use more Ray Osborne's. Some specialty's such as human resources have e-mail based methods (Listserv) available to receive job leads. Also provides a list of job hot lines that you can obtain. Ray manages four sites at present and has some interesting things to say.

Hap Hiring Assistant

Commercial Resume Site
www.sonic.net/~richw/zjobapps.html#top

Rich Wingerter Zip Consulting & Design
PO Box 66682, Scotts Valley, CA 95067
Phone: 408-336-9285 Fax: 408-336-9283 e-mail: rich@sonic.net

Jobs? No
- Cost to post jobs: N/A
- Cost to see jobs: N/A
- Specialty: Rates Applicants Resumes
- Industry: All
- Country/Region/State/City: US

Resumes? Yes
- Cost to post resumes: Free
- Cost to see resumes: Fee

Links to Jobs? No

Career Advice? No

Resume database that takes the process one step further by rating the skills of each applicant against your job criterion.

Hard@Work

Career Management
www.hardatwork.com

Dennis Murphy Hard @Work, Inc.
210 Commerce Boulevard, Round Rock, TX 78664
Phone: 800-580-5421 e-mail: demwit@hardatwork.com

Jobs? No
- Cost to post jobs: N/A
- Cost to see jobs: N/A
- Specialty: Career Management
- Industry: N/A
- Country/Region/State/City: US

Resumes? No
- Cost to post resumes: N/A
- Cost to see resumes: N/A

Links to Jobs? No

Career Advice? Yes

Fun site with good intentions. Has great employee relations questions/answers with interesting career advice. Interesting articles and special sections where you can e-mail questions to stump the mentor on employee related issues. This is like having an interactive human resource department. Unique site that is definitely worth visiting.

Harry's BBS and Internet Job Hotlist

Lists &/or Links
rescomp.stanford.edu/jobs-bbs.html

Harry Lemon
e-mail: hlemon@netcom.com

Jobs? No
- Cost to post jobs: N/A
- Cost to see jobs: N/A
- Specialty: N/A
- Industry: N/A
- Country/Region/State/City: US

Resumes? No
- Cost to post resumes: N/A
- Cost to see resumes: N/A

Links to Jobs? Yes

Career Advice? Yes

Another icon, Harry Lemon's list of Job Bulletin Boards is among the most comprehensive of any on the net. Gives you some idea of how many direct dial job databases are still working to connect to the internet. Many have already come online.

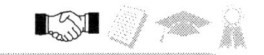

Hartford Courant

Publisher/Newspaper
www.courant.com

285 Broad Street, Hartford, CT 06115
Phone: 800-524-4242 Fax: 860-241-3864

Jobs? Yes
- Cost to post jobs: Fee
- Cost to see jobs: Free
- Specialty: All
- Industry: N/A
- Country/Region/State/City: US/NE/CT

Resumes? No
- Cost to post resumes: N/A
- Cost to see resumes: N/A

Links to Jobs? No

Career Advice? No

Help wanted classifieds printed in Sunday's newspaper are posted. This publisher participates in CareerPath (See CareerPath).

Health Careers Online

Commercial Job Site
www.healthcareers-online.com

Richard Sierra
PO Box 6103, Hollywood, CA 33081
Phone: 800-322-1463 Fax: 954-680-0995 e-mail: rsierra@interpoint.net

Jobs? Yes
- Cost to post jobs: Fee
- Cost to see jobs: Free
- Specialty: Health Care
- Industry: Health Care
- Country/Region/State/City: US

Resumes? No
- Cost to post resumes: N/A
- Cost to see resumes: N/A

Links to Jobs? Yes

Career Advice? Yes

Positions listed in all health care fields. Applicants can respond to a position listing while conducting their search via e-mail to most jobs listed. Cost to employer is $125 per position (30 days) with packages for multiple listings. Positions are up on the net within 24 hours of receipt. The site advertises through Valley Forge Publications (PT&OT Today, RT IMAGE and MT Today, Pharmacy Today and the Journal of the APHA, Health Careers Online) to attract a broad range of allied health care jobseekers.

Heart Career Connections

Career Hub
www.career.com

Sandhya Dave   Heart Advertising
5150 El Camino Real, Ste D33, Los Altos, CA 94022
Phone: 415-903-5800   Fax: 415-903-5848   e-mail: webmaster@career.com

Jobs? Yes
- Cost to post jobs: Fee
- Cost to see jobs: Free
- Specialty: All
- Industry: All
- Country/Region/State/City: US

Resumes? Yes
- Cost to post resumes: Free
- Cost to see resumes: Fee

Links to Jobs? Yes

Career Advice? Yes

Conducts on-line Virtual job Fairs (CyberFair) charging $5000 (check data available on success rates before trying this) but you would be hard pressed to find a better job site design with a vision of the possibilities. Heart deserves a look. Future CyberFair dates listed at the site. Jobs posted by companies are searchable by Company, Location and Discipline. Separate category for New Graduates. Nice feature is that the site is reachable by telnet, ftp, gopher and as a direct dial up. Additional services include full range job postings for $150/2 weeks, hyperlinks and home pages. Resumes posted free and available to client companies via e-mail.

Help Wanted

Commercial Job Site
www.helpwanted.com

Recruitment On_Line, Inc.
771 Boston Post Road, Marlboro, MA 01752
Phone: 508-485-1230   Fax: 508-481-9616   e-mail: editor@helpwanted.com

Jobs? Yes
- Cost to post jobs: Fee
- Cost to see jobs: Free
- Specialty: All
- Industry: helpwanted.com
- Country/Region/State/City: US

Resumes? Yes
- Cost to post resumes: Free
- Cost to see resumes: Fee

Links to Jobs? Yes

Career Advice? No

Lot of jobs, resumes. $1200 for a 1 year membership to list 15 jobs per month ($15 for extra). Other packages available. Free to post resumes that can be accessed by member companies.

Help Wanted-USA

Career Hub
iccweb.com/employ.html

James Gonyea Gonyea and Associates, Inc.
3543 Enterprise Road East, Safety Harbor, Florida 34695
Phone: 813-725-9600

Jobs? Yes
- Cost to post jobs: Fee
- Cost to see jobs: Free
- Specialty: All
- Industry: All
- Country/Region/State/City: US

Resumes? Yes
- Cost to post resumes: Fee
- Cost to see resumes: Free

Links to Jobs? Yes

Career Advice? Yes

Internet Career Connection
A Service of Gonyea & Associates, Inc.

New and improved - now with blazing fast search engines!

HW-USA is a centralized database of jobs and resumes at the Internet Career Connection site. Key word searched by applicants, the database is built through a network of interdependent sites in cties throughout the country. Accessible from America Online as well as the internet, James Gonyea is one of the pioneers in electronic recruiting. Site claims weekly listings of 10,000 jobs. Employers pay $75 for a 2 week posting.

High Technology Career Centre

Job Fair/Trade Magazine
hightechcareers.com/

West Tech
4701 Patrick Henry Drive, #1901, Santa Clara, CA 95054
Phone: 408-970-8800 e-mail: webmaster@vjf.com

Jobs? Yes
- Cost to post jobs: Fee
- Cost to see jobs: Free
- Specialty: IT
- Industry: All
- Country/Region/State/City: US

Resumes? Yes
- Cost to post resumes: Free
- Cost to see resumes: Fee

Links to Jobs? Yes

Career Advice? Yes

This site links directly into West Tech's (a well known West Coast Job Fair organization) resume database and the job postings from the owner's High Tech Careers Magazine. If you want to advertise in their magazine, prices start from about $1,500. The site also has a career resouce center with links to career sites, articles, etc. Site states it has a resume tracking system and will also be your agent to match your requirements for your jobs.

High Technology Careers/Links

Links/Diversity
www.vjf.com/pub/docs/jobsearch.html

Cynthia Chin-Lee West Tech
4701 Patrick Henry Drive, #1901, Santa Clara, CA 95054
Phone: 408-970-8800 e-mail: cchinlee@aol.com

Jobs? No
- Cost to post jobs: N/A
- Cost to see jobs: N/A
- Specialty: N/A
- Industry: N/A
- Country/Region/State/City: US

Resumes? No
- Cost to post resumes: N/A
- Cost to see resumes: N/A

Links to Jobs? Yes

Career Advice? Yes

Links to numerous minority sites for jobs and career guidance. Nice lists of links. This site is part of Westech Career Expo.

Hong Kong Jobs

Commercial Job Site
www.hkjobs.com

Hong Kong

Jobs? Yes
- Cost to post jobs: Fee
- Cost to see jobs: Free
- Specialty: All
- Industry: All
- Country/Region/State/City: Int'l/Hong Kong

Resumes? Yes
- Cost to post resumes: Free
- Cost to see resumes: Fee

Links to Jobs? No

Career Advice? No

Direct company contact/information is present on site to see for technical/non-technical positions. Also has listing of headhunters for Hong Kong as well. You can post your resume to this site for free and it stay on the site for six months. You will need to register to get additional info as we cosuld not find an e-mail address or other contact info.

Hong Kong Standard

Publisher/Newspaper
www.hkstandard.com/online/job/english/engjob.htm

Hongkong Standard Newspapers Ltd.
Hongkong
Phone: 852-279-82647 e-mail: jobmarket@hkstandard.com

Jobs? Yes
- Cost to post jobs: Fee
- Cost to see jobs: Free
- Specialty: All
- Industry: All
- Country/Region/State/City: Int'l/HongKong

Resumes? Yes
- Cost to post resumes: Free
- Cost to see resumes: Fee

Links to Jobs? No

Career Advice? No

Hong Kong newspaper that allows you to fill out a resume form that goes directly to the company that posted the advertisement for the position you are interested in. Also has direct contact information. A newspaper ahead of its time.

Hospital Web

College/University
www.132.183.145.103/hospitalweb.html

John Lester
e-mail: lester@helix.mgh.harvard.edu

Jobs? No
- Cost to post jobs: N/A
- Cost to see jobs: N/A
- Specialty: Health Care
- Industry: Health Care
- Country/Region/State/City: Health Care

Resumes? No
- Cost to post resumes: N/A
- Cost to see resumes: N/A

Links to Jobs? Yes

Career Advice? No

Large list of hospitals and links. Many with jobs. It will take time to wade through however.

Hospitality Net

Commercial Job Site
www.hospitalitynet.nl

Henri Roelings Hospitality Net
Akersteenweg 31, Maastricht, Netherlands 6226 HR
Phone: 314-336-26600 Fax: 314-336-26770 e-mail: henri@hospitalitynet.nl

Jobs? Yes
- Cost to post jobs: Free
- Cost to see jobs: Free
- Specialty: All
- Industry: Hospitality
- Country/Region/State/City: Hospitality

Resumes? Yes
- Cost to post resumes: Free
- Cost to see resumes: Free

Links to Jobs? No

Career Advice? No

Online service for hospitality professionals. Employers can post jobs directly and review applicant profiles online. Site provides demographics of its 15,000 visitors/per month which include: hotel execs (60%), consultants (10%) and students (10%). About 50% are US based. Jobs posted range from chefs to CEOs. International scope. Student internships listed as well. Easy to see and use. Applicants post resumes for free.

Hot Jobs

Commercial Job Site
www.hotjobs.com

Otec Inc.
24 West 40th Street, 11th floor, New York, New York 10128
Phone: 212-840-8600 Fax: 212-768-8309 e-mail: ginna@hotjobs.com

Jobs? Yes
- Cost to post jobs: Fee
- Cost to see jobs: Free
- Specialty: Information Systems
- Industry: Information Systems
- Country/Region/State/City: US

Resumes? Yes
- Cost to post resumes: Free
- Cost to see resumes: Fee

Links to Jobs? No

Career Advice? Yes

Computer related jobs listed. Nice search engine for scanning open positions or you can look at all of their openings going down a long list. They had 413 jobs listed from major corporations when we last visited. Can send your resume direct via e-mail as jobs are coded. Resumes go directly to member companies who pay $500 per month to post positions.

Houston Chronicle Interactive

Publisher/Newspaper
www.chron.com

Houston Chronicle
801 Texas Avenue, Houston, TX 77002
Phone: 800-669-4600

Jobs? Yes
- Cost to post jobs: Fee
- Cost to see jobs: Free
- Specialty: All
- Industry: N/A
- Country/Region/State/City: US/SW/TX/Houston

Resumes? No
- Cost to post resumes: N/A
- Cost to see resumes: N/A

Links to Jobs? No

Career Advice? No

Employers pay an additional $25 to the cost of the ad placed in the Houston Chronicle Sunday Classified pages. Another paper that only has classified advertisements up on the net.

HR World

Commercial Job Site
www.hrworld.com

David Mahal DGM Associates
P.O.Box 10639, Marina del Rey, CA 90295-6639
e-mail: dgm@hrworld.com

Jobs? Yes
- Cost to post jobs: Free
- Cost to see jobs: Free
- Specialty: Human Resources
- Industry: N/A
- Country/Region/State/City: US

Resumes? Yes
- Cost to post resumes: Free
- Cost to see resumes: Free

Links to Jobs? No

Career Advice? No

Owner publishes HR/PC Quarterly. Good human resource links, articles and association information. Employers post ings for free.

HRIM Mall

Commercial Job Site/Agent
www.hrimmall.com

Jim Morrone PeoplePros, Inc.
5603-B W. Friendly Ave. #269, Greensboro, NC 27410
Phone: 910-643-8241 Fax: 910-643-9519 e-mail: info@hrimmall.com

Jobs? Yes
- Cost to post jobs: Free
- Cost to see jobs: Free
- Specialty: Human Resources/HRIS
- Industry: All
- Country/Region/State/City: US

Resumes? No
- Cost to post resumes: N/A
- Cost to see resumes: N/A

Links to Jobs? Yes

Career Advice? Yes

Register your e-mail with the site and the owners will send you updates when new jobs are posted. This site is well laid out with tons of current information on the different areas of HR. Jobs are posted within 48 hours of receipt.

Human Element

Placement/Search/Temp
mindlink.net/vci/thehp.htm

Virtual Connections Inc.
4043 Shone Road, N. Vancouver, British Columbia, Canada V7G2N3
Phone: 604-929-2262 e-mail: vci@vciglobal.com

Jobs? No
- Cost to post jobs: N/A
- Cost to see jobs: N/A
- Specialty: Recruitment/Assessment
- Industry: All
- Country/Region/State/City: Int'l/Canada

Resumes? Yes
- Cost to post resumes: Free
- Cost to see resumes: Fee

Links to Jobs? Yes

Career Advice? Yes

Interesting site as it tries to be all things to recruiting. Pre-screens resumes or you can go into their database and if you hire someone you owe the site 3.5% for a WWW search, or 5.0% of the annual first year's compensation if the candidate is pulled from their database. They also will do newsgroup postings of jobs for $30 each. Some interesting concepts and may be a site to watch.

Hyper Media Resumes & Career Center

Career Hub
www.webcom.com/resumes/

Interactive Executive Professionals
e-mail: siteadmin@webcom.com

Jobs? Yes
- Cost to post jobs: Fee
- Cost to see jobs: Free
- Specialty: All
- Industry: All
- Country/Region/State/City: US

Resumes? Yes
- Cost to post resumes: Fee
- Cost to see resumes: Free

Links to Jobs? Yes

Career Advice? Yes

Interesting place in that they will post your resume to their site as well as other web sites, add sound to your copy if you wish. Costs run from $29.95 +. For employers resume search is free and it can be done by a key word search engine. Site has a recruiters forum where you can ask questions or obtain answers regarding your career search.

ICS NY Job Listings

Association
www.iicsny.org/jobs

Thiery Sansaricq International Interactive Comm. Soc. of NY
Phone: 212-736-4427 e-mail: theory@walrus.com

Jobs? Yes
- Cost to post jobs: Free
- Cost to see jobs: Free
- Specialty:
- Industry: Publishing
- Country/Region/State/City: USNY

Resumes? No
- Cost to post resumes: N/A
- Cost to see resumes: N/A

Links to Jobs? Yes

Career Advice? Yes

The International Interactive Communications Society (IICS) is the nation's oldest professional organization for interactive arts and technology professionals. They have 30 US chapters and 5 in foreign countries. They bring together people in multimedia /publishing/entertainment and related professions.

Have you found a site that isn't listed in CAREERXROADS?

Have you REGISTERED to receive FREE updates?

Keep us informed.

We'll keep you informed.

CAREERXROADS
Where Talent and Opportunity Connect on the Internet

IEEE

Association
www.ieee.org

William R. Anderson Institute of Electrical and Electronic Eng.
445 Hoes Lane, Po Box 1331, Piscataway, NJ 08855-1331
Phone: 800-678-3222 Fax: 202-785-0835 e-mail: rossr@ix.netcom.com

Jobs? Yes
- Cost to post jobs: Fee
- Cost to see jobs: Free
- Specialty: Engineering/Electrical/Electronic
- Industry: All
- Country/Region/State/City: US

Resumes? No
- Cost to post resumes: N/A
- Cost to see resumes: N/A

Links to Jobs? Yes

Career Advice? Yes

IEEE UNITED STATES ACTIVITIES

Promoting the Career and Public Policy Interests of IEEE's U.S. Members

Institute of Electrical and Electronics Engineers, Inc.
United States Activities

Welcome to IEEE-USA

315,000 electrical/electronic engineers belong to the IEEE. This site has openings categorized on regional basis. Members can request future job postings be forwarded by e--mail. Employer cost is $15-25 per posting. Newest service is a free resume database for members (See ResumeLink). A "salary calculator", job site links and job fair information are provided. Top site for the profession.

IHRIM Chapter/Pacific Northwest

Association
www.ihrim.org/chapters/pacificnorthwest/index.html

Christopher Platz IHRIM Pacific NW Chapter
PO Box 21345, , Seattle, Washington 98111-3345
Phone: 206-464-8130   e-mail: moreinfo@ihrim.org

Jobs? Yes
- Cost to post jobs: Free
- Cost to see jobs: Free
- Specialty: Human Resources
- Industry: HRIS
- Country/Region/State/City: US/Pacific Northwest

Resumes? No
- Cost to post resumes: N/A
- Cost to see resumes: N/A

Links to Jobs? Yes

Career Advice? Yes

Human Resource Information Management site providing knowledge of the use of technology /systems to HR folks. Only had 1 job posted when we visited. Lots of interestinge links such as salary surveys, international sites and others on numerous HR topics. Good starting point for HR info for Pacific Northwest.

Imcor-Provides Top-Level Executives

Placement/Search/Temp
www.webdirect.com/ct/imcor

Laura Copeland
100 Prospect Street, North Tower, Stamford, CT 06901
Phone: 203-975-8000 Fax: 203-975-8199 e-mail: info@imcor.com

Jobs? Yes
- Cost to post jobs: Fee
- Cost to see jobs: Free
- Specialty: All
- Industry: N/A
- Country/Region/State/City: US

Resumes? No
- Cost to post resumes: N/A
- Cost to see resumes: N/A

Links to Jobs? No

Career Advice? No

Imcor is one of the larger executive temporary firms whose clients are looking to try out key executives and then hire them on a permanent basis. They also handle temporary assignments, which is their forte. Typically high level positions in all fields. Applicants send their resume directly to Imcor via snail mail and then they match you with their current openings. Had numerous openings when we visited their site.

Impact Online

Commercial
www.impactonline.com

715 Colorado Avenue. Ste. 4, Palo Alto, CA 94303
Phone: 415-327-2389 Fax: 415-327-1395 e-mail: respond@impactonline.com

Jobs? Yes
- Cost to post jobs: Free
- Cost to see jobs: Free
- Specialty: All
- Industry: Non-Profit
- Country/Region/State/City: US

Resumes? No
- Cost to post resumes: N/A
- Cost to see resumes: N/A

Links to Jobs? Yes

Career Advice? Yes

Impact Online seeks to foster involvement with nonprofits by informing potential volunteers about nonprofit organizations and how to get involved with them. For someone looking for the balance in their career.

Info Louisiana

Government
state.la.us/

State of Louisiana
e-mail: webmaster@doc.state.la.us

Jobs? Yes
- Cost to post jobs: Free
- Cost to see jobs: Free
- Specialty: All
- Industry: Government
- Country/Region/State/City: US/S/LA

Resumes? No
- Cost to post resumes: N/A
- Cost to see resumes: N/A

Links to Jobs? Yes

Career Advice? No

Home Page for the State of LA. Select Job Information Search (JIS) to search jobs within the state and region by occupational category. Links to America's Job Bank/Fed World / US Dept. of Labor etc.

Infoseek

Links
www.infoseek.com

Bill Peck Infoseek Corporation
2620 Augustine Drive, Ste 250, Santa Clara, CA 95054
Phone: 408-982-4450 Fax: 408-986-1889 e-mail: corpsales@infoseek.com

Jobs? No
- Cost to post jobs: N/A
- Cost to see jobs: N/A
- Specialty: All
- Industry: All
- Country/Region/State/City: N/A

Resumes? No
- Cost to post resumes: N/A
- Cost to see resumes: N/A

Links to Jobs? Yes

Career Advice? Yes

One of the better Search Engines to retrieve new sites and updates on your search criteria. Plug in employment. Site can also be viewed in several foreign languages.

InJersey

Publisher/Newspaper
www.injersey.com

Asbury Park Press
3601 Highway 66, Neptune, NJ 07754
Phone: 908-922-6000

Jobs? Yes
- Cost to post jobs: Fee
- Cost to see jobs: Free
- Specialty: All
- Industry: N/A
- Country/Region/State/City: US/E/NJ/Asbury

Resumes? No
- Cost to post resumes: N/A
- Cost to see resumes: N/A

Links to Jobs? No

Career Advice? No

100% in-col, Display N/A Newspaper Help Wanted Classifieds. Help Wanted Display Ads are not included. No extra charges. Employers must pay for ad in Newspaper.

Insurance Career Center

Commercial Resume Site
www.connectyou.com:80/talent

Bob Taylor Connect You, Inc.
Phone: 410-266-1460 Fax: 800-394-6140 e-mail: connect@connectyou.com

Jobs? Yes
- Cost to post jobs: Fee
- Cost to see jobs: Free
- Specialty: Insurance
- Industry: Insurance
- Country/Region/State/City: US

Resumes? Yes
- Cost to post resumes: Fee
- Cost to see resumes: Fee

Links to Jobs? Yes

Career Advice? Yes

Interactive employment center dedicated to the insurance industry. Search job postings by title and salary level. Some direct e-mail links to send resume. Some career advice and insurance industry information. Limited links to other sites. Employers pay $75 for posting 2 months. Candidates pay $25 to post- graduates/students free. Only member companies ($550/year) can view resumes.

Have you found a site that isn't listed in CAREERXROADS?

Have you REGISTERED to receive FREE updates?

Keep us informed.

We'll keep you informed.

CAREERXROADS

Where Talent and Opportunity Connect on the Internet

CAREERXROADS©
Job, Resume & Career Management Sites on the World Wide Web
• The 1997 Directory •

Intellimatch

Commercial Resume/Agent
www.intellimatch.com

Kim La Barber Intellimatch
2107 N. First Street, San Jose, CA 95131
Phone: 408-441-1947 Fax: 408-441-7048 e-mail:

Jobs? No
- Cost to post jobs: N/A
- Cost to see jobs: N/A
- Specialty: All
- Industry: N/A
- Country/Region/State/City: US

Resumes? Yes
- Cost to post resumes: Fee
- Cost to see resumes: Fee

Links to Jobs? No

Career Advice? No

Intellimatch's sophistication and technology is very appealing despite the costs. Job seekers will spend approximately 30 minutes using a form based application called Power Resume Builder to input. Prospective employers use the site's Candidate Finder application to search for unlimited number of applicants and are charged about $50 per candidate to download. Privacy filters let candidates block which employers can see their resumes or opt for prior approval to release their personal (Name, address, etc.) information if a company expresses interest. Intellimatch has been very active partnering with numerous other job services, publications and even outplacement organizations. They claim about 100 (mostly technology-related) companies work with them and that their resume database contains 50,000 resumes and is growing at the rate of 10,000 resumes a month.

CAREERXROADS©
Job, Resume & Career Management Sites on the World Wide Web
• The 1997 Directory •

International Dental Connection

Commercial Job Site
unixg.ubc.ca:880/leighton/idc/contents.htm

Christina Leighton Int'l Dental Connections
Phone: 604-241-3020 Fax: 604-241-2725 e-mail: leighton@unixg.ubc

Jobs? Yes
- Cost to post jobs: Fee
- Cost to see jobs: Free
- Specialty: Health Care/DDS
- Industry: Health Care
- Country/Region/State/City: Health Care

Resumes? Yes
- Cost to post resumes: Free
- Cost to see resumes: Fee

Links to Jobs? Yes

Career Advice? Yes

Under construction. Employer subscription needed to review resumes.

Internet Business Network

Links
www.interbiznet.com/ibn

Internet Business Network
Mill Valley, CA 94914

Jobs? No
- Cost to post jobs: N/A
- Cost to see jobs: N/A
- Specialty: All
- Industry: All
- Country/Region/State/City: US

Resumes? No
- Cost to post resumes: N/A
- Cost to see resumes: N/A

Links to Jobs? Yes

Career Advice? No

Market Research Firm lists the top 25 job sites with reviews and sells a job site survey for hundreds of dollars. Also maintains an electronic daily recruiting newsletter and a directory of professional associations for recruiters.

Internet Career Interest Assesment

Career Management
www.ksu.edu/~dangle/icia

Dennis Angle Kansas Careers
2323 Anderson Ave., Manhattan, KS 66502
Phone: 913-532-6540 Fax: 913-532-7732 e-mail: dangle@ksu.edu

Jobs? No
- Cost to post jobs: N/A
- Cost to see jobs: N/A
- Specialty: All
- Industry: N/A
- Country/Region/State/City: US

Resumes? No
- Cost to post resumes: N/A
- Cost to see resumes: N/A

Links to Jobs? No

Career Advice? Yes

Career information includes an interest assessment orginally designed for women. The interest assessment includes 246 occupations within 12 clusters. Click a cluster to read about it, click an occupation and get a full narrative report.

Internet Fashion Exchange

Commercial Job Site
www.fashionexch.com

Gilbert Career Resources Ltd.
275 Madison Avenue, NY, NY 10016
Phone: 800-967-3846 e-mail: career@tiac.net

Jobs? Yes
- Cost to post jobs: Free
- Cost to see jobs: Free
- Specialty: All
- Industry: Retail/Fashion
- Country/Region/State/City: US/E/NY

Resumes? Yes
- Cost to post resumes: Free
- Cost to see resumes: Free

Links to Jobs? Yes

Career Advice? Yes

Site owner provides a marketplace for resumes and job postings for the fashion and retail industries at no charge. Option to maintain confidentiality. Direct contact information can be found. Unique niche.

Internet Job Locator

Commercial Job Site
www.joblocator.com/jobs/

Brett Tabin Travelers Online
PO Box 4981, Winter Park, Fl 32793
Phone: 407-672-1669 e-mail: webmaster@joblocator

Jobs? Yes
- Cost to post jobs: Fee
- Cost to see jobs: Free
- Specialty: All
- Industry: N/A
- Country/Region/State/City: US

Resumes? Yes
- Cost to post resumes: Free
- Cost to see resumes: Free

Links to Jobs? Yes

Career Advice? No

Lots of jobs posted, good search engine by title with direct contact information at site, can also e-mail company direct to post resume. Short resume profile, has job locator that allows recruiters the ability to post jobs to over 150 news groups. Nice simple site, easy to use, good access features. To post positions site charges $1.00 for 2 months; pay as you go, as you need to send in a check by 15 days after you post the job.

Internet Job Surfer

Links
www.eng.rpi.edu/dept/cdc.jobsurfer/joba.html

Jasmit Singh Kochhar
e-mail: kochhj@rpi.edu

Jobs? No
- Cost to post jobs: N/A
- Cost to see jobs: N/A
- Specialty: N/A
- Industry: N/A
- Country/Region/State/City: US

Resumes? No
- Cost to post resumes: N/A
- Cost to see resumes: N/A

Links to Jobs? Yes

Career Advice? No

Links, links and more links to job sites. Once you arrive at the Internet Job Surfer, you are faced with choosing your favorite letter of the alphabet and linking to a long list of site names starting with that letter. A great place to check if you think you know the name of the site but don't have the address.

CAREERXROADS©
Job, Resume & Career Management Sites on the World Wide Web
• The 1997 Directory •

Internet Resume Registry

Commercial Resume Site
amsquare.com/cgi-bin/poo?order_resload.html

Wayne Gonyea Online Solutions, Inc.
1584 Rt. 22B, Morrisville, NY 12962
Phone: 518-643-0321 Fax: 518-643-2873 e-mail: online@ns.cencom.net

Jobs? No
- Cost to post jobs: N/A
- Cost to see jobs: N/A
- Specialty: Resume distribution
- Industry: All
- Country/Region/State/City: Int'l/US

Resumes? Yes
- Cost to post resumes: Fee
- Cost to see resumes: N/A

Links to Jobs? No

Career Advice? No

Site charges $59.95 to load your resume to 20 web sites, (most of the sites are not the major players in the game.) We had trouble linking to see what you are paying for. One of many in this game so be careful when it comes to paying to place your resume on the web. Check sites out and be careful.

IPMA HR Job Pool

Association
www.ipma-hr.org

IPMA HR Job Pool
Association

Jobs? Yes
- Cost to post jobs: Free
- Cost to see jobs: Free
- Specialty: Human Resources
- Industry: Public/Government
- Country/Region/State/City: US

Resumes? No
- Cost to post resumes: N/A
- Cost to see resumes: N/A

Links to Jobs? Yes

Career Advice? No

The IPMA is an association whose members are local, state and national personnel professionals. 20-30 listings. Nice thing about these jobs is they all have a salary range included.

CAREERXROADS©
Job, Resume & Career Management Sites on the World Wide Web
• The 1997 Directory •

iWorld

Publisher/Trade Magazine
www.iworld.com

Mecklermedia
e-mail: feedback@iworld.com

Jobs? Yes
- Cost to post jobs: Fee
- Cost to see jobs: Free
- Specialty: IT/Internet
- Industry: High Technology
- Country/Region/State/City: Int'l/

Resumes? No
- Cost to post resumes: N/A
- Cost to see resumes: N/A

Links to Jobs? No

Career Advice? No

Excellent search engine for career articles. Primarily this site provides links to 500 magazines and trade publications. Many have help wanted sections and many do not.

Have you found a site that isn't listed in CAREERXROADS?

Have you REGISTERED to receive FREE updates?

Keep us informed.

We'll keep you informed.

CAREERXROADS

Where Talent and Opportunity Connect on the Internet

I-Search

Commercial Resume Site
www.isearch.com

John Reese Interactive Search
5959 West Century Blcd #1122, Los Angeles, CA 90045
Phone: 310-641-1600   e-mail: info@isearch.com

Jobs? No
- Cost to post jobs: N/A
- Cost to see jobs: N/A
- Specialty: N/A
- Industry: N/A
- Country/Region/State/City: US

Resumes? No
- Cost to post resumes: N/A
- Cost to see resumes: Fee

Links to Jobs? No

Career Advice? No

Welcome to...

I-SEARCH

Internet power for job seekers and employers

The New VJF Resume Center. I-Search and Westech Career ExpoCorp recently announced that we've joined forces to provide a powerful new job seeker-employer matching tool on the Internet... the NEW Virtual Job Fair (VJF) Resume Center. For details see our press release.

Private Reserve℠

Private Reserve Customers
Exclusively for Private Reserve customers. Here is your gateway to your private password-protected database.

Features and Capabilities

A unique recruitment service that combines a broad based resume processing service with a sophisticated, searchable web-based database. Focusing on companies with high-volume staffing needs and limited or overloaded applicant tracking systems, I-Search comes to the rescue by accepting resumes via fax, e-mail or snail mail, scanning them and then making them available to be searched and viewed on the Web within 24-48 hours. Recruiters can surf from anywhere to their "Private Reserve" and search the applicant database on any combination of criteria. A great front-end to a company's sourcing strategy, I-Search's only weakness is its inability to track applicant flow. Reasonably priced (setup approximately $5000 plus a per resume processing cost) compared to high-end optical scanning systems, this web model pushes the limits of what is possible on the Net.

Jaeger's Interactive Career Center

Private site
www.apk.net:80/cmd/jaeger/

Jaeger Advertising
Cleveland, OH
Phone: 216-243-8700 Fax: 216-243-1888

Jobs? Yes
- Cost to post jobs: Fee
- Cost to see jobs: Free
- Specialty: All
- Industry: All
- Country/Region/State/City: US

Resumes? No
- Cost to post resumes: N/A
- Cost to see resumes: N/A

Links to Jobs? Yes

Career Advice? No

Search jobs posted by several dozen clients of this recruitment advertising company by title or company.

JAMA

Publisher/Trade Magazine
ama-assn.org

American Medical Association
515 North State Street, Chicago, IL 60610
Phone: 800-262-2260 e-mail: webadmin@ama-assn.org

Jobs? Yes
- Cost to post jobs: Fee
- Cost to see jobs: Free
- Specialty: Health Care/MD
- Industry: Health Care
- Country/Region/State/City: US

Resumes? No
- Cost to post resumes: N/A
- Cost to see resumes: N/A

Links to Jobs? Yes

Career Advice? No

All Physician recruitment ads in JAMA appear at this site. Lots of articles on the profession out of their latest publication.

Job Bank USA

Career Hub
www.jobbankusa.com

Brett Warner JobBank USA
3232 Cobb Parkway, Suite 611, Atlanta, GA 30339
Phone: 770-971-1971   Fax: 770-971-7788   e-mail: webmaster@jobbankusa.com

Jobs? Yes
- Cost to post jobs: Fee
- Cost to see jobs: Free
- Specialty: All
- Industry: All
- Country/Region/State/City: US

Resumes? Yes
- Cost to post resumes: Free
- Cost to see resumes: Fee

Links to Jobs? Yes

Career Advice? Yes

Multiple services for job seekers including a strong searchable database (keyword, company, field and location). Limited international positions and links to job databases. Online entry of job opportunities is available. Tie-ins exist between JobBank USA and other sites in specific geographic niches (See Georgia JobBank). Employer packages available to post positions for 60 days.

Quick Review Rating for each site.

- Has jobs:
- Has resumes:
- Has career advice:
- One of the best in class:

You'll also see a reduced version of the home page for the sites with the best value on the 'Net..

CAREERXROADS©
Job, Resume & Career Management Sites on the World Wide Web
• The 1997 Directory •

Job Board

College/University
wfscnet.tamu.edu:80/jobs.html

Dept. Of Wildlife and Fisheries Science
Texas A&M University

Jobs? Yes
- Cost to post jobs: Free
- Cost to see jobs: Free
- Specialty: Science
- Industry: Government
- Country/Region/State/City: US

Resumes? No
- Cost to post resumes: N/A
- Cost to see resumes: N/A

Links to Jobs? Yes

Career Advice? No

Great collection of summer jobs, internships, volunteer jobs and full time opportunities for graduates with degrees in this area. Links to other State and Government Departments offering careers information. Site states that it is updated on a daily basis.

Job Center

Commercial Job Site/Agent
jobcenter.com/

Christopher McQueeney Job Center Employment Services, Inc.
2 Fennell Street, P.O. Box 125, Skaneateles, NY 13152
Phone: 315-673-0122 Fax: 315-673-1820

Jobs? Yes
- Cost to post jobs: Fee
- Cost to see jobs: Free
- Specialty: All
- Industry: N/A
- Country/Region/State/City: US

Resumes? Yes
- Cost to post resumes: Fee
- Cost to see resumes: N/A

Links to Jobs? No

Career Advice? No

Site acts as an agent for candidates by matching ads posted to key words in resume and sending it to the applicant. Resumes that match the employers keywords are also sent automatically. Employers pay $5/ ad per week Applicants pay $60 for 6 months ($20 for a month) to post their resume. Resumes are also posted to various newsgroups as part of the service.

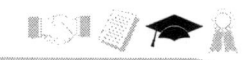

Job Find

Commercial Job Site/Agent
www.dicwest.com/~comdata/jobfind.htm

Commercial Data Systems Ltd.
16 Emerald Place, Emerald Park, SK, Canada S4L1A7
Phone: 800-499-4488 Fax: 306-781-2808 e-mail: comdata@dicwest.com

Jobs? No
- Cost to post jobs: N/A
- Cost to see jobs: N/A
- Specialty: All
- Industry: All
- Country/Region/State/City: N/A

Resumes? No
- Cost to post resumes: N/A
- Cost to see resumes: N/A

Links to Jobs? N/A

Career Advice? Yes

Job Find allows you to test their software for 7 days for free. The price is then $29.95. Site states that it searches thousands of job postings each day from newsgroups discarding those that don't fit your background and zeroing in on only those that are a match for your qualifications. CareerXroads will test this site and place more info on our web site as if this has what it reports they are way ahead of the curve.

Job Hunt: On-Line Job Meta-List

Links
www.job-hunt.org

Dane Spearing Stanford U.
e-mail: dave@job-hunt.org

Jobs? No
- Cost to post jobs: N/A
- Cost to see jobs: N/A
- Specialty: All
- Industry: All
- Country/Region/State/City: N/A

Resumes? No
- Cost to post resumes: N/A
- Cost to see resumes: N/A

Links to Jobs? Yes

Career Advice? No

Links to job sites, resume sites, job services and publications. One of the very best as each site is presented with an accurate mini-review. Listings cross referenced as Academia, General, Science etc., Classified Ads, Recruiting Agencies, Companies and Newsgroup Searches. You can do almost all of it from here. A must to bookmark on your travels.

Job Listings in Academia

College/University
volvo.gslis.utexas.edu~acadres/jla.html

Dan Knauft
e-mail: dknauft@.gslis.utexas.edu

Jobs? Yes
- Cost to post jobs: Free
- Cost to see jobs: Free
- Specialty: All/College
- Industry: Education
- Country/Region/State/City: Int'l/US

Resumes? No
- Cost to post resumes: N/A
- Cost to see resumes: N/A

Links to Jobs? Yes

Career Advice? Yes

Collection of internet resources for the academic job hunter. Has other than teaching positions listed. Positions listed at colleges /universities by US, Canada, Australia, UK or alpha listing. In US good search engine by state for college teaching positions. Links to college sites for open jobs. Simple site but effective.

Job Navigator

Commercial Job Site
www.jobs.co.za

Vanessa Wallace
South Africa
e-mail: vanessaw@systems.co.za

Jobs? Yes
- Cost to post jobs: Fee
- Cost to see jobs: Free
- Specialty: All
- Industry: All
- Country/Region/State/City: Int'l/South Africa

Resumes? Yes
- Cost to post resumes: Free
- Cost to see resumes: N/A

Links to Jobs? No

Career Advice? No

Job contact information can be seen directly as the site states they have 1,255 jobs listed. Interesting search engine which you can also utilize to see affirmative action applicable job postings only (first time we have seen that statement). Site has potential depending on costs and if they can get the technology right. Site has an agency recruitment directory.

Job Net

College/University
westga.edu:80/~coop/index.html

Dr. Bruce Brewer State U. of West Georgia
Career Services Office, Carrollton, GA
Phone: 770-836-6638 Fax: 770-836-6431 e-mail: bbrewer@westga.edu

Jobs? Yes
- Cost to post jobs: Free
- Cost to see jobs: Free
- Specialty: All
- Industry: All
- Country/Region/State/City: US/SE/GA

Resumes? Yes
- Cost to post resumes: Free
- Cost to see resumes: Free

Links to Jobs? Yes

Career Advice? Yes

Collection of job-related resources including career manuals, job descriptions and job-hunting strategies. Also contains newsgroup lists, web sites and listservs. Browse jobs by state. Some areas restricted to alumni. Resumes can be posted for free for 6 months. Employers can post jobs and search resumes for free.

Job Net San Diego

Commercial Job Site
www.eghjobnet.com/

EGH Corporation
PO Box 712465, San Diego, CA 92171
Phone: 619-276-5627 e-mail: jobnet@eghjobnet.com

Jobs? Yes
- Cost to post jobs: Fee
- Cost to see jobs: Free
- Specialty: All
- Industry: N/A
- Country/Region/State/City: US

Resumes? No
- Cost to post resumes: N/A
- Cost to see resumes: N/A

Links to Jobs? Yes

Career Advice? Yes

Information on jobs, job fairs. Direct job information is easy accessable. Cost to post jobs is $11.00 per job if you want to post Sunday - Thursday or Wednesday - Saturday. $20.00 to post Sunday - Saturday. Can see job categories in text only to save time. Can link directly to co's that advertise on site to obtain more info. Nice west coast site.

Have you found a site that isn't listed in CAREERXROADS?

Have you REGISTERED to receive FREE updates?

Keep us informed.

We'll keep you informed.

CAREERXROADS

Where Talent and Opportunity Connect on the Internet

Job Net Work: Your Total Employment Connection

Commercial Job Site
www.conquest-prod.com/resume.html

Job Net Work
P.O. Box 715, Blacksburg, VA 24063
Phone: 540-961-9336 e-mail: inetwork@conquest.prod.com

Jobs? Yes
- Cost to post jobs: Free
- Cost to see jobs: Free
- Specialty: All
- Industry: All
- Country/Region/State/City: US

Resumes? Yes
- Cost to post resumes: Free
- Cost to see resumes: Free

Links to Jobs? Yes

Career Advice? Yes

For extended service this site will post your resume to several other (free) sites for you. Employers can post jobs and review resumes for free. Site has potential but needs to simplify.

Job Net & Online Opportunities

Commercial Job Site
www.jobnet.com

Ward Christman Online Opportunities
422 W. Lincoln Highway, Suite 124, Exton, PA 19341
Phone: 610-973-6811 e-mail: info@jobnet.com

Jobs? Yes
- Cost to post jobs: Fee
- Cost to see jobs: Free
- Specialty: All
- Industry: All
- Country/Region/State/City: US/PA/NJ/DE

Resumes? Yes
- Cost to post resumes: Fee
- Cost to see resumes: Fee

Links to Jobs? Yes

Career Advice? Yes

Lots of links to PA/NJ/DE companies' job pages. Site will sell you a package for advertising jobs to Help Wanted-USA, Online Career Center, Career Web, E-Span and this site for $350 per month per job. Direct employer information is available. Site states it has a resume bulletin board database of 17,000 resumes but they cannot be accessed from this site. You need to dialup their BBS or jobnet.com telnet site. Working on bringing their resumes to the web at this time.

Job Resources by US Region

College/University
www.wm.edu/csrv/career/stualum/jregion.html#top...orcrsv

College of William & Mary
Williamsburg, VA 23187
Phone: 757-221-3240 Fax: 757-221-3329

Jobs? No
- Cost to post jobs: N/A
- Cost to see jobs: N/A
- Specialty: All
- Industry: N/A
- Country/Region/State/City: US

Resumes? No
- Cost to post resumes: N/A
- Cost to see resumes: N/A

Links to Jobs? Yes
Career Advice? No

Comprehensive list of links to jobs, set by region of the US, by field of work, summer jobs, internships, or by alpha listings. Also has a good search engine to take you to the sight of your choice. Simple site that is done well.

Job Scape

Commercial Job /Diversity
www.jobscape.com/occupational

Scott Lipton Occupational Resources Corporation
5694 Mission Center Rd., Suite 310, San Diego, CA 92108
Phone: 619-338-4455 Fax: 619-592-1411 e-mail: or@jobscape.com

Jobs? Yes
- Cost to post jobs: Fee
- Cost to see jobs: Free
- Specialty: All
- Industry: All
- Country/Region/State/City: US//W/CA/San Diego

Resumes? No
- Cost to post resumes: N/A
- Cost to see resumes: N/A

Links to Jobs? Yes
Career Advice? No

Company profiles, jobs etc. are made available for students. Comments at the site imply they are the only ones emphasizing EEO criteria. Not likely. Employer costs range from $100 per month and up. Free to job seeker. Majority of postings and listings are Southern California.

Job Search

Commercial Job Site
www.ventura.com/isearch/ishome2.html

137 East Thousand Oaks Blvd., Suite 203, Thousand Oaks, CA 91360
Phone: 805-496-9908 Fax: 805-496-5512 e-mail: jobsearch@adnetsol.com

Jobs? Yes
- Cost to post jobs: Fee
- Cost to see jobs: Fee
- Specialty: All
- Industry: All
- Country/Region/State/City: US/Southern California

Resumes? Yes
- Cost to post resumes: Fee
- Cost to see resumes: Fee

Links to Jobs? No

Career Advice? Yes

Site brings together the job seeker and the employer/agency for a fee. Membership for the job seeker is $25, while for the employer/agency there is a on-time registration of $25 and a $50 charge for each job listing. If you want to be in the Southern CA area or want t o employ people in this highly competitive market, this is an inexpensive way to test the area. Nice search engine that really goes into detail. Site states it reaches 40,000 employers and over 100,000 potential job seekers. Site also gives you the ability to search info on local corporations.

Job Search Materials for Engineers

Career Management
www.www.englib.cornell.edu/elib_instruction//jobsearch.html

Cornell University Engineering Library
Phone: 315-255-5935 e-mail: englib@cornell.edu

Jobs? No
- Cost to post jobs: N/A
- Cost to see jobs: N/A
- Specialty: Engineering
- Industry: All
- Country/Region/State/City: US

Resumes? No
- Cost to post resumes: N/A
- Cost to see resumes: N/A

Links to Jobs? Yes

Career Advice? Yes

Describes Cornell's Engineering Library and contents related to job seekers including directories, Journals and conferences. A few links. Highly focused engineering career resources

Job Search & Employment Opportunities-Best Bets

Links
www.personal.umich.edu

Philip Ray
e-mail: job-guide@umich.edu

Jobs? No
- Cost to post jobs: N/A
- Cost to see jobs: N/A
- Specialty: N/A
- Industry: N/A
- Country/Region/State/City: US

Resumes? No
- Cost to post resumes: N/A
- Cost to see resumes: N/A

Links to Jobs? Yes

Career Advice? No

Long list of job related links with a brief explanation of each.

Job Serve: IT Vacancies in the UK

Commercial Job Site/Agent
www.jobserve.com

John Witney JobServe Ltd.
Haland House, 66 York Road, Weybridge, Surrey, England KT139DY
Phone: 441-932-829525 Fax: 441-932-829527 e-mail: sales@jobserve.com

Jobs? Yes
- Cost to post jobs: Fee
- Cost to see jobs: Free
- Specialty: IT
- Industry: All
- Country/Region/State/City: Int'l/UK

Resumes? No
- Cost to post resumes: N/A
- Cost to see resumes: N/A

Links to Jobs? Yes

Career Advice? No

4,021 jobs posted with 643 new the day of our visit. JobServe sends out free daily e-mail messages to nearly 20,000 subscribing jobseekers which include hundreds of new listings. Owner claims JobServe is the largest source of IT vacancies in the UK advertising more than 13,000 openings each month. Over 500 IT recruitment agencies and companies use Jobserve and about 30 have links from its site to their home page. All candidates need to do is send a blank e-mail message to: "subscribe@jobserve.com" and the listings begin almost immediately.

CAREERXROADS©
Job, Resume & Career Management Sites on the World Wide Web
• The 1997 Directory •

Job Source

Commercial Job Site
www.jobsource.com/

Market Source Corporation Attn:Dave Mevorah
2 Commerce Drive, Cranbury, NJ 08512
Phone: 609-860-5341 e-mail: mevorah@marketsource.com

Jobs? Yes
- Cost to post jobs: Free
- Cost to see jobs:
- Specialty: All
- Industry:
- Country/Region/State/City: US

Resumes? Yes
- Cost to post resumes: Yes
- Cost to see resumes:

Links to Jobs? Yes

Career Advice? Yes

Owner makes a few outlandish claims about being the largest most popular internet site for college students. Unlikely, but still a nicely designed site with useful information.

Quick Review Rating for each site.

- Has jobs:
- Has resumes:
- Has career advice:
- One of the best in class:

You'll also see a reduced version of the home page for the sites with the best value on the 'Net..

CAREERXROADS©
Job, Resume & Career Management Sites on the World Wide Web
• The 1997 Directory •

Job Smart

Publisher/Newspaper/Agent
www.jobsmart.com

Community Newspaper Company
Phone: 617-433-6868 e-mail: jobsmart@cnc.com

Jobs? Yes
- Cost to post jobs: Fee
- Cost to see jobs: Free
- Specialty: All
- Industry: All
- Country/Region/State/City: US/NE/MA

Resumes? Yes
- Cost to post resumes: Free
- Cost to see resumes: Free

Links to Jobs? Yes

Career Advice? Yes

Could be one of the smartest moves by a publisher since CareerPath. Nearly 100 local weekly and daily papers in the Boston Market include a common Publication "Job Smart" each week as a special stand alone help wanted section. All the ads are available on the 'Net. In addition, you can post to the site direct for just a few dollars. Resumes use the same technology available at CareerSite (see CareerSite) to provide agent like capability for both the employer and applicant while protecting the

JOBTRAK

Commercial Job/College
www.jobtrak.com

Ken Ramberg
1990 Westwood Blvd, Ste 260, Los Angeles, CA 90025
Phone: 310-474-3377 Fax: 310-475-7912 e-mail: kramberg@jobtrak.com

Jobs? Yes
- Cost to post jobs: Fee
- Cost to see jobs: Free
- Specialty: All
- Industry: N/A
- Country/Region/State/City: US

Resumes? Yes
- Cost to post resumes: Free
- Cost to see resumes: Fee

Links to Jobs? Yes

Career Advice? Yes

Site advertises extensively in college newspapers to attract students to use the service. Claims exclusive agreements with more than 500 Colleges and Universities. Employers calling most major colleges are referred by the career centers to JOBTRAK. Has large number of hypertext links to companies with openings. To get access to the jobs, students & Alumni need to have a password. This site deserves high marks for its effort to successfully market its services to some of the best colleges in the country. Employers can post jobs for as little as $15-25/job/1 college. Resume services are just getting started

Job Tree

Career Hub
peace.netnation.com/joblink/

Richard Lawson   NetNation Internet Inc.
Canada
Phone: 609-688-8946   e-mail: webmaster@netnation.com

Jobs? Yes
- Cost to post jobs: Free
- Cost to see jobs: Free
- Specialty: All
- Industry: All
- Country/Region/State/City: Int'l/Canada/US

Resumes? Yes
- Cost to post resumes: Free
- Cost to see resumes: Free

Links to Jobs? Yes

Career Advice? Yes

Career Hub that gives all services for free. Posts jobs in 24 hours and also has direct contact info posted. Can post your resume using their search engine that makes it easy to imput. Also has corporate profiles that you need to download. Has jobs posted in the US and Canada. Great job, worth a visit. Long term objective of site is to move it to a non-profit society so that it can be run on a shareware basis.

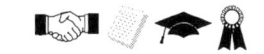

JobWeb

Association/College
www.jobweb.org/

Tom Flood National Association of Colleges and Employers
62 Highland Avenue, Bethlehem, PA 18017
Phone: 800-544-5272 Fax: 610-868-1421 e-mail: tom@jobweb.com

Jobs? Yes
- Cost to post jobs: Fee
- Cost to see jobs: Free
- Specialty: All/College
- Industry: N/A
- Country/Region/State/City: US

Resumes? No
- Cost to post resumes: N/A
- Cost to see resumes: N/A

Links to Jobs? Yes

Career Advice? Yes

NACE provides an extensive job opportunity bank for college students to peruse as well as helpful diversity information (INROADS is just one example). A forum and news info for college career professionals, a career and human resource bibliography, events calendar and links to human resource associations round out one of the webs most valuable databases. NACE claims 3 million visitors a month making it one of the most trafficked sites for job hunting. For approx. $500, companies can list descriptive information about their company (Profile), including a logo and hypertext links to their site for a year. More extensive Home pages available. Recently, NACE took over responsibility for Catapult. (See Catapult). In March '96 JobWeb introduced a new streamlined look to assist recruiters, career planning specialists and college seniors as well as experienced job seekers find their way through the site's labyrinth with a helpful map showing various routes to information. JobWeb has developed an array of services allowing companies direct posting capability. Costs are in the $10-50 range for 4 weeks. Volume packages are available to reduce costs further. Even the company profiles can be searched for keyword skills. Look to JobWeb as a major force with the ability to broaden from their college base. They are among the few sites with the staying power to dominate their segment of this emerging marketplace. Best job value on the net.

CAREERXROADS©
Job, Resume & Career Management Sites on the World Wide Web
• **The 1997 Directory** •

JOBS

Links
ageninfo.tamu.edu/jobs.html

Texas A&M

Jobs? No
- Cost to post jobs: N/A
- Cost to see jobs: N/A
- Specialty: All
- Industry: All
- Country/Region/State/City: US

Resumes? No
- Cost to post resumes: N/A
- Cost to see resumes: N/A

Links to Jobs? Yes

Career Advice? No

Solid listings of links including several for the Southwest that aren't on any other list. Several links will be inactive. Best used for its links to colleges.

Jobs Mathematics

Links
www.cs.dartmouth.edu/~gdavis/policy/jobmarket.html

Geoff Davis Dartmouth College
210 Sudikoff Lab, Math Dept., Bradley Hall, Hanover, NH 03755
Phone: 603-646-1618 Fax: 603-646-1672 e-mail: gdavis@cs.dartmouth.edu

Jobs? No
- Cost to post jobs: N/A
- Cost to see jobs: N/A
- Specialty: All
- Industry: N/A
- Country/Region/State/City: Int'l/US

Resumes? No
- Cost to post resumes: N/A
- Cost to see resumes: N/A

Links to Jobs? Yes

Career Advice? No

Links to numerous jobs that are math related. Internships, jobs in academia and also links to job sites all over the world. Great list of links.

Jobs OnLine

Commercial Job Site/Agent
JobsOnLine.com/emp_enter.cgi

e.m.a.n.a.t.e. Div. of Physicomp Corp.
e-mail: jolaemanate.com

Jobs? Yes
- Cost to post jobs: Fee
- Cost to see jobs: Free
- Specialty: IT
- Industry: IT
- Country/Region/State/City: US

Resumes? Yes
- Cost to post resumes: Free
- Cost to see resumes: N/A

Links to Jobs? Yes

Career Advice? No

Site states that it plays the part of the middle person between the potential employee/contract and the corporation/agency. Jobs are coded as site has a good search engine but not many posted. Concentrates on IT positions. Could not see resumes although you can post to the different positions.

Jobs.CZ

Commercial Job Site
www.cz/english

Dekuji Vam
VysocanskA234, 19000 Praha9, Czech Republic
Phone: 060-341-0920 Fax: 422-800-935 e-mail: www_us@jobs.cz

Jobs? Yes
- Cost to post jobs: Fee
- Cost to see jobs: Free
- Specialty: All
- Industry: All
- Country/Region/State/City: Int'l/Czech Republic

Resumes? Yes
- Cost to post resumes: Free
- Cost to see resumes: Fee

Links to Jobs? No

Career Advice? Yes

This site claims to be the first server in the Czech Republic. You can post your resume and find open positions. We are waiting for costs to do these things but have to believe there is one. Site states country has zero unemployment but that you must speak Czech to get a job. Jobs listed in all fields.

Journalism-Related Jobs

College/University
eb,journPaul Grabowicz Louisiana Tech

e-mail: grab@ix.netcom.com.latech.edu/jobs/jobs_home.html

Jobs? Yes
- Cost to post jobs: Free
- Cost to see jobs: Free
- Specialty: All
- Industry: Journalism
- Country/Region/State/City: US

Resumes? No
- Cost to post resumes: N/A
- Cost to see resumes: N/A

Links to Jobs? Yes

Career Advice? No

Job banks at Gannett, Editor & Publisher Magazine and other newspapers can be linked. Listings of jobs in journalism at all levels. Direct contact info is available by week of issue. Simple sight that gets the job done. You can e-mail posting directly.

JWT Specialized Communications

Private site
www.jwtworks.com

Chuck Robbins JWT Specialized Communications
466 Lexington Ave., 4th Floor, NY, NY 10017
Phone: 212-856-0045 Fax: 212-210-1097 e-mail: webhot@jwtworks.com

Jobs? Yes
- Cost to post jobs: Fee
- Cost to see jobs: Free
- Specialty: All
- Industry: All
- Country/Region/State/City: US

Resumes? No
- Cost to post resumes: N/A
- Cost to see resumes: N/A

Links to Jobs? Yes

Career Advice? Yes

JWT Specialized Communications is a division of J.Walter Thompson. Has added a section called HR Live that advises recruiters who is laying off, what areas of the country are going through large hiring cycles and lists of current job fairs. Also has a link to OCC.

K3 & Company

Commercial Job Site
www.k3k3k3.com/index.html

Katie Keane K3 & Company
P.O. Box 27054, Concord, CA 94527
Phone: 510-370-7006 Fax: 510-370-1986 e-mail: info@k3k3k3.com

Jobs? Yes
- Cost to post jobs: Fee
- Cost to see jobs: Free
- Specialty: All
- Industry: N/A
- Country/Region/State/City: US/W/CA/San Francisco

Resumes? Yes
- Cost to post resumes: Free
- Cost to see resumes: Fee

Links to Jobs? Yes

Career Advice? Yes

Straightforward resume database for the S.F. Bay area. Includes a calendar of events, resume tips, resume templates and other links to bay area resources and support groups. Employers pay $50 for a 30 day listing.

Kansas Careers

College/Diversity
www-personal.ksu.edu/~dangle/

Kansas University
e-mail: dangle@ksu.ksu.edu

Jobs? No
- Cost to post jobs: N/A
- Cost to see jobs: N/A
- Specialty: All
- Industry: N/A
- Country/Region/State/City: US/MW/KS

Resumes? No
- Cost to post resumes: N/A
- Cost to see resumes: N/A

Links to Jobs? Yes

Career Advice? Yes

Many minority and gender links for career and job information. Excellent diversity career information with an internet asessment link especially for women. Highly focused site that is definitely worth a look.

Kansas City Star

Publisher/Newspaper
www.kansascity.com

Kansas City Star
1729 Grand Boulevard, Kansas City, MO 54108
Phone: 816-234-4000

Jobs? Yes
- Cost to post jobs: Fee
- Cost to see jobs: Free
- Specialty: All
- Industry: N/A
- Country/Region/State/City: US/MW/MO/Kansas City

Resumes? No
- Cost to post resumes: N/A
- Cost to see resumes: N/A

Links to Jobs? No

Career Advice? No

Help wanted advertising from this paper's Sunday classified section. Employers pay for space in the newspaper only.

Latino Web

Diversity
www.catalog.com/favision/latnoweb

PO Box 3852, Montebello, CA 90640
Phone: 818-300-8445 e-mail: support@latinoweb.com

Jobs? Yes
- Cost to post jobs: Free
- Cost to see jobs: Free
- Specialty: All
- Industry: N/A
- Country/Region/State/City: US

Resumes? No
- Cost to post resumes: N/A
- Cost to see resumes: N/A

Links to Jobs? Yes
Career Advice? Yes

Latino Web is a virtual information center geared toward the Latino population. Jobs are posted with links to other company sites. Seems to be a new site with a lot of diversity information.

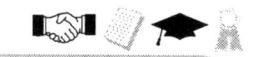

Law Employment Center

Publisher/Trade
www.lawjobs.com/

Frank Fitts New York Law Publishing Company
Phone: 212-545-5959 Fax: 212-481-8075

Jobs? Yes
- Cost to post jobs: Fee
- Cost to see jobs: Free
- Specialty: Law
- Industry: Legal
- Country/Region/State/City: US/E/NY

Resumes? No
- Cost to post resumes: N/A
- Cost to see resumes: N/A

Links to Jobs? No

Career Advice? Yes

Info includes salary survey of legal profession, lists of legal headhunters and links to them. Visitors can ask questions and an "expert" will answer them. Q & A's are retained. Employers pay for advertising in publications. List of the nation's top 250 law firms is also included.

Law Mall

Commercial Resume Site
www.lawmall.com/resumes/resumes/html

e-mail: webmaster@lawmall.com

Jobs? No
- Cost to post jobs: N/A
- Cost to see jobs: N/A
- Specialty: Law
- Industry: All
- Country/Region/State/City: US

Resumes? Yes
- Cost to post resumes: Free
- Cost to see resumes: Free

Links to Jobs? Yes

Career Advice? No

Law Mall will post your resume for free on their site. Easy alpha listing of resumes to see Design your own resume with minimal effort. Nice set of legal links to find other legal sites.

Layover

Commercial Job Site
www.layover.com

Bruce Martin
Phone: 717-859-4546 e-mail: layover@ptd.net

Jobs? Yes
- Cost to post jobs: Fee
- Cost to see jobs: Free
- Specialty:
- Industry: Trucking
- Country/Region/State/City: US

Resumes? No
- Cost to post resumes: N/A
- Cost to see resumes: N/A

Links to Jobs? Yes

Career Advice? No

Who says all sites deal with technical positions? Job opportunities for over the road truckers abound on this site. Long list of jobs listed by company with links to those organizations. Good articles on what's going on in the industry.

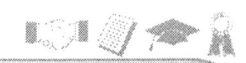

Le Web Cafe Career

Links to Jobs
www.lewebcafe.com/pages/career.htm

Le Web Cafe, Inc.
PO Box 611144, San Jose, CA 95161
Phone: 408-259-5974 Fax: 408-923-1462 e-mail: feedback@lewebcafe.com

Jobs? No
- Cost to post jobs: N/A
- Cost to see jobs: N/A
- Specialty: Links
- Industry: All
- Country/Region/State/City: US

Resumes? No
- Cost to post resumes: N/A
- Cost to see resumes: N/A

Links to Jobs? Yes

Career Advice? No

Listing of major links/newsgroups as well as resume job banks. The company that owns this site creates web pages and charges $50-$80 an hour to do so.

Lee Hecht Harrison

Career Management
www.careerlhh.com

Lee Hecht Harrison
200 Park Ave, 26th Fl, New York, NY 10166
Phone: 212-557-0009 Fax: 212-455-8518 e-mail: infollh@ix.netcom.com

Jobs? Yes
- Cost to post jobs: Free
- Cost to see jobs: Free/Clients
- Specialty: N/A
- Industry: N/A
- Country/Region/State/City: US

Resumes? Yes
- Cost to post resumes: Free/Clients
- Cost to see resumes: Free

Links to Jobs? No

Career Advice? Yes

Employers can post jobs to this outplacement firms clients, review client resumes (coded) and review a nationwide survey of corporate severance practices. Little help for the job-seeker who is not a client. LHH is one of several outplacement industry firms developing specialized internet and intranet services for their clients.

Lendman's Recruiting Resources Gateway

Job Fair
www.lendman.com

The Lendman Group
141 Business Park Drive, Virginia Beach, VA 23462
Phone: 804-473-2450

Jobs? No
- Cost to post jobs: N/A
- Cost to see jobs: N/A
- Specialty: All
- Industry: All
- Country/Region/State/City: US

Resumes? No
- Cost to post resumes: N/A
- Cost to see resumes: N/A

Links to Jobs? Yes

Career Advice? Yes

As one of the largest firms involved in the running of job fairs, job seekers will find a schedule of job fairs, advice and other services.

Life Goes On

Publisher/Newspaper
www.lifegoeson.com

Patuxent Publishing Company
10750 Little Patuxent Parkway, Columbia, MD 21044
Phone: 410-730-3990 Fax: 410-730-7050 e-mail: webmaster@lifegoeson.com

Jobs? Yes
- Cost to post jobs: Fee
- Cost to see jobs: Free
- Specialty: All
- Industry: N/A
- Country/Region/State/City: US/E/MD

Resumes? No
- Cost to post resumes: N/A
- Cost to see resumes: N/A

Links to Jobs? No

Career Advice? No

If you are seeking opportunities in the Chesapeake Bay area (MD), the 13 weekly papers that make up Life Goes On have created a single searchable database for their helpwanted classified ads. Employers pay for the print ads and get the Internet as added value.

Links on the Web

Links
www.cob.ohio-state.edu/other/other.html#jobs

Ohio State Univ. Fisher College of Business
Ohio

Jobs? No
- Cost to post jobs: N/A
- Cost to see jobs: N/A
- Specialty: All
- Industry: All
- Country/Region/State/City: US

Resumes? No
- Cost to post resumes: N/A
- Cost to see resumes: N/A

Links to Jobs? Yes

Career Advice? No

Interesting list of links to get you started in your job search. Has companies, business info, telephone directory links as well as a few job related sites.

Los Angeles Times

Publisher/Newspaper
www.latimes.com

Nancy Massa Los Angeles Times
145 S. Spring Street, Los Angeles, CA 90012
Fax: 213-237-3181 e-mail: nancy.massa@latimes.com

Jobs? Yes
- Cost to post jobs: Fee
- Cost to see jobs: Free
- Specialty: All
- Industry: N/A
- Country/Region/State/City: US/W/CA/Los Angeles

Resumes? No
- Cost to post resumes: N/A
- Cost to see resumes: N/A

Links to Jobs? No

Career Advice? No

Newspaper help wanted classifieds. Help wanted display ads are extra ($1.90/line and $190 per ad for display). In addition, employers must pay for ad in the newspaper. This publisher also participates in CareerPath (See CareerPath)

MacTemps

Placement/Search/Temp
www.mactemps.com.jobs.html

Phone: 800-622-8367

Jobs? Yes
- Cost to post jobs: Fee
- Cost to see jobs: Free
- Specialty: Contract/Contingent
- Industry: All
- Country/Region/State/City: Int'l/US

Resumes? No
- Cost to post resumes: N/A
- Cost to see resumes: N/A

Links to Jobs? No

Career Advice? No

Temporary/Contract agency with locations throughout the world. Search jobs by office. Positions range from professional/technical to administrative. Job seekers provided with ability to e-mail for more info. Nice touch.

MedSearch

Commercial Job Site/Agent
www.medsearch.com

Larry Bouchard
15254 NE 95th Street, Redmond, WA 98052
Phone: 206-883-7252 Fax: 206-883-7465 e-mail: office@medsearch.com

Jobs? Yes
- **Cost to post jobs: Fee**
- Cost to see jobs: Free
- Specialty: All
- Industry: Health Care
- Country/Region/State/City: US

Resumes? Yes
- Cost to post resumes: Free
- Cost to see resumes: Fee

Links to Jobs? No

Career Advice? Yes

Developed by a physician recruiting network, this site focuses on opportunities in healthcare for pharmaceutical companies, sports medicine clinics, health care centers and insurance companies. Search by discipline or state. Resume database. Of course the applicants are coded. Annual fee $700+ to hiring companies includes a company profile. Employers can post jobs for $125 each. Site has attracted a lot of attention for quality of candidates it has in it's database.

CAREERXROADS©
Job, Resume & Career Management Sites on the World Wide Web
• The 1997 Directory •

Medical Device Link

Publisher/Trade
www.devicelink.com

Canon Communications, Inc.
e-mail: feedback@canon.com

Jobs? No
- Cost to post jobs: N/A
- Cost to see jobs: N/A
- Specialty: Health Care/MD
- Industry: Health Care
- Country/Region/State/City: US

Resumes? No
- Cost to post resumes: N/A
- Cost to see resumes: N/A

Links to Jobs? No

Career Advice? Yes

Jobs and resumes will soon be posted on this site. Has a salary estimator for health care positions. Site to watch in a very specific industry.

Medical Jobs

Commercial Job Site
www.MEDJOB.com

Impact Publications
e-mail: info@medjob.com

Jobs? Yes
- Cost to post jobs: Fee
- Cost to see jobs: Free
- Specialty: Health Care/MD
- Industry: Health Care
- Country/Region/State/City: US/SE

Resumes? No
- Cost to post resumes: N/A
- Cost to see resumes: N/A

Links to Jobs? No

Career Advice? No

Site lists positions in the medical field from doctors to office administrators. Currently concentrates on the Southeast but is attempting to broaden their market. One to watch as several sections are under construction.

Medical Web

Commercial Job Site
www.medical-web.com/med_web/medical_web.html

Tim Thomas
Phone: 607-844-3447 e-mail: medweb@web-foundry.com

Jobs? Yes
- Cost to post jobs: Fee
- Cost to see jobs: Free
- Specialty: Health Care/MD
- Industry: Health Care
- Country/Region/State/City: US

Resumes? No
- Cost to post resumes: N/A
- Cost to see resumes: N/A

Links to Jobs? Yes

Career Advice? No

Direct contact information for physician/faculty positions throughout the US. Has a fast search engine with specific fields so you can narrow down your field of expertise. Site has lots of technical information that anyone can use.

Medical/Health Care Jobs Page

Commercial Job Site/Agent
www.nationjob.com

Bob Levenstein NationJob, Inc.(See NationJob)
2010 Ankeny Blvd., Ankeny, IA 50021
Phone: 515-964-6794

Jobs? Yes
- Cost to post jobs: Fee
- Cost to see jobs: Free
- Specialty: Health Care
- Industry: Health Care/Agent
- Country/Region/State/City: US/MW

Resumes? Yes
- Cost to post resumes: Free
- Cost to see resumes: Fee

Links to Jobs? Yes

Career Advice? Yes

Job seekers will find flexibility to search and scan among manufacturing, aviation, engineering and many other "breakouts" in addition to this medical sectors. Excellent added free service for registering in the form of "P.J. Scout," an agent which monitors the site and returns new postings to you by e-mail. See Nationjob listing for full information.

Mercury Center Web

Publisher/Newspaper
www.sjmercury.com

Janet Huebner San Jose Mercury News
750 Ridder Park Drive, San Jose, CA 95190
Phone: 408-920-5585 e-mail: jehuebner@sjmercury.com

Jobs? Yes
- Cost to post jobs: Fee
- Cost to see jobs: Free
- Specialty: All
- Industry: N/A
- Country/Region/State/City: US/W/CA/San Jose

Resumes? No
- Cost to post resumes: N/A
- Cost to see resumes: N/A

Links to Jobs? No

Career Advice? No

Help Wanted ads from the San Jose Mercury News. One of the first publishers to provide classifieds on the Internet. A model for many that came later. One of the best designed overall resources by a publisher. Recently developed a partnership with Intellimatch called Free Agent to provide sophisticated resume matching for applicants and employers. (See Intellimatch). This publisher also participates in CareerPath (See CareerPath)

Metroworld

Publisher/Trade Magazine
metroworld.com

Montgomery Newspapers
290 Commerce Drive, Fort Washington, PA 19034
Phone: 215-283-25555 Fax: 215-283-2335

Jobs? Yes
- Cost to post jobs: Fee
- Cost to see jobs: Free
- Specialty: All
- Industry: All
- Country/Region/State/City: US/E/PA

Resumes? No
- Cost to post resumes: N/A
- Cost to see resumes: N/A

Links to Jobs? Yes

Career Advice? Yes

Local Philadelphia, PA (Montgomery County) papers. In-column ads automatically placed online

Michigan Employment

Government
www.mesc.state.mi.us/techjobs.htm

e-mail: help@mesc.sate.mi.us

Jobs? No
- Cost to post jobs: N/A
- Cost to see jobs: N/A
- Specialty: All
- Industry: All
- Country/Region/State/City: US/MW/MI

Resumes? Yes
- Cost to post resumes: Free
- Cost to see resumes: Free

Links to Jobs? Yes

Career Advice? Yes

Site is getting started and parts are still under construction. Great idea to have a map of each state that takes you to each one's job information center. Under construction is a resume feedback section. Career info is also available. Link to employers did not work on our vist and no jobs are posted at present. Asks for your resume but employers cannot see them at this time. As usual states have the beaurocratic process to go through and even now they still do not get the power of the web. We give them points for trying and will follow this site as it matures.

Milwaukee Journal (Help Wanted)

Publisher/Newspaper
www.adquest.com

Milwaukee Journal
333 W. State Street, Milwaukee, WI 53203
Phone: 414-224-2000

Jobs? Yes
- Cost to post jobs: Fee
- Cost to see jobs: Free
- Specialty: All
- Industry: N/A
- Country/Region/State/City: US/MW/WI/Mil

Resumes? No
- Cost to post resumes: N/A
- Cost to see resumes: N/A

Links to Jobs? No

Career Advice? No

Newspaper help wanted classifieds. All ads placed cost $.59/line. In addition, employers must pay for ad in newspaper.

Minneapolis Star-Tribune

Publisher/Newspaper
www.startribune.com

425 Portland Avenue
Minneapolis, MN 55488
Phone: 800-827-8742

Jobs? Yes
- Cost to post jobs: Fee
- Cost to see jobs: Free
- Specialty: All
- Industry: N/A
- Country/Region/State/City: US/MW/MI/Minn.

Resumes? No
- Cost to post resumes: N/A
- Cost to see resumes: N/A

Links to Jobs? No

Career Advice? No

Help wanted classifieds printed in Sunday's newspaper are posted. This publisher participates in CareerPath (See CareerPath). Help wanted display ads are not included on the Internet site.

Mississippi Careers Online

Commercial Job Site
www.whipcomm.com/whipcomm/mscareer

Whippoorwill Communications P. O. Box 4870
University, Mississippi 38677
Phone: 800-662-5621 Fax: 601-234-9980 e-mail: bafitts@sunset.backbone.olemis

Jobs? Yes
- Cost to post jobs: Yes
- Cost to see jobs: Free
- Specialty: All
- Industry: N/A
- Country/Region/State/City: US/S/MS

Resumes? Yes
- Cost to post resumes: Fee
- Cost to see resumes: Free

Links to Jobs? Yes

Career Advice? Yes

This service links you to not only Mississippi opportunities, but also other nationwide opportunities. Resumes are also posted in 25 different nationally distributed databases. All resume postings have a fee ranging from $30.00 to $75.00 based on its distribution.

MMWire Online

Publisher/Trade
www.mmwire.com

Allison Dollar Phillips Business Information
1201 Seven Locks Road, Suite 300, Potomac, MD 20854
Phone: 301-340-3338 Fax: 301-309-3847 e-mail: adollar@phillips.com

Jobs? Yes
- Cost to post jobs: Fee
- Cost to see jobs: Free
- Specialty: IT
- Industry: Entertainment/Interactive
- Country/Region/State/City: US

Resumes? No
- Cost to post resumes: N/A
- Cost to see resumes: N/A

Links to Jobs? Yes

Career Advice? No

Employers pay $49.95 to place jobs on this uniue site for web masters. The advertisement is only up for 5 days so you may want to check on packages for longer lengths of time. Site seems to have recently merged with another so keep watching for changes. Dozens of organizations listing IS, Marketing and design positions.

Have you found a site that isn't listed in CAREERXROADS?

Have you REGISTERED to receive FREE updates?

Keep us informed.

We'll keep you informed.

CAREERXROADS
Where Talent and Opportunity Connect on the Internet

CAREERXROADS©
Job, Resume & Career Management Sites on the World Wide Web
• The 1997 Directory •

The Monster Board

Career Hub/Agent
www.monster.com

Peter Steiner
2 Kendall Street, Suite 301 PO Box 586, Framingham, MA 01701
Phone: 508-879-4641 Fax: 508-879-4651 e-mail:

Jobs? Yes
- Cost to post jobs: Fee
- Cost to see jobs: Free
- Specialty: All
- Industry: All
- Country/Region/State/City: Int'l./US

Resumes? Yes
- Cost to post resumes: Free
- Cost to see resumes: Fee

Links to Jobs? Yes

Career Advice? Yes

This commercial service owned by TMP, a recruitment advertising firm, offers improving design and contains 1000s of postings (claims 50,000+ in one spot) in its database. Career info, links to other sites and flexible search of postings makes this a useful site. Employers also have a flexible way to post openings and receive resumes. "Monster" recruiters will even do your work for you on an hourly basis. Prices for posting range from under $100 to thousands. The sites alliance with Restrac, allow employers to download resumes form applicants (who respond to their job posting) directly into their corporate resume databases for scanning and searching. The Monster has also added an international component to see jobs in several countries. Recently announced is Resume City, a monsterboard service selling a searchable database of "70,000". Employer costs were quoted at the $1900 for a three month trial. This may change.

CAREERXROADS©
Job, Resume & Career Management Sites on the World Wide Web
• The 1997 Directory •

Montgomery Newspapers

Publisher/Newspaper
www.montnews.com

Tom Cole Montgomery Newspapers
290 Commerce Drive, Fort Washington, PA 19034
Phone: 215-646-5100 Fax: 215-643-0166

Jobs? Yes
- Cost to post jobs: Fee
- Cost to see jobs: Free
- Specialty: All
- Industry: N/A
- Country/Region/State/City: US/E/PA

Resumes? No
- Cost to post resumes: N/A
- Cost to see resumes: N/A

Links to Jobs? No

Career Advice? No

Straightforward newspaper help wanted classified site covering Montgomery County (North Philadelphia). Includes ads from 15 weekly newspapers owned by the publisher.

Multimedia News Stand

Links
www.mmnewsstand.com

Hearst Corp

Jobs? No
- Cost to post jobs: N/A
- Cost to see jobs: N/A
- Specialty: N/A
- Industry: N/A
- Country/Region/State/City: US

Resumes? No
- Cost to post resumes: N/A
- Cost to see resumes: N/A

Links to Jobs? Yes

Career Advice? No

An online resource for magazines, annual reports and more. Great tool for researching companies. Could be outstanding if annual reports were to expand. We had some difficulty continually getting to this site but keep trying.

Music Exchange

Commercial Job Site
www.scsn.net/~musex/

Jobs? Yes
- Cost to post jobs: Free
- Cost to see jobs: Free
- Specialty: Music
- Industry: Entertainment
- Country/Region/State/City: US

Resumes? Yes
- Cost to post resumes: Free
- Cost to see resumes: Free

Links to Jobs? Yes

Career Advice? No

Looking for musicians or a job with a band. Here is a classified marketplace for posting resumes or jobs at no cost. Site needs to be updated as, on our recent visit, a date of June 14, 1996 was the last time this was done.

NAACB Job Board and Resume Bank

Assocation
http://computerwork.com

National Association of Computer Consulting Bus.

Jobs? Yes
- Cost to post jobs: Free
- Cost to see jobs: Free
- Specialty: IT
- Industry: Computer
- Country/Region/State/City: US

Resumes? Yes
- Cost to post resumes: Free
- Cost to see resumes: Free

Links to Jobs? Yes

Career Advice? Yes

Two hundred and fifty computer consulting firms, members of the NACCB could be using this site...but they aren't. Job seekers trying to find what they want may have some difficulty with the keyword search which works best when you know specifically what project or skill area you want to consider. Resume posting is free and easy and even includes an optional form with prompts and clickable skill sets.

CAREERXROADS©
Job, Resume & Career Management Sites on the World Wide Web
• The 1997 Directory •

Nando Times

Publisher/Newspaper
www.nando.net

Raleigh News & Observer
127 West Hargett Street, Suite 406, Raleigh, NC 27601
Phone: 919-829-4610

Jobs? Yes
• Cost to post jobs: Fee
• Cost to see jobs: Free
• Specialty: All
• Industry: N/A
• Country/Region/State/City: US/E/NC/Raleigh

Resumes? No
• Cost to post resumes: N/A
• Cost to see resumes: N/A

Links to Jobs? No

Career Advice? No

Newspaper help wanted classifieds. Help wanted display ads cost $.50-$1.00 extra in addition to the cost of newspaper space. Links to newspapers in Modesto, CA; Sacramento, CA; Tacoma, WA and Anchorage, AK.

National Business Employment Weekly

Pub/Career Management
www.nbew.com

Mary LaMagna Dow Jones & Company, Inc.
US Rte. 1 at Ridge Road, , South Brunswick, NJ 08852
Phone: 800-323-6239 Fax: 609-520-7315

Jobs? No
• Cost to post jobs: N/A
• Cost to see jobs: N/A
• Specialty: N/A
• Industry: N/A
• Country/Region/State/City: US

Resumes? No
• Cost to post resumes: N/A
• Cost to see resumes: N/A

Links to Jobs? No

Career Advice? Yes

The NBEW is a weekly career guidance and job search publication that includes job advertising placed in the Wall Street Journal as well as directly. While the site does not include jobs at this time (See Wall Street Journal), the career management articles available are excellent.

National Diversity Journalism Job Bank

Publisher/Trade Magazine
www.newsjobs.com

Jody Kestler Florida Times-Union
One Riverside Ave., Jacksonville, FL 32202
Phone: 904-359-4079 Fax: 904-359-4478 e-mail: news@newsjobs.com

Jobs? Yes
- Cost to post jobs: Free
- Cost to see jobs: Free
- Specialty: Journalism
- Industry: Publishing
- Country/Region/State/City: US

Resumes? No
- Cost to post resumes: N/A
- Cost to see resumes: N/A

Links to Jobs? Yes

Career Advice? Yes

If you are looking for a journalism position in a newspaper, this is a free service to all employers (mostly newspapers) who post jobs (coded). Candidates can get listings several different ways. Applicants can fill out an online form indicating areas of interest. If there is a match, candidates are advised and can contact employers directly. Job links to other journalism job banks and related professional sites are maintained. Student interns from Edward Waters College help service the site.

National Educators Employment Review

Publisher/Trade
www.teacherjobs.com/

PO Box 60309, Colorado Springs, CO 80960
Phone: 719-632-5877 Fax: 800-377-1146 e-mail: info@netgraftx.ocm

Jobs? Yes
- Cost to post jobs: Free
- Cost to see jobs: Free
- Specialty: Teaching
- Industry: Teaching
- Country/Region/State/City: US

Resumes? Yes
- Cost to post resumes: Free
- Cost to see resumes: Free

Links to Jobs? No

Career Advice? Yes

Educators magazine that provides a web site with everything for free. You can post a job, a resume, or you can see resumes and obtain career information in a format that is easy to find and easy to understand. Has hundreds of employment opportunities throughout the US in the education field. We recommend you visit this site if teaching is your field.

National Physician Job Listing Directory

Commercial Job Site
www.njnet.com/~embbs/job/jobs.html

M.D. Ash Nashed Triple Star Systems
7 Hickory Court, Middlesex, NJ 08846
Phone: 908-469-7129 e-mail: ashrafn@aol.com

Jobs? Yes
- Cost to post jobs: Fee
- Cost to see jobs: Free
- Specialty: Health Care/MD
- Industry: Health Care
- Country/Region/State/City: US

Resumes? No
- Cost to post resumes: N/A
- Cost to see resumes: N/A

Links to Jobs? No

Career Advice? No

Postings for physicians and other medical specialties cost $20/month. Search jobs by state and contact source directly. A simple site with a few jobs.

National Society of Black Engineers

Association
www.nsbe.com

NSBE
1454 Duke Street, Alexandria, VA 22314
Phone: 703-549-2207 Fax: 703-683-5312

Jobs? Yes
- Cost to post jobs: Fee
- Cost to see jobs: Free
- Specialty: All
- Industry: All
- Country/Region/State/City: US

Resumes? No
- Cost to post resumes: N/A
- Cost to see resumes: N/A

Links to Jobs? Yes

Career Advice? Yes

Site provides classifieds from NSBE, a monthly publication. Career Fair information is also provided with interesting articles on career management.

National Society of Professional Engineering HP

Association
www.nspe.org

NSPE
1420 King Street, Alexandria, VA 22314
Phone: 703-684-4811 e-mail: customer.service@nspe.org

Jobs? Yes
- Cost to post jobs: Free
- Cost to see jobs: Free
- Specialty: Engineering/PE
- Industry: Construction
- Country/Region/State/City: US

Resumes? No
- Cost to post resumes: N/A
- Cost to see resumes: N/A

Links to Jobs? Yes

Career Advice? Yes

Represents licensed engineers across all disciplines. Links to engineer related jobs, guide for choosing engineering as a career and career development issues for young engineers.

The National (Int'l) Home Workers Association

Association
www.homeworkers.com/homeworkers

e-mail: iha@homeworkers.com

Jobs? Yes
- Cost to post jobs: Fee
- Cost to see jobs: Fee
- Specialty: All
- Industry: Work at Home
- Country/Region/State/City: US

Resumes? No
- Cost to post resumes: N/A
- Cost to see resumes: N/A

Links to Jobs? Yes

Career Advice? Yes

News, information and resource for homeworkers. Claims to be a telecommuting association. Job seekers must join to be able to view jobs. Cost is $79.95 + to be a member.

CAREERXROADS©
Job, Resume & Career Management Sites on the World Wide Web
• The 1997 Directory •

NationJob Network

Career Hub/Agent
www.nationjob.com

Bob Levenstein NationJob, Inc.
2010 Ankeny Blvd., Ankeny, IA 50021
Phone: 800-292-7731 Fax: 515-965-6737 e-mail: njsales@nationjob.com

Jobs? Yes
- Cost to post jobs: Fee
- Cost to see jobs: Free
- Specialty: All
- Industry: All
- Country/Region/State/City: US

Resumes? Yes
- Cost to post resumes: Free
- Cost to see resumes: N/A

Links to Jobs? Yes

Career Advice? Yes

NationJob Online Jobs Database
Current weekly update is 11-22

Welcome to NationJob Network, an on-line job search service with thousands of current job listings and company profiles. Job listings are from around the U.S. with a Midwest focus. About NationJob.

Search for a Job now...

...and sign up P.J. Scout to continue your job search for you!
(e-mail address required). A free service now serving over 70,000 people!

Search for a Job now (no e-mail required).
Search for a Company that meets your custom criteria.
Directory of all Companies available in NationJob.

Thousands of current positions, company profiles, specialized job pages for many discplines and a personal agent (PJ Scout), make NationJob one of the better places to land a job or get the word out. Strong Midwest presence. This site has an excellent design for both Employers and Jobseekers. Sophisticated search, listing and download criteria. A directory of companies allows all ads from that company to be viewed. Links to company site provided. Employer costs are $75 for a 30 day listing but many packages are available. Job seekers will find tremendous flexibility to search among special job groupings that highlight manufacturing, aviation, medical as well as the more traditional engineering and computer areas. Job Seekers should register with "P.J. Scout", an agent which monitors the site and returns new postings to you by e-mail. One of the best sites to watch. NationJob also serves as the classified repository for several newspapers including: Des Moines Register, Cedar Rapids Gazette, Sioux City Journal, Waterloo Courier, Dubuque Telegraph-Herald.

CAREERXROADS©
Job, Resume & Career Management Sites on the World Wide Web
• The 1997 Directory •

Navy

Government
www.navyjobs.com

Phone: 800-872-6289 e-mail: 857_at_fmso.navy.mil

Jobs? Yes
- Cost to post jobs: N/A
- Cost to see jobs: Free
- Specialty: "See the World"
- Industry: Armed Services
- Country/Region/State/City: US

Resumes? No
- Cost to post resumes: N/A
- Cost to see resumes: N/A

Links to Jobs? No

Career Advice? Yes

Even the Navy has a site where you can submit your application on-line and learn more about a careers with the military. Easy to use, cleanly implemented and it gets the job done. Why can't other government agencies look at this site? It could be a model for state employment services.

Net Jobs Information Services

Commercial Job Site
www.netjobs.com

6695 Millcreek Drive, Unit 1, Mississauga, Canada L5N5R8
Phone: 905-542-9484 Fax: 905-542-9479

Jobs? Yes
- Cost to post jobs: Fee
- Cost to see jobs: Free
- Specialty: All
- Industry: All
- Country/Region/State/City: Int'l./Canada

Resumes? Yes
- Cost to post resumes: Fee
- Cost to see resumes: Free

Links to Jobs? Yes

Career Advice? Yes

Canadian employment site with positions listed by company. Contact information is provided so you can e-mail your resume directly. Many links to Canadian companies. Interesting articles on preparing your resume along with interview tips. Employer cost to post jobs is $100 per month and applicant cost to post a resume is $30 for six months. Simple site with lots of information.

Netshare

Commercial Job Site
www.netshare.com

Barbara Blosses
2 Commercial Boulevard, Ste. 200, Novato, CA 94949
Phone: 415-883-1700 Fax: 415-883-1799

Jobs? Yes
- Cost to post jobs: Free
- Cost to see jobs: Fee
- Specialty: All
- Industry: N/A
- Country/Region/State/City: US

Resumes? No
- Cost to post resumes: N/A
- Cost to see resumes: N/A

Links to Jobs? No

Career Advice? Yes

Subscriber service that provides mid-to senior-level job openings to its members in the broad areas of general management, marketing & sales, finance & IS or human resources twice a month through snail mail. Positions can be posted for free. Postings must be limited to positions in 70K area and above. Members are not identified. Positions can be viewed by members through this Internet site. Subscriptions cost $175 for 6 months.

Network World Fusion

Publisher/Trade
www.nwfusion.com

Network World
The Meadows, 161 Worcester Rd., , Framingham, MA 01701
Phone: 508-875-6400 Fax: 508-875-3090 e-mail: webmaster@nwfusion.com

Jobs? Yes
- Cost to post jobs: Fee
- Cost to see jobs: Free
- Specialty: IT/Network
- Industry: N/A
- Country/Region/State/City: US

Resumes? No
- Cost to post resumes: N/A
- Cost to see resumes: N/A

Links to Jobs? No

Career Advice? Yes

Monthly publication focuses on network engineering professionals and provides tools, articles and resources like a help desk forum to attract them to the site. Positions form the publication's classified section are listed online.

New England Journal of Medicine

Publisher/Trade
www.nejm.org/nejm/webmate?nejm/form/nejm/welcome

New England Journal of Medicine
1440 Main Street, Waltham, MA 02154
Phone: 617-893-3800 Fax: 617-893-7729

Jobs? Yes
- Cost to post jobs: Fee
- Cost to see jobs: Free
- Specialty: Health Care/MD
- Industry: Health Care
- Country/Region/State/City: US

Resumes? No
- Cost to post resumes: N/A
- Cost to see resumes: N/A

Links to Jobs? No

Career Advice? No

No added charge to employers who pay for ads in this medical publication. Both line and display ads are posted.

New Jersey Online

Publisher/Newspaper
www.nj.com

Madhavi Saifee Advance Internet
Star Ledger, 30 Journal Square, Jersey City, NJ 07306
Phone: 201-459-2871

Jobs? Yes
- Cost to post jobs: Fee
- Cost to see jobs: Free
- Specialty: All
- Industry: All
- Country/Region/State/City: US/E/NJ

Resumes? No
- Cost to post resumes: N/A
- Cost to see resumes: N/A

Links to Jobs? Yes

Career Advice? No

The classified ads from NJ's "Newark Star Ledger" and "Trenton Times" are extensive and will be available from this site in an easily searchable format...eventually.

CAREERXROADS©
Job, Resume & Career Management Sites on the World Wide Web
• The 1997 Directory •

New York Law Journal

Publisher/Trade
www.lextra.com/classifieds

Leonie Christie
345 Park Avenue, NY, NY 10010
Phone: 212-545-5933

Jobs? Yes
- Cost to post jobs: Fee
- Cost to see jobs: Free
- Specialty: Law
- Industry: Legal
- Country/Region/State/City: US/E/NY

Resumes? No
- Cost to post resumes: N/A
- Cost to see resumes: N/A

Links to Jobs? No

Career Advice? No

Lawyers, paralegals and legal secretaries looking for opportunities in the NYC area will find the classified section of the weekly NY Law Journal readily available. Employers pay for space in the print version and get the Internet as added value.

New York Times

Publisher/Newspaper
www.nytimes.com

Kerrie Gillis New York Times
229 W. 43rd Street, New York, NY 10036
Phone: 212-237-3181 e-mail: kerrie@nytimes

Jobs? Yes
- Cost to post jobs: Fee
- Cost to see jobs: Free
- Specialty: All
- Industry: N/A
- Country/Region/State/City: US/E/NY/NYC

Resumes? No
- Cost to post resumes: N/A
- Cost to see resumes: N/A

Links to Jobs? No

Career Advice? No

Newspaper help wanted classifieds. Help wanted display ads are not included. No extra charges as the employers must pay for advertising in the classified section of the newspaper. This publisher also participates in CareerPath (See CareerPath).

News Link

Publisher/Trade
www.newslink.org

AJR Newslink
8701 Adelphi Road, Adelphi, MD 20783-1716
Phone: 301-431-4771   e-mail: feedback@newslink.org

Jobs? Yes
- Cost to post jobs: Free
- Cost to see jobs: Free
- Specialty: Journalism
- Industry: Journalism
- Country/Region/State/City: Int'l./US

Resumes? Yes
- Cost to post resumes: Free
- Cost to see resumes: Free

Links to Jobs? Yes

Career Advice? No

Positions in journalism can be found with direct contact information. Excellent search engine where you plug in specific data and it finds the opening in your area of journalism expertise. Newspaper links provide direct contact to more than 3,500 on-line newspapers, magazines, broadcasting concerns, news services and other journalistic sites. Opportunity to search papers with classified ads throughout the world at no charge.

NJ Job Search

Government
nj.jobsearch.org

Fred Cantwell   State of New Jersey
Phone: 609-530-3481

Jobs? Yes
- Cost to post jobs: Free
- Cost to see jobs: Free
- Specialty: All
- Industry: All
- Country/Region/State/City: US/NJ

Resumes? Yes
- Cost to post resumes: Free
- Cost to see resumes: Free

Links to Jobs? Yes

Career Advice? Yes

New key word search capability is still a problem for the state of NJ. Site is to complicated and continues to take you to places other then what you wanted. How a state site can allow third party recruiters to link to it is beyond us. Why not have corporations link for free and stop wasting time between the state employment offices and the job seeker. Some day the states will get it, like Wisconsin has, but until that time this site needs a lot of work.

NJ JOBS

Commercial
www.njjobs.com

Robert Peters Advanced Interactive Communications
Phone: 908-303-9333 Fax: 908-303-8614 e-mail: info@njjobs.com

Jobs? Yes
- Cost to post jobs: Fee
- Cost to see jobs: Free
- Specialty: All
- Industry: All
- Country/Region/State/City: US/E/NJ

Resumes? Yes
- Cost to post resumes: Fee
- Cost to see resumes: Free

Links to Jobs? Yes

Career Advice? No

Costs $100 (per position/month) to post ads. Limited openings (40). Some links to other NJ sites with jobs. Employers might consider just registering to this site with a hypertext link. NY Jobs listed as well. Resumes posted for 1 month ($20)- 6 months ($60). Employers can search resumes for free.

NMAA'S Job Banker

Association
www.nmaa.org/jobbank.htm

Nat'l Multimedia Assoc. of America
4920 Niagara Road, 3rd floor, College Park, MD 20740
Phone: 800-819-1335 Fax: 301-513-9466 e-mail: webmaster@nmaa.org

Jobs? Yes
- Cost to post jobs: Free
- Cost to see jobs: Free
- Specialty: Multimedia
- Industry: Multimedia
- Country/Region/State/City: US

Resumes? No
- Cost to post resumes: N/A
- Cost to see resumes: N/A

Links to Jobs? No

Career Advice? No

Jobs can be posted directly to the site. Has a good search engine for posting as well as finding a position in multimedia. In future will have a resume database that will be searchable.

The Nonprofit/Fundraising Jobnet

Community Service
www.philanthropy-journal.org

e-mail: tcohen@nando.net

Jobs? Yes
- Cost to post jobs: Free
- Cost to see jobs: Free
- Specialty: N/A
- Industry: Non-Profit
- Country/Region/State/City: US

Resumes? No
- Cost to post resumes: N/A
- Cost to see resumes: N/A

Links to Jobs? Yes

Career Advice? Yes

Information about opportunities and organizations in the non-profit sector. The Philanthropy Journal Online is the digital effort of this organization. This site has been upgraded since our last visit and is striving to be the leader in this area.

Norfolk Virginian-Pilot Online

Publisher/Newspaper
www.infi.net/pilot

Norfolk Virginian-Pilot
150 W. Brambleton Ave., Norfolk, VA 23510
Phone: 800-446-2004

Jobs? Yes
- Cost to post jobs: Fee
- Cost to see jobs: Free
- Specialty: All
- Industry: N/A
- Country/Region/State/City: US/E/VA/Norfolk

Resumes? No
- Cost to post resumes: N/A
- Cost to see resumes: N/A

Links to Jobs? No

Career Advice? No

Newspaper help-wanted classifieds. Help wanted display ads are not included. No extra charges to employers as they must pay for ad in classified section to gain the web.

No. Carolina Career & Employment

Commercial Job Site
www.webcom.com/~nccareer/

Rich Schreyer Career Connectons of the Cent. Carolinas
8508 Park Road #308, Charlotte, NC 28210
Phone: 704-543-1317 e-mail: nccareer@aol.com

Jobs? Yes
- Cost to post jobs: Fee
- Cost to see jobs: Free
- Specialty: All
- Industry: All
- Country/Region/State/City: US/SE/NC

Resumes? Yes
- Cost to post resumes: Fee
- Cost to see resumes: Fee

Links to Jobs? Yes

Career Advice? Yes

Help Wanted USA network. Ads submitted online by employers for $75 are posted for 2 weeks on America OnLine and The Internet Career Connection and several newsgroups. Information and links for individuals seeking employment in North Carolina is provided. Resume preparation assistance and database at a cost ($30). Nice feature is a package that, for $75, will take your resume and post it on 25 databases. All 25 are listed and include some of the best.

NYC Headhunter's Mall

Placement/Search/Temp
jobs-nyc.com

Kevin McIntyre
175 West 4th Street, New York, NY 10014
Phone: 212-242-2191 e-mail: birt@gramercy.ios.com

Jobs? Yes
- Cost to post jobs: Fee
- Cost to see jobs: Free
- Specialty: All
- Industry: All
- Country/Region/State/City: US

Resumes? No
- Cost to post resumes: Free
- Cost to see resumes: N/A

Links to Jobs? Yes

Career Advice? No

Group of New York headhunters who have gotten together to have their own site. Nice list of links to other resources. Also has a "suggest a link" automatic entry form which gives the site something others have not thought of.

O Hayo Sensei

Publisher/Newspaper
www.ohayosensei.com/~ohayo/

Editor
1032 Irving Street, Suite 508, San Francisco, CA 94122
Fax: 415-731-1113 e-mail: position@ohayosensei.com

Jobs? Yes
- Cost to post jobs: Free
- Cost to see jobs: Free
- Specialty: Teaching
- Industry: Education
- Country/Region/State/City: Int'l./Japan

Resumes? No
- Cost to post resumes: N/A
- Cost to see resumes: N/A

Links to Jobs? No

Career Advice? No

O-Hayo Sensei is a bi-weekly newsletter that lists teaching positions in Japan for public school, colleges & universities. You can see their latest issue for free when you go to their site. They allow schools to post openings for free with direct e-mail contact for you to apply for positions. Ads are in english.

Oasys Network

Commercial Job Site
www.oasysnet.com/home.html

Phone: 800-367-5457 e-mail: info@oasysnet.com

Jobs? Yes
- Cost to post jobs: Fee
- Cost to see jobs: Free
- Specialty: All
- Industry: Advertising
- Country/Region/State/City: US

Resumes? Yes
- Cost to post resumes: Free
- Cost to see resumes: Fee

Links to Jobs? Yes

Career Advice? No

Artists can upload their portfolio for free to this creative site. The employer pays $200 per month for access to this talent bank. If you would like a taste of what this site has to offer try their freelancer of the month screen which will show you a standard format of an artists background with direct contact info.

OfficeNet

Placement/Search/Temp
www.officenet1.com

OfficeNet, Inc.
502 Cutwater Lane, Foster City, CA 94404
Phone: 415-574-7558 Fax: 415-574-3825 e-mail: sales@officenet.com

Jobs? Yes
- Cost to post jobs: N/A
- Cost to see jobs: N/A
- Specialty: Contract/Contingent
- Industry: All
- Country/Region/State/City: US/W

Resumes? No
- Cost to post resumes: N/A
- Cost to see resumes: N/A

Links to Jobs? No

Career Advice? No

This unique temporary services firm is offering to coordinate special projects, do translations, marketing presentations, engineering assignments etc. over the internet with contract employees who work only from their computer. Job seekers can apply by e-mailing their resume.

Omicron Personal Career Center

Association
www.omicronet.com/career/resume.htm#top

e-mail: resumes@omicronet.com

Jobs? No
- Cost to post jobs: N/A
- Cost to see jobs: N/A
- Specialty: IT
- Industry: IT
- Country/Region/State/City: US

Resumes? Yes
- Cost to post resumes: Free
- Cost to see resumes: Free

Links to Jobs? No

Career Advice? Yes

Easy to see list of resumes, (18) present on our visit, which is free of charge to IT professionals which are posted for 90 days. Directory of events for this organization, but as far as the job seeker, that's all folks.

Online Career Center

Career Hub
www.occ.com

Gina Gioe Online Career Center
2780 Waterfront Pkwy. E. Dr., Suite 100, Indianapolis, IN 46214
Phone: 317-293-6499 Fax: 317-293-6692 e-mail: occ@occ.com

Jobs? Yes
- Cost to post jobs: Fee
- Cost to see jobs: Free
- Specialty: All
- Industry: N/A
- Country/Region/State/City: US

Resumes? Yes
- Cost to post resumes: Free
- Cost to see resumes: Fee

Links to Jobs? Yes

Career Advice? Yes

A top site in everyone's book. OCC is highly rated and offers its annual subscribers unlimited job postings. Annual cost is near $3000. Applicants can post resumes for free. Many extras offered from hosting home pages to links. Well designed and executed, this site offers job applicants an outstanding array of information about job fairs, conferences, links to 800 colleges, career related articles from well known authors in addition to jobs and a resume data base. Single ads can be placed through recruitment advertising firms in the $125 range for 4 weeks. Virtual agents, capability to add, post and delete jobs directly online, a recruiter's forum and more are available.

CAREERXROADS©
Job, Resume & Career Management Sites on the World Wide Web
• The 1997 Directory •

OnLine Opportunities

Commercial Job Site
www.jobnet.com

Ward Christman OnLine Opportunities
422 W. Lincoln Hghwy, Ste 124, Exton, PA 19341
Phone: 610-873-6811 Fax: 610-873-4022 e-mail: info@jobnet.com

Jobs? Yes
- Cost to post jobs: Fee
- Cost to see jobs: Free
- Specialty: All
- Industry: N/A
- Country/Region/State/City: US/E/PA

Resumes? Yes
- Cost to post resumes: Free
- Cost to see resumes: Fee

Links to Jobs? Yes

Career Advice? No

Excellent regional site posting to numerous local BBSs in the PA area in addition to Help Wanted-USA Network (See Help Wanted USA). Ward Christman can also help with postings to E-Span, CareerWEB, Microsoft Network and more. Packages range from low hundreds to much more. Ward has been in this business for several years and is extremely knowledgeable about electronic recruiting strategies. He has been giving local courses and provides local recruiters with some unique and valuable hands-on assistance. Employer packages start at less than $100 to post and range upward for company profiles and annual packages. Local Bulletin Board Direct Dial 610-873-7170.

Online Sports Career Center

Placement/Search/Temp
www.onlinesports.com:80/pages/careercenter.html

Sports Management Enterprises
e-mail: resumes@onlinesports.com

Jobs? Yes
- Cost to post jobs: Fee
- Cost to see jobs: Free
- Specialty: Sports
- Industry: Entertainment/Recreation
- Country/Region/State/City: US

Resumes? No
- Cost to post resumes: N/A
- Cost to see resumes: N/A

Links to Jobs? Yes

Career Advice? No

A unique niche to providing sporting goods and recreation industry related positions.

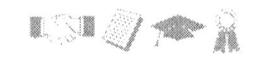

Open Market Comercial Sites Index

Links
www.directory.net/

Open Market, Inc.
245 First Street, Cambridge, MA 02142
e-mail: editors@directory.net

Jobs? No
- Cost to post jobs: N/A
- Cost to see jobs: N/A
- Specialty: N/A
- Industry: N/A
- Country/Region/State/City: US

Resumes? No
- Cost to post resumes: N/A
- Cost to see resumes: N/A

Links to Jobs? Yes

Career Advice? No

This is the "mother lode" of links to companies. From the very large to to the very small, from those you'll recognize in a second to some that you've never heard of, search to your hearts content by using keywords, or by industry, or specialty, etc. This site is updatded daily. If you are in a contest to find the weirdest site, Open Market is a good starting point.

Orlando Sentinel

Publisher/Newspaper
www.orlandosentinel.com

P.O.Box 2833, 633 N. Orange Ave., Orlando, FL 32801
Phone: 407-420-5179

Jobs? Yes
- Cost to post jobs: Fee
- Cost to see jobs: Free
- Specialty: All
- Industry: N/A
- Country/Region/State/City: US/SE/FL
  /Orlando

Resumes? No
- Cost to post resumes: N/A
- Cost to see resumes: N/A

Links to Jobs? No

Career Advice? No

Help-wanted classifieds printed in Sunday's newspaper are posted. Employers will pay an additional $1/line for display ads and $.50/line for regular classified. This publisher participates in CareerPath (See CareerPath).

Packinfo-world

Association
www.packinfo.world.org

World Packaging Organization

Jobs? Yes
- Cost to post jobs: Fee
- Cost to see jobs: Free
- Specialty: Engineering/Packaging
- Industry: Packaging
- Country/Region/State/City: US

Resumes? Yes
- Cost to post resumes: Free
- Cost to see resumes: Fee

Links to Jobs? US

Career Advice? Yes

The Institute of Packaging Professionals and the World Packaging Organization with Dupont Co. have developed a site for reaching packaging engineers and other professionals. We had trouble contacting this site but it will attract attention for companies seeking candidates with these highly specialized skills.

Parksville/Qualicum Career Center

Commercial Job Site
qb.island.net/~careers/

e-mail: ccrdg@9B.island.net

Jobs? No
- Cost to post jobs: N/A
- Cost to see jobs: N/A
- Specialty: All
- Industry: All
- Country/Region/State/City: Int'l./Canada

Resumes? No
- Cost to post resumes: N/A
- Cost to see resumes: N/A

Links to Jobs? Yes

Career Advice? Yes

Articles on finding a job in Canada along with a great list of links to Canadian job sites. Nice graphics make this an easy to use site. Job listings were not found even though an icon points you to the spot. May be a new site getting started.

Passport Access

Commercial Resume Site
www.passportaccess.com

John Malone Passport Access
3470 Mt. Diablo Blvd., Ste. 150, Lafayette, CA 94549
Phone: 510-552-1000 Fax: 510-552-1010 e-mail: webboy@passportaccess.com

Jobs? Yes
- Cost to post jobs: Fee
- Cost to see jobs: Free
- Specialty: All
- Industry: All
- Country/Region/State/City: US

Resumes? Yes
- Cost to post resumes: Free
- Cost to see resumes: Fee

Links to Jobs? Yes

Career Advice? No

Online resume database boasts 50,000 technical resumes and an equal number non-technical. Employers can request and obtain a demo disk to help assess the databases value. Resumes are primarily West Coast demographics. Efforts are made by the owners to source fresh resumes from companies that are downsizing or from outplacement firms, universities etc. We recently spoke to John who advised us that his site would be under going major changes in the near future and would appreciate that we re-look at him after the holiday. We will do an update on our site as this one has great potential.

Perioperative Online Employment Opps

Publisher/Trade
www.aorn.org

Association of Operating Room Nurses
Phone: 800-755-2676

Jobs? Yes
- Cost to post jobs: Fee
- Cost to see jobs: Free
- Specialty: Health Care/Nursing
- Industry: Health Care
- Country/Region/State/City: US

Resumes? No
- Cost to post resumes: N/A
- Cost to see resumes: N/A

Links to Jobs? No

Career Advice? No

This association updates weekly, the nursing positions listed in three publications: Opportunity: AORN Perioperative Referral Service, AORN Journal, and Surgical Services Management. The design is excellent. Applicants select preferred states and use a pull-down window to select from among a dozen nursing specialties and administrtive titles.

Peterson's Education Center

Career Management/College
www.petersons.com

Cris Maloney Peterson's
202 Carnegie Center, Princeton, NJ 08540
Phone: 609-243-9111 Fax: 609-243-9150 e-mail: crism@petersons.com

Jobs? Yes
- Cost to post jobs: Fee
- Cost to see jobs: Free
- Specialty: All
- Industry: N/A
- Country/Region/State/City: US

Resumes? No
- Cost to post resumes: N/A
- Cost to see resumes: N/A

Links to Jobs? Yes

Career Advice? Yes

Career and education information. Positions listed for all levels of educational institutions and summer camps. Jobs are presently listed in alpha order but changes are coming at this major site. Has good articles on writing your resume and many others that can help you in your job serach. Does a great job for the college market and wants to do more.

CAREERXROADS©
Job, Resume & Career Management Sites on the World Wide Web
• **The 1997 Directory** •

Physician Recruit Net

Publisher/Trade
www.physiciannet.com/index.html

Transcontinental Publishing
PO Box 45454, Phoenix, AZ 85064-5454
Phone: 602-331-8448 Fax: 602-331-8448

Jobs? Yes
- Cost to post jobs: Fee
- Cost to see jobs: Free
- Specialty: Health Care/MD
- Industry: Health Care
- Country/Region/State/City: Int'l./US

Resumes? No
- Cost to post resumes: N/A
- Cost to see resumes: N/A

Links to Jobs? No

Career Advice? No

You can see jobs for free but they are coded so you need to e-mail the magazine who in turn sends your info to the employer. With that said some have direct contact info yet all have the ability to e-mail responses to the magazine. Confusing site! Has international as well as US openings. Nice map of US so you can focus on what area you wish to locate to. Search engine concentrates on your specialty which saves you time.

Physicians Employment

Commercial Job Site
www.physemp.com

Robert Truog
58 1/2 Main Street 200, Fairfield, IA 52556
Phone: 515-472-0998 Fax: 515-472-3007 e-mail: truog@lisco.com

Jobs? Yes
- Cost to post jobs: Fee
- Cost to see jobs: Free
- Specialty: Health Care
- Industry: Health Care
- Country/Region/State/City: US

Resumes? No
- Cost to post resumes: N/A
- Cost to see resumes: N/A

Links to Jobs? Yes

Career Advice? Yes

Physicians positions can be posted for free. If you are running multiple ads then there is a charge. Recruitment firms pay a fee for all ads. Site gives direct contact information while also listing fellowship openings around the country. Links to other medical sites. You have to register to get into the jobs directory. Nice search engine with ability to e-mail responses to posted jobs.

CAREERXROADS©
Job, Resume & Career Management Sites on the World Wide Web
• The 1997 Directory •

Physics Jobs On-Line

College/University
www.tp.umu.se/TIPTOP/

Kenneth Holmlund Umea University
Dept. Theoretical Physics, S-901 87 Umea, Sweden
Phone: 460-901-67717 e-mail: kenneth.holmlund@tp.umu.se

Jobs? Yes
- Cost to post jobs: Free
- Cost to see jobs: Free
- Specialty: Physics
- Industry: Education
- Country/Region/State/City: Int'l/US

Resumes? Yes
- Cost to post resumes: Free
- Cost to see resumes: Free

Links to Jobs? No

Career Advice? No

Information on jobs in Physics supported by university departments from around the world. Many post-doc position openings with links to the employer are provided. Jobs go up as soon as soon as they are received. Site has over 100 openings with 69 resumes posted on our last visit. Simple site that gets the job done.

Pioneer Press

Publisher/Newspaper
www.pioneerlocal.com

Pioneer Press
,Phone: 708-256-9286 Fax: 708-251-7606

Jobs? Yes
- Cost to post jobs: Fee
- Cost to see jobs: Free
- Specialty: All
- Industry: N/A
- Country/Region/State/City: US/MW/IL

Resumes? No
- Cost to post resumes: N/A
- Cost to see resumes: N/A

Links to Jobs? No

Career Advice? No

Help wanted section from 45 Chicago suburban newspapers classified pages.

Planet Jobs-Phil. On-Line Classifieds

Publisher/Newspaper
www.phillynews.com/programs/ads/SUNHLP

Dennis Wichterman Philadelphia Inquirer
400 N.Broad Street, Philadelphia, PA 19101
Phone: 215-563-5000 e-mail: adsmanager@phillynews.com

Jobs? Yes
- Cost to post jobs: Fee
- Cost to see jobs: Free
- Specialty: All
- Industry: N/A
- Country/Region/State/City: US/E/PA/Phil.

Resumes? No
- Cost to post resumes: N/A
- Cost to see resumes: N/A

Links to Jobs? No

Career Advice? No

Help Wanted advertising in the Philadelphia Inquirer.

Plasma Laboratory Wis

College/University
plasma-gate.weizman.ac.il/jobs.html

Prof Yitzhak Maron
Phone: 972-893-44055 Fax: 972-893-44106

Jobs? Yes
- Cost to post jobs: Free
- Cost to see jobs: Free
- Specialty: Physics
- Industry: Biotechnology/Pharmaceutical
- Country/Region/State/City: Int'l.

Resumes? No
- Cost to post resumes: N/A
- Cost to see resumes: N/A

Links to Jobs? No

Career Advice? No

Post-doc/research/lectureship positions listed for all over the world opportunities. Site allows you to post jobs directly with contact information available in a very specific niche- Atomic & Plasma Physics. E-mail for site is: fnevgeny@plasma-gate.weizmann.ac.il

PolySort

Commercial Job Site
www.polysort.com

Carolyn Reed-Dickson
4040 Embassy Parkway Ste.180, Akron, OH 44333
Phone: 800-326-8666 Fax: 330-665-5152 e-mail: crd@polysort.com

Jobs? Yes
- Cost to post jobs: Fee
- Cost to see jobs: Free
- Specialty: Chemistry
- Industry: Rubber and Plastics
- Country/Region/State/City: US/E/NY

Resumes? No
- Cost to post resumes: N/A
- Cost to see resumes: N/A

Links to Jobs? No

Career Advice? No

Employers pay $150 range per month to post ads at this highly specialized site serving the rubber and plastics industries. For first time clients you can post a job for $99. Extensive industry news, discussion groups for injection molding, packaging, recycling professional and links to more than 450 company web sites including BASF, DOW, DuPont and Monsanto, as well as links to worldwide industry and association sites, are a great attraction. Excellent niche site.

Pop Jobs

Commercial Job Site
www.popjobs.com

Kelly O'Leary Hoyt Publishing Company
7400 Skokie Blvd., Skokie, IL 60097
Phone: 847-675-7494 Fax: 847-675-7400 e-mail: hoytpub@interaccess.com

Jobs? Yes
- Cost to post jobs: Fee
- Cost to see jobs: Fee
- Specialty: Advertising
- Industry: Advertising
- Country/Region/State/City: US

Resumes? No
- Cost to post resumes: N/A
- Cost to see resumes: N/A

Links to Jobs? No

Career Advice? No

Site offers access to jobs and resumes in the "point of purchase advertising industry". Applicants are charged approx $100 for posting resumes that are on the web for 8 weeks. Employers pay in the $250 range and up, adding a logo, e-mail link, web site link etc. Rate sheet is available for downloading. Nice niche.

Positions in Psychology

College/University/Agent
www.anu.edu.au/psychology/PiP/pip.htm

Austrailian National University

Jobs? Yes
- Cost to post jobs: Free
- Cost to see jobs: Free
- Specialty: Psychology
- Industry: N/A
- Country/Region/State/City: Int'l

Resumes? No
- Cost to post resumes: N/A
- Cost to see resumes: N/A

Links to Jobs? No

Career Advice? No

Positions in Psychology maintains openings worldwide. To register and have new position announcements sent directly via e-mail. Send blank message to:lubosh.hanuska @anu.edu.au

Potpourri Shoppers

Publisher/Newspaper
www.netview.com/pp/employ/

Harte-Hanks Communications
e-mail: mksview@netview.com

Jobs? Yes
- Cost to post jobs: Fee
- Cost to see jobs: Free
- Specialty: N/A
- Industry: All
- Country/Region/State/City: US/W/CA

Resumes? No
- Cost to post resumes: N/A
- Cost to see resumes: N/A

Links to Jobs? No

Career Advice? No

Employment opportunities in the Silicon Valley of California. Few jobs posted but has direct access information, and the price is right to see opportunities (free) on the web.

Princeton 1 Info (US 1)

Publisher/Newspaper
www.princetoninfo.com

Barbara Figge Fox US 1 Newspapers
12 Roszel Road, Princeton, NJ 08540
Phone: 609-452-0033 Fax: 609-452-0038 e-mail: reply@princetoninfo.com

Jobs? Yes
- Cost to post jobs: Fee
- Cost to see jobs: Free
- Specialty: All
- Industry: All
- Country/Region/State/City: US/E/NJ

Resumes? Yes
- Cost to post resumes: Free
- Cost to see resumes: Free

Links to Jobs? No

Career Advice? Yes

Cental NJ newspaper that allows job seekers to post a brief on themselves for free. Good local information with a survival guide for businesses to help you grow your company.

Princeton Review Online

Career Management
www.review.com

Steven Hodas 2315 Broadway
NY, NY 10024
Phone: 212-874-8282 Fax: 212-874-0775 e-mail: steven@review.com

Jobs? No
- Cost to post jobs: N/A
- Cost to see jobs: N/A
- Specialty: N/A
- Industry: N/A
- Country/Region/State/City: US

Resumes? No
- Cost to post resumes: N/A
- Cost to see resumes: N/A

Links to Jobs? US

Career Advice? Yes

Downloadable advice for entry-level college grads on how to obtain a job. Includes America's top 100 internships and job seminar info. Articles from Princeton Review books.

Pro Net Search

Commercial Job Site
bisinc.com/pronet/ccc/

Buck Information Systems, Inc.
22 Orchard Hill, Hamilton, Ontario, Canada L8P2V8
Phone: 800-355-2666 Fax: 905-777-0383 e-mail: psmail@inforamp.net

Jobs? Yes
- Cost to post jobs: Fee
- Cost to see jobs: Free
- Specialty: IT
- Industry: All
- Country/Region/State/City: Int'l./Canada

Resumes? Yes
- Cost to post resumes: Free
- Cost to see resumes: Fee

Links to Jobs? Yes

Career Advice? No

Cost to post jobs is $65 per job which sounds like you can see the resumes the site collects as well. If you want an advertisement to be blind it is $15 a week extra. All job ads are on the site in 24-48 hours. Site is for computer professionals while being dedicated to the Canadian computing industry. What we do not understand is that the site is also a recruiting agency. Which is it, free or minimal cost or an agency fee ? Hard to tell.

Proctor & Gamble Career Center

Company
www.pg.com/docCareers/index9.html

PO Box 599 TN-4, Department WWW, Cincinnati, OH 45201-0599
e-mail: careers@pg.com

Jobs? Yes
- Cost to post jobs: N/A
- Cost to see jobs: Free
- Specialty: All
- Industry: Consumer Products
- Country/Region/State/City: Int'l./US

Resumes? No
- Cost to post resumes: Free
- Cost to see resumes: N/A

Links to Jobs? No

Career Advice? Yes

One of the few company sites we have listed. We added P&G because they did an interesting thing with their job information-they outsourced it to OCC. Takes away a lot of headache and gives it to a group that knows what they are doing. They still post generic domestic and international jobs at their site but for more specific position information you should go to OCC. Can send your resume via e-mail direct to apply.

Programmers Available

Commercial Job Site
www.qldnet.com.au/web.users/programmers

Captive Data
PO Box 8005, Southport   QLD 4215, Australia
Phone: 617-553-77304   Fax: 617-553-76489   e-mail: captive@xenios.qldnet.com.au

Jobs? Yes
- Cost to post jobs: Free
- Cost to see jobs: Free
- Specialty: Part time work.
- Industry: IT
- Country/Region/State/City: Int'l./US

Resumes? Yes
- Cost to post resumes: Free
- Cost to see resumes: Free

Links to Jobs? No

Career Advice? No

Site is designed to help companies locate programmers who would like to program from home via the Internet. No charge to post jobs (only had 1 on our visits) but expect it will get more. Easy to find info.

Psych

Association
psych.hanover.edu:80%-zfaps/

American Psychological Society

Jobs? Yes
- Cost to post jobs: Fee
- Cost to see jobs: Free
- Specialty: Psychology
- Industry: All
- Country/Region/State/City: US

Resumes? No
- Cost to post resumes: N/A
- Cost to see resumes: N/A

Links to Jobs? Yes

Career Advice? No

Next to mind games being played on the internet, you'll find key opportunities for this profession...requiring PhDs of course. Cost to employers based on placing ad in their publication. Had difficulty finding job opportunities on our last visit but know they are there via the magazine.

PT Net (Physical Therapy)

College/University
bob.coe.uga.edu/%7escott/pt.html

e-mail: scott@coe.uga.edu

Jobs? No
- Cost to post jobs: N/A
- Cost to see jobs: N/A
- Specialty: Physical Therapy
- Industry: Health Care
- Country/Region/State/City: US

Resumes? No
- Cost to post resumes: N/A
- Cost to see resumes: N/A

Links to Jobs? Yes

Career Advice? No

List of links to other physical therapy sites as well as a selection of information on career management. Did not see jobs posted as we have in the past. Extensive list of listserves for the field.

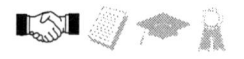

Purchasing NAPM

Association
catalog.com/napmsv/jobs.htm

Nat'l Assoc. of Purchasing Mgmt.
PO Box 32156, San Jose, CA 95152-2156
Phone: 408-929-6276 Fax: 408-929-6277 e-mail: info@napmsv.com

Jobs? Yes
- Cost to post jobs: Free
- Cost to see jobs: Free
- Specialty: Purchasing
- Industry: All
- Country/Region/State/City: US/W/CA

Resumes? No
- Cost to post resumes: N/A
- Cost to see resumes: N/A

Links to Jobs? No

Career Advice? No

Numerous purchasing and materials management positions are listed here free to see by the National Association of Purchasing Management out of California. Direct contact information is available with good job descriptions on the open positions.

Purdue's Job List

Links/College
www.ups.purdue.edu/student/jobsites.htm

Purdue Universit

Jobs? No
- Cost to post jobs: N/A
- Cost to see jobs: N/A
- Specialty: All
- Industry: All
- Country/Region/State/City: US

Resumes? No
- Cost to post resumes: N/A
- Cost to see resumes: N/A

Links to Jobs? Yes

Career Advice? No

Placement Service — **Student Info**

Internet Sites for Job Seekers and Employers

A listing of over 955 On-Line Job-Search Resources and Services, brought to you by Purdue University Placement Service

Last Updated November 8, 1996

Best set of Job Site links maintained by a college. Great service and very few errors. Recruiters should treat this site as a treasure trove. Forget the links and look at what Purdue Placement operation is providing you. We don't want to say any more for fear of killing the golden goose.

Pursuit Net Jobs

Commercial Resume Site
www.tiac.net/users/jobs/index.html

David Jaynes PursuitNet, Inc.
60 Franklin Road, Winchester, MA 01890
Phone: 617-729-2814 e-mail: jobs@pusuitnet.com

Jobs? Yes
- Cost to post jobs: Fee
- Cost to see jobs: Fee
- Specialty: All
- Industry: All
- Country/Region/State/City: Int'/Canada/US

Resumes? Yes
- Cost to post resumes: Free
- Cost to see resumes: Fee

Links to Jobs? Yes

Career Advice? No

Employers post opportunities and pay a "success" fee to match against database of potential applicants. Applicants aren't charged for posting their resume using an online form.

Have you found a site that isn't listed in CAREERXROADS?

Have you REGISTERED to receive FREE updates?

Keep us informed.

We'll keep you informed.

CAREERXROADS
Where Talent and Opportunity Connect on the Internet

CAREERXROADS©
Job, Resume & Career Management Sites on the World Wide Web
• The 1997 Directory •

Radio DJ's Unemployed

Commercial Job Site
www.icnet.net/users/wwhite/urdjhome.htm

Matt Michaels
e-mail: wwhite@icnet.net

Jobs? Yes
- Cost to post jobs: Free
- Cost to see jobs: Free
- Specialty: Communications/Radio
- Industry: Comunications
- Country/Region/State/City: Int'l/US

Resumes? Yes
- Cost to post resumes: Free
- Cost to see resumes: Free

Links to Jobs? Yes

Career Advice? No

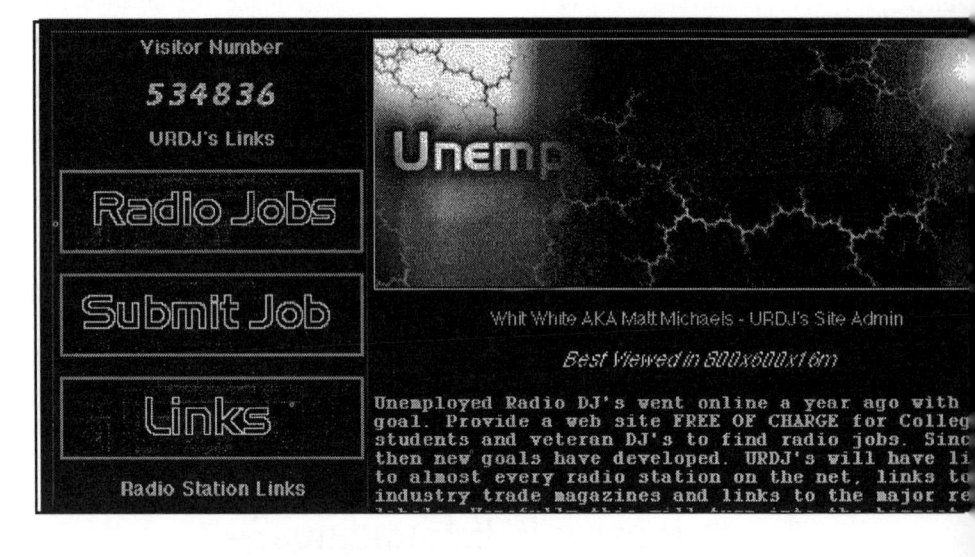

Site has jobs, resumes, links to the world's radio stations so you can contact them for career information. If you want a job as a disc jockey, this is the place to look as it has it all. Site where you can post your resume directly and makes it easy for you to do. Nice set up, easy to find information make this a top site to visit.

Real Bank

Commercial Job Site/Agent
www.realbank.com

RealBank
429 East 52nd Street, Suite 6-D, New York, NY 10022
Phone: 212-355-6159 Fax: 212-751-3797 e-mail: webmaster@realbank.com

Jobs? Yes
- Cost to post jobs: Free
- Cost to see jobs: Free
- Specialty: Real Estate
- Industry: Real Estate
- Country/Region/State/City: US

Resumes? Yes
- Cost to post resumes: Free
- Cost to see resumes: Free

Links to Jobs? No

Career Advice? No

Site owner posts profiles of Real Estate candidates with titles ranging from Property Managers and Real Estate Attorneys to Directors of Real Estate Development. The profiles do not include names and contact information. Instead, the owner will forward company information to the candidate. Employers can also post positions directly to a jobs database. All activity takes place through online forms. Free in 1996, expect some form of fee eventually.

Real Jobs

College/University
www.real-jobs.com

Dr. Norm Miller
Phone: 513-556-7088 e-mail: real.jobs@horandata.net

Jobs? Yes
- Cost to post jobs: Free
- Cost to see jobs: Free
- Specialty: Real Estate
- Industry: Real Estate
- Country/Region/State/City: US

Resumes? Yes
- Cost to post resumes: Free
- Cost to see resumes: Free

Links to Jobs? No

Career Advice? No

Information on Real Estate professional positions. Need to gain a password to see jobs/resumes posted. Jobs/resumes stay posted for 3 months. Originally set up to support real estate programs in universities around the country, but now also supports alumni, professionals and trade associations.

Recruit Net

Publisher/Newspaper
recruitnet.guardian.co.uk/

The Guardian Media Group
e-mail: feedback@guardian.co.uk

Jobs? Yes
- Cost to post jobs: Fee
- Cost to see jobs: Free
- Specialty: N/A
- Industry: N/A
- Country/Region/State/City: Int'l/UK

Resumes? No
- Cost to post resumes: N/A
- Cost to see resumes: N/A

Links to Jobs? No

Career Advice? No

Publication classifieds are nicely organized by category. Each category has an indication of how many ads are listed. When you click on a category, each opening is a brief description with full text and contact information immediately available. But the best is yet to come. As far as we can see this is the first newspaper that also acts as your (jobseek) assistant. Register at the site and you'll have openings e-mailed to you. US media take note.

Recruiters Online Network

Placement/Search Firm
www.ipa.com

Bill Vick
3325 Landershire Lane, Suite 1001, Plano, TX 75023
Phone: 972-612-8425 Fax: 972-612-1924 e-mail: info@ipa.com

Jobs? Yes
- Cost to post jobs: Fee
- Cost to see jobs: Free
- Specialty: YES
- Industry: All
- Country/Region/State/City: Employment/Search

Resumes? Yes
- Cost to post resumes: Free
- Cost to see resumes: Fee

Links to Jobs? Yes

Career Advice? Yes

Bill Vick has created a network of recruiter members (not employers) who share openings they are working on or tap the site's database of resumes. A bookstore is open and additional recruiter related services and partnerships.

Recruitex Technologies

Commercial Job Site
www.recruitex.com/

Greg Scott
1434 Johnston Road, White Rock, BC, Canada
Phone: 604-899-2224 Fax: 604-538-4841 e-mail: gregs@recruitex.com

Jobs? Yes
- Cost to post jobs: Fee
- Cost to see jobs: Free
- Specialty: All
- Industry: All
- Country/Region/State/City: US

Resumes? Yes
- Cost to post resumes: Free
- Cost to see resumes: Fee

Links to Jobs? Yes

Career Advice? Yes

Site provides the ability to send your resume directly via e-mail to a listing of employment agencies and read their profiles on their field of expertise. Links to numerous sites with career links as well. Cannot see if this site is an agency (although they say they are not) but I could not find cost information for posting jobs. Site when we went to press, is still under construction but will be open January 1997. Check it out as it seems to have potential.

Recruiting Links

Links
www.recruiting-links.com/

Skillsearch Corporation
3354 Perimeter Hill Drive, Suite 235, Nashville, TN 37211-4129
Phone: 800-252-5665 Fax: 615-834-9453 e-mail: skillsearch@internet-is.com

Jobs? No
- Cost to post jobs: N/A
- Cost to see jobs: N/A
- Specialty: All
- Industry: All
- Country/Region/State/City: US

Resumes? No
- Cost to post resumes: N/A
- Cost to see resumes: N/A

Links to Jobs? Yes

Career Advice? No

Internet Link service that provides a search engine that allows applicants to search for your site by location, business profile and jobs. Can search by function, discipline or specialty. Nice idea, worth a visit as from the employers standpoint you can update your profile monthly to post new positions. You select from 700 specific categories. Cost is $1,615 per year for your site to link to this one. Site to watch. From a job seeker's perspective this is the pot of gold at the end of the world wide web rainbow. No more spending hours looking. It is new, so let's see what time brings.

Red Guide to Temporary Agencies

Links
www.best.com/~ezy/redguide/intro.html

Angus B. Grieve-Smith
e-mail: grvsmth@panix.com

Jobs? No
- Cost to post jobs: N/A
- Cost to see jobs: N/A
- Specialty: All
- Industry: All
- Country/Region/State/City: US/W/CA/San Fran

Resumes? No
- Cost to post resumes: N/A
- Cost to see resumes: N/A

Links to Jobs? Yes

Career Advice? Yes

Directory of San Francisco temporary employment agencies. This business has fast become the mainstay for most of America's income what with righ/down sizings. Done in alpha order with contact info, it is plain vanilla and gets the job done. Nice work from someone who does this as a good will gesture.

Resources for Students of Color

College/Diversity
www.alumni.wesleyan.edu/WWW/Info/CPC/soc.html

Michael Sciola Wesleyan University
284 High Street, Middletown, CT 06459
Phone: 860-685-2180 e-mail: msciola@wesleyan.edu.

Jobs? Yes
- Cost to post jobs: Free
- Cost to see jobs: Free
- Specialty: All
- Industry: All
- Country/Region/State/City: US

Resumes? No
- Cost to post resumes: N/A
- Cost to see resumes: N/A

Links to Jobs? Yes

Career Advice? Yes

Numerous internships are listed for people of color as well as career programs/conference information. Problem we have with this site is that one has to call/go in to get the contact information for the internship positions. It seems they are only open to the students of Wesleyan University.

Restrac

Recruiting Services
www.restrac.com

Greg Morse Restrac, inc.
3 Allied Drive, Dedham, MA 02026
Phone: 617-320-5600 Fax: 617-320-5630 e-mail: greg@restrac.com

Jobs? No
- Cost to post jobs: N/A
- Cost to see jobs: N/A
- Specialty: N/A
- Industry: All
- Country/Region/State/City: US

Resumes? No
- Cost to post resumes: N/A
- Cost to see resumes: N/A

Links to Jobs? Yes

Career Advice? No

Indirectly, this site can enlighten the sophisticated job seeker about how recruiters are using emerging technology. Restrac sells, installs and supports staffing automation and skills management systems for high volume recruitment. They have developed alliances with several WWW career hub sites including, Monsterboard and Intellimatch toward the goal of "seamless" electronic recruiting and searching. With a recent alliance with the Hunter Group they can assist your corporation with implementation and recruiting process improvement.

Resumatch, Inc.

Commercial Resume Site
resumatch.com

PO Box 434, Gainesville, FL 32602
e-mail: david@resumatch.com

Jobs? No
- Cost to post jobs: N/A
- Cost to see jobs: N/A
- Specialty: Resumes
- Industry: All
- Country/Region/State/City: US

Resumes? Yes
- Cost to post resumes: Fee
- Cost to see resumes: Free

Links to Jobs? No

Career Advice? No

Resume posting service that allows you to see the contact info on candidates directly. Has hundreds of resumes posted. Will have a search engine in the future, as for now it is a tedious process.

The Resume Hut

Career Management
www.penlan.com/penlan

The PenLan Career Group
743 View Street, Victoria, BC V8W1J9
Phone: 604-383-3983 Fax: 604-383-1580

Jobs? No
- Cost to post jobs: N/A
- Cost to see jobs: N/A
- Specialty: N/A
- Industry: N/A
- Country/Region/State/City: US

Resumes? Yes
- Cost to post resumes: Free
- Cost to see resumes: Free

Links to Jobs? Yes

Career Advice? Yes

An experienced supplier of career management services offers some unique information and a wide variety of career service advice. Offers resume writing, coaching, cover letters, etc. by e-mail, fax, phone etc. Costs range from a few dollars and up. Has recently added links to job sites. Resumes are now available to see as well.

Resumes on the Web

Commercial Resume Site
www.resweb.com

Sharon Das Resumes on the Web
959 Severin Drive, Bridgewater, NJ 08807
Phone: 908-429-9141 Fax: 908-828-4700 e-mail: sdas@ifu.net

Jobs? Yes
- Cost to post jobs: Fee
- Cost to see jobs: Free
- Specialty: All
- Industry: All
- Country/Region/State/City: US

Resumes? Yes
- Cost to post resumes: Fee
- Cost to see resumes: Free

Links to Jobs? No

Career Advice? No

Primarily a resume writing service, Resumes on the Web charges in the $25 range. The site sells higher priced packages for publicizing applicant resumes elsewhere. Offers to post positions e-mailed by employers for $8 per position. You can now see resumes for free on this site, while it also has a search engine to assist you with numerous categories. Contact information is available. Clean and simple service.

Resume-Link

Commercial Resume Site
resume-link.com

Susan Ross
P.O. Box 218, 3960 Brown Park Drive, Hillaird, OH 43026
Phone: 614-529-0429 Fax: 614-771-5708 e-mail: sross@resume-link

Jobs? No
- Cost to post jobs: N/A
- Cost to see jobs: N/A
- Specialty: All
- Industry: All
- Country/Region/State/City: US

Resumes? Yes
- Cost to post resumes: Free
- Cost to see resumes: Fee

Links to Jobs? No

Career Advice? No

This site has an agreement with the IEEE, SAE, SPE, ASME, ACM where members can register and send a resume on-line (free) which will be added to their database within 48 hours. Employers pay $275 to search the database once or $1395 to get a years subscription with monthly updates. Employers receive software that allows them to search whenever they want. Site now has an agent that matches jobs/candidates.

Resumix

Private Site
www.resumix.com

Resumix Inc.
2953 Bunker Hill Lane, Santa Clara, CA 95054
Phone: 800-988-0003 Fax: 408-727-9893 e-mail: info@resumix.com

Jobs? No
- Cost to post jobs: N/A
- Cost to see jobs: N/A
- Specialty: N/A
- Industry: N/A
- Country/Region/State/City: US

Resumes? No
- Cost to post resumes: N/A
- Cost to see resumes: N/A

Links to Jobs? Yes

Career Advice? Yes

How to prepare a resume-electronically, to increase an applicant's chances that their resume will be viewed after being optically scanned. One of the pioneers in the development of optical scanning systems for high volume recruiting.

Right Management Consultants, Inc.

Career Management
www.right.com

1818 Market Street, Thirty-third floor, Philadelphia, PA 19103
Phone: 800-237-4448 Fax: 215-988-0081 e-mail: info@right.com

Jobs? Yes
- Cost to post jobs: Free
- Cost to see jobs: Fee
- Specialty: All
- Industry: All
- Country/Region/State/City: US

Resumes? No
- Cost to post resumes: N/A
- Cost to see resumes: N/A

Links to Jobs? No

Career Advice? Yes

Right Associates is one of the major players in the career management arena. Most of this site is presently under construction. Seeing jobs is limited to their candidates at this time. In the future resume briefs will be posted for recruiters to see for free.

The Riley Guide

Links
www.jobtrak.com/jobguide/

Margaret Riley Margaret Riley
3726 Nimitz Rd., Kensington, MD 20895
Phone: 301-946-1917 Fax: 301-933-9529 e-mail: mfriley@erols.com

Jobs? No
- Cost to post jobs: N/A
- Cost to see jobs: N/A
- Specialty: NO
- Industry: N/A
- Country/Region/State/City: N/A

Resumes? No
- Cost to post resumes: N/A
- Cost to see resumes: N/A

Links to Jobs? Yes

Career Advice? Yes

Co-author of the PLA Guide to Internet Job Searching (VGM Career Horizons, April, 1996). A true Icon when it comes to recruiting information on the net. Margaret was one of the very first to catalog the recruiting sites. Definitely the queen of the job links. Look for Margaret's columns in National Business Employment Weekly. Site is filled with annotated information about the links.

Roanoke Times Online

Publisher/Newspaper
www.infi.net/roatimes/index.html

Roanoke Times & World News
201-09 W. Campbell Street, Roanoke, VA 24010
Phone: 800-346-1234 Fax: 540-981-3365 e-mail: roatimes@infi.net

Jobs? Yes
- Cost to post jobs: Fee
- Cost to see jobs: Free
- Specialty: All
- Industry: N/A
- Country/Region/State/City: US/E/VA/Roanoke

Resumes? No
- Cost to post resumes: N/A
- Cost to see resumes: N/A

Links to Jobs? No

Career Advice? No

Help wanted advertising from Sundays' paper. Ads remain searchable by keyword for 1 week.

Rocky Mountain News

Publisher/Newspaper
www.denver-rmn.com

400 West Colfax Ave., Denver, CO 80204
Phone: 303-892-2676

Jobs? Yes
- Cost to post jobs: Fee
- Cost to see jobs: Free
- Specialty: All
- Industry: N/A
- Country/Region/State/City: US/W/CO/Denver

Resumes? No
- Cost to post resumes: N/A
- Cost to see resumes: N/A

Links to Jobs? No

Career Advice? No

Classified advertisements are published on this site for all to see.

RPI Career Resource Home Page

College/University
www.rpi.edu:80/dept/cdc

Jasmit Singh Kochhar Renssalear Polytechnic Institute
Career Development Center, Troy, NY 12180
Phone: 518-276-2952 e-mail: kochhj@rpi.edu

Jobs? Yes
- Cost to post jobs: Free
- Cost to see jobs: Free
- Specialty: All
- Industry: All
- Country/Region/State/City: US

Resumes? Yes
- Cost to post resumes: Free
- Cost to see resumes: Free

Links to Jobs? Yes

Career Advice? Yes

Good college model. Everything from student resumes, jobs database and employer profiles. Jasmit has been busy working on other sites as this one has not been updated since July, 1996. Still has some interesting things you can learn.

RS/6000 Employment Page

Commercial Job Site
www.s6000.com/job.html

Donohue Consulting, Inc.
Phone: 202-362-8144 e-mail: dci@s6000.com

Jobs? Yes
- Cost to post jobs: Free
- Cost to see jobs: Free
- Specialty: RS 6000
- Industry: IT
- Country/Region/State/City: US

Resumes? Yes
- Cost to post resumes: Free
- Cost to see resumes: Free

Links to Jobs? No

Career Advice? No

Site that provides a free service by posting jobs and resumes for people interested in RS/6000 (the world of IT). Basic site that gets it done. Direct contact information is available.

Sacramento Bee

Publisher/Newspaper
www.sacramentobee.com

2100 Q Street, Sacramento, CA 95816
Phone: 916-321-1234

Jobs? Yes
- Cost to post jobs: Fee
- Cost to see jobs: Free
- Specialty: All
- Industry: N/A
- Country/Region/State/City: US/W/CA/Sacramento

Resumes? No
- Cost to post resumes: N/A
- Cost to see resumes: N/A

Links to Jobs? No

Career Advice? No

Help wanted classifieds printed in Sunday's newspaper are posted. This publisher participates in CareerPath (See CareerPath). Help wanted display ads are not included on the Internet site.

Saludos Career Web

Publisher/Diversity
www.wenet.nt/saludos/

Erika Christiansen Saludos Hispanos
41-550 Eclectic Street, Suite 260, Palm Desert, CA 92260
Phone: 619-776-1206 Fax: 619-776-1214 e-mail: erikac@saludos.com

Jobs? Yes
- Cost to post jobs: Fee
- Cost to see jobs: Free
- Specialty: All
- Industry: All
- Country/Region/State/City: US/W/CA

Resumes? Yes
- Cost to post resumes: Free
- Cost to see resumes: Fee

Links to Jobs? Yes

Career Advice? Yes

Hispanic focus for career information and positions in the SF Bay area. Supported by Saludos Hispanos magazine. Excellent material. Post resumes for free. Employers can search resumes and contact candidates directly. Costs to employers range upward from $50 for posting an ad to several hundred for web pages and higher for sponsorship opportunities.

San Francisco Bay Area Job Lines

Links
www.webcom.com:80/~rmd/bay_area/joblines.html

Gina di Gualco
e-mail: regina@netcom.com

Jobs? No
- Cost to post jobs: N/A
- Cost to see jobs: N/A
- Specialty: All
- Industry: All
- Country/Region/State/City: US/W/CA

Resumes? No
- Cost to post resumes: N/A
- Cost to see resumes: N/a

Links to Jobs? Yes

Career Advice? No

Links to job telephone hot lines in the SF Bay area. Links to sites so you can see what jobs are available. Nice idea for links in one specific area of the country.

San Francisco Chronicle-Classified on the Gateway

Publisher/Newspaper
www.sfgate.com/classifieds/

San Francisco Chronicle
San Francisco, CA

Jobs? Yes
- Cost to post jobs: Fee
- Cost to see jobs: Free
- Specialty: All
- Industry: All
- Country/Region/State/City: US/W/CA/San Francisco

Resumes? No
- Cost to post resumes: N/A
- Cost to see resumes: N/A

Links to Jobs? No

Career Advice? No

Help wanted advertising from the San Francisco Chronicle. Several weeks worth of openings are maintained.

Sanford Rose Associates

Placement/Search/Temp
www.sanfordrose.com/

Sanford Rose Associates
Phone: 800-731-7724

Jobs? Yes
- Cost to post jobs: Fee
- Cost to see jobs: Free
- Specialty: All
- Industry: All
- Country/Region/State/City: US

Resumes? No
- Cost to post resumes: N/A
- Cost to see resumes: N/A

Links to Jobs? Yes

Career Advice? No

This home page is used by dozens of offices throughout the country associated with the SRA franchise. Quite a few jobs are listed. Check out the listing of offices and their specialties.

SC WIST Work Pathfinder

Association
www.harbour.sfu.ca/scwist/pathfinder/index.htm

Women in Science & Technology
Canada
e-mail: scwist@sfu.ca

Jobs? No
- Cost to post jobs: N/A
- Cost to see jobs: N/A
- Specialty: All
- Industry: All
- Country/Region/State/City: Int'l/Canada

Resumes? No
- Cost to post resumes: N/A
- Cost to see resumes: N/A

Links to Jobs? Yes

Career Advice? Yes

Links to many Canadian companies that have jobs posted. Good career advice, articles on resume writing tips and on networking. Lists of work finder clubs/associations to e-mail to join to help your career. Easy to use site that is trying to assist women in science & technology get ahead and break the glass ceiling.

Science Global Career Network

Publisher/Trade Magazine
www.aaas.org

Janice Crowley Science Magazine
1200 NY Avenue N.W., Washington, DC 20005
Phone: 212-326-6400 Fax: 202-682-0816 e-mail: science_classifieds@aaas.org

Jobs? Yes
- Cost to post jobs: Fee
- Cost to see jobs: Fee
- Specialty: Science
- Industry: Science
- Country/Region/State/City: Int'l/US

Resumes? No
- Cost to post resumes: N/A
- Cost to see resumes: N/A

Links to Jobs? Yes

Career Advice? Yes

Science Magazine provides internet exposure for all employer paid classifieds (including display ads). Science has 163,000 weekly circulation and is the flagship publication of the American Assoc. for the Advancement of Science

SEACnet Southeastern Atlantic Coast Career Network

College/University
minerva.acc.Virginia.EDU/~seacnet/

Jobs? Yes
- Cost to post jobs: Free
- Cost to see jobs: Free
- Specialty: All
- Industry: All
- Country/Region/State/City: US

Resumes? Yes
- Cost to post resumes: Free
- Cost to see resumes: Free

Links to Jobs? Yes

Career Advice? Yes

Contact e-mail is seacnet@minerva.acc.virginia.edu Unique "consortium of Career Placement Offices from 21 schools: Alabama, Arkansas, Auburn, Clemson, Duke, Florida, Florida State, Georgia, Georgia Tech, Kentucky, LA. State, Maryland, Mississippi, Mississippi State, North Carolina, NC State, South Carolina, Tennessee, Vanderbilt, Virginia and Wake Forest. Employers can search which schools have programs they are interested in and then tap a student resume database in the 400,000 + range. Site also offers video conferencing capability. This deserves a very close look as a model for the future.

Seamless Web: Legal Job Center

Commercial Job Site
www.seamless.com/jobs/

Kelli Geehan TSW Ltd
300 Montgomery Street, 4th Flo, San Francisco, CA 94104
Phone: 415-732-5600 Fax: 415-732-5606 e-mail: access@seamless.com

Jobs? Yes
- Cost to post jobs: Free
- Cost to see jobs: Free
- Specialty: Law
- Industry: All
- Country/Region/State/City: US/W/CA

Resumes? Yes
- Cost to post resumes: Free
- Cost to see resumes: Free

Links to Jobs? Yes

Career Advice? Yes

Site provides opportunity for positions to be posted as well as positions "wanted". Not an easy site to use but free.

Seattle Times

Publisher/Newspaper
www.seatimes.com/classified/

Seattle Times
1120 John Street, Seattle, WA 98111
Phone: 206-464-2994

Jobs? Yes
- Cost to post jobs: Fee
- Cost to see jobs: Free
- Specialty: All
- Industry: N/A
- Country/Region/State/City: US/NW/WA/Seattle

Resumes? No
- Cost to post resumes: N/A
- Cost to see resumes: N/A

Links to Jobs? No

Career Advice? No

Newspaper help wanted classifieds. Help wanted display ads are not included. No extra charges as employers must pay for advertisement in the newspaper.

CAREERXROADS©
Job, Resume & Career Management Sites on the World Wide Web
• The 1997 Directory •

Seniors On-Line Job Bank

Commercial Job/Diversity
www.seniorsnet.com/jobbank.htm

Seniors Web Design Services
Phone: 416-522-2601

Jobs? Yes
- Cost to post jobs: Fee
- Cost to see jobs: Fee
- Specialty: All
- Industry: All
- Country/Region/State/City: US

Resumes? Yes
- Cost to post resumes: Free
- Cost to see resumes: Fee

Links to Jobs? Yes

Career Advice? Yes

There is now a charge to post jobs on this site. Employers need password to search. Jobs listed have a 50 word limit. Nice niche but Seniors is difficult to operate and needs help for the future.

SenseMedia Job Board

Links
sensemedia.net/getajob/

SenseMedia

Jobs? No
- Cost to post jobs: N/A
- Cost to see jobs: N/A
- Specialty: N/A
- Industry: N/A
- Country/Region/State/City: US

Resumes? Yes
- Cost to post resumes: Free
- Cost to see resumes: Free

Links to Jobs? Yes

Career Advice? No

Lots of college site links can now be viewed. This is a place to find hypermedia professionals. Many links to job sites that have been nicely chosen.

CAREERXROADS©
Job, Resume & Career Management Sites on the World Wide Web
• The 1997 Directory •

The Shaker Edge

Private Site
www.shaker.com

Mike Temkin Shaker Advertising Agency
Shaker Bldg., 1100 Lake Street, Oak Park, IL 60301
Phone: 800-323-5170 e-mail: info_shaker.com

Jobs? No
- Cost to post jobs: N/A
- Cost to see jobs: N/A
- Specialty: All
- Industry: All
- Country/Region/State/City: US

Resumes? No
- Cost to post resumes: N/A
- Cost to see resumes: N/A

Links to Jobs? Yes

Career Advice? Yes

Recruitment advertising firm provides customized services to recruiters of client companies. These specialized services are password protected. Some content is open to the public including links to the company job pages of all of the agency's clients.

SHRM HR Jobs

Association/Publisher
www.shrm.org

SHRM
606 North Washington Street, Alexandria, VA 22314
Phone: 800-283-7476

Jobs? Yes
- Cost to post jobs: Fee
- Cost to see jobs: Free
- Specialty: Human Resources
- Industry: N/A
- Country/Region/State/City: US

Resumes? No
- Cost to post resumes: N/A
- Cost to see resumes: N/A

Links to Jobs? Yes

Career Advice? Yes

The Society for Human Resource Management has 70,000 members. HRNews is a monthly publication for human resource members. Positions placed in help wanted section are up on the net within a few days.

Silicon Valley Technical Employment Agencies

Links

www.sease.com/jobs.html

Jim Sease Sease Associates
P.o. Box 390576, Mountain View, CA 94039
Phone: 415-964-3348 e-mail: jim@sease.com

Jobs? No
- Cost to post jobs: N/A
- Cost to see jobs: N/A
- Specialty: IT
- Industry: High Technology
- Country/Region/State/City: US/W/CA/San Francisco

Resumes? No
- Cost to post resumes: N/A
- Cost to see resumes: N/A

Links to Jobs? Yes

Career Advice? No

List and contact information for 200+ technical employment agencies in the Silicon Valley. This site is intended for technical writers, engineers and computer jockeys. Alpha list of recruitment firms.

Quick Review Rating for each site.

- Has jobs:

- Has resumes:

- Has career advice:

- One of the best in class:

You'll also see a reduced version of the home page

CAREERXROADS©
Job, Resume & Career Management Sites on the World Wide Web
• The 1997 Directory •

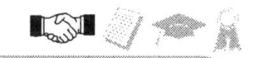

Singapore On Line

www.singapore.com/jobs.htm

Richard Goh Accel Infotech (S) Pte Ltd.
111 North Bridge Road #04-27, , Peninsula Plaza, Singapore 17908
Phone: 615-799-1126 Fax: 657-916-377 e-mail: accel@technet.sg

Jobs? Yes
- Cost to post jobs: Fee
- Cost to see jobs: Free
- Specialty: All
- Industry: All
- Country/Region/State/City: Int'l/Singapore

Resumes? No
- Cost to post resumes: N/A
- Cost to see resumes: N/A

Links to Jobs? Yes

Career Advice? No

Site will post jobs for Singapore companies only and it costs $200 per posting regardless of the number of jobs. Singapore On Line wants to provide all information necessary for doing business in this country. Good search engine and easy access to all information.

SkillBank

Commercial Resume/Agent
www.laps.com/skillbank

Lapis software Associates, LLC
601 Jefferson Road, Suite 207, Parsippany, NJ 07054
Phone: 201-844-4006 Fax: 201-884-4233 e-mail: skillinfo@lapis.com

Jobs? No
- Cost to post jobs: N/A
- Cost to see jobs: N/A
- Specialty: All
- Industry: All
- Country/Region/State/City: US

Resumes? Yes
- Cost to post resumes: Free
- Cost to see resumes: Free

Links to Jobs? No

Career Advice? No

This supplier of software services provides free skill/job matching for employers and applicants. The database presents applicants with skill choices (the site is still building and improving the "universe" of skill choices available). Employers then select and search for the skills they require. Employers can contact applicants directly, or if the applicant chooses, he or she can keep their information private. Using this confidentiality feature, the employer's interest is forwarded to the applicant.

Snelling Staffing Services

Placement/Search Firm
www.clark.net/network/

Snelling & Snelling
20 East Timonium Rd, Timonium, MD 21903
Phone: 410-561-5701 Fax: 410-561-0542 e-mail: network@clark.net

Jobs? Yes
- Cost to post jobs: Fee
- Cost to see jobs: Free
- Specialty: All
- Industry: All
- Country/Region/State/City: US

Resumes? Yes
- Cost to post resumes: Free
- Cost to see resumes: Fee

Links to Jobs? No

Career Advice? No

Jobs, internships and co-ops from network site of this large employment agency. Employment opportunities link to the office with the order. Candidates can e-mail resume.

Society of Women Engineers

Association/Diversity
www.swe.org

Society of Women Engineers
120 Wall Street, 11th Floor, New York, NY 10005
Phone: 212-509-9577 Fax: 212-509-0224 e-mail: vp-special.services@swe.org

Jobs? Yes
- Cost to post jobs: Fee
- Cost to see jobs: Free
- Specialty: Engineering
- Industry: All
- Country/Region/State/City: US

Resumes? No
- Cost to post resumes: N/A
- Cost to see resumes: N/A

Links to Jobs? No

Career Advice? Yes

Employers can place ads in SWE publication and receive a disk of resumes from Resume-Link. SWE members can post their resumes for free. Site has recently been under construction so look for an interesting 1997 from one of the major engineering associations.

Software Contractors Guild

Association
www.scguild.com/

David Keeney
PO Box 257, Nottingham, NH 03290-0257
e-mail: keeney@mv.mv.com

Jobs? Yes
- Cost to post jobs: Free
- Cost to see jobs: Free
- Specialty: IT
- Industry: IT
- Country/Region/State/City: US

Resumes? Yes
- Cost to post resumes: Free
- Cost to see resumes: Free

Links to Jobs? Yes

Career Advice? No

Site posts resumes of software contractors who pay $12.00 a year to join this organization of which they claim to have 260 members. Resumes are posted by skill and by alpha order. For recruiters the price is right so, pay them a visit.

The Software Jobs Home Page

Placement/Search/Temp
www.softwarejobs.com

Allen Davis & Associates

Jobs? Yes
- Cost to post jobs: Fee
- Cost to see jobs: Free
- Specialty: IT
- Industry: All
- Country/Region/State/City: US

Resumes? No
- Cost to post resumes: N/A
- Cost to see resumes: N/A

Links to Jobs? No

Career Advice? No

Search Firm with a twist. Job seekers can view "newsletters" in each of four separate skill areas: SAP, Windows, GUI and DBMS. The newsletters include a mix of editorial and jobs. Don't expect to apply directly to the listing companies. If you submit your resume, you'll get a call if the agency feels you might be a match. Nice design for a site that is a little better than the average model for the permanent and temp placement industry.

CAREERXROADS©
Job, Resume & Career Management Sites on the World Wide Web
• The 1997 Directory •

SPIE's Employment Center

Association
optics.org/employment/employment.html

Mark Mugittroyd SPIE
1000 20th Street, Bellingham, WA 98226
Phone: 360-676-3290 Fax: 360-647-1445 e-mail: advertising@spie.org

Jobs? Yes
- Cost to post jobs: Fee
- Cost to see jobs: Free
- Specialty: Physics
- Industry: N/A
- Country/Region/State/City: US

Resumes? Yes
- Cost to post resumes: Free
- Cost to see resumes: Free

Links to Jobs? No

Career Advice? No

SPIE-The International Society for Optical Engineering contains a small number of quality positions related to the optical instrumentation and engineering field that are published in the society's monthly newsletter (27,000 members). Members can post resumes free for 60 days and they are available to employers for free. The job database is linked from http://www.spie.org and http://optics.org. Employers pay $250 for a 4 week listing. All transactions are conducted from a web interface.

SPTimes

Publisher/Newspaper
www.sptimes.com

St. Petersburg Times
490 First Avenue, St. Petersburg, FL 33701
Phone: 813-893-8554

Jobs? Yes
- Cost to post jobs: Fee
- Cost to see jobs: Free
- Specialty: All
- Industry: N/A
- Country/Region/City: US/SE/FL/St. Petersburg

Resumes? No
- Cost to post resumes: N/A
- Cost to see resumes: N/A

Links to Jobs? No

Career Advice? No

Ads placed in the St. Petersburg Times are put on the Internet for an additional $1-$10.

Student Center

Links
studentcenter.com

Eve Yohelem StudentCenter LLC
31 West 21st Street, Suite 1102, New York, NY 10010
Phone: 212-929-7980 Fax: 212-255-6357 e-mail: advisory@studentcenter.com

Jobs? No
- Cost to post jobs: N/A
- Cost to see jobs: N/A
- Specialty: N/A
- Industry: N/A
- Country/Region/State/City: US

Resumes? No
- Cost to post resumes: N/A
- Cost to see resumes: N/A

Links to Jobs? Yes

Career Advice? Yes

StudentCenter.com

Welcome to StudentCenter. The job search begins here!

Easy to use database of 35,000 companies. Regular columnist on job issues and extra services oriented to entry level students looking to get into the job market. Several unusual and entertaining features like a career generator. Employers can expand their company information. A "Virtual" and "Informational" interview featured.

St. Louis Area Companies on the Net

Government
www.st-louis.mo.us/st-louis/companies.html

Brian Smith Washington University
School of Engineering, St.Louis, MO
Phone: 314-935-4850 e-mail: brians@cait.wustl.edu

Jobs? No
- Cost to post jobs: N/A
- Cost to see jobs: N/A
- Specialty: N/A
- Industry: N/A
- Country/Region/State/City: US/MW/MO/St. Louis

Resumes? No
- Cost to post resumes: N/A
- Cost to see resumes: N/A

Links to Jobs? Yes

Career Advice? No

Solid list of and links to local companies.

St. Paul Pioneer Press

Publisher/Newspaper
www.stpaulpp.com

345 Cedar Street, St. Paul, Minnesota 55101
Phone: 612-222-5011

Jobs? Yes
- Cost to post jobs: Fee
- Cost to see jobs: Free
- Specialty: All
- Industry: N/A
- Country/Region/State/City: US/MW/MN/St. Paul

Resumes? No
- Cost to post resumes: N/A
- Cost to see resumes: N/A

Links to Jobs? No

Career Advice? No

Classified advertising can be seen on this site for the St. Paul Minnesota area.

St. Thomas Human Resource Centre

Government
ein.ccia.st-thomas.on.ca/agencies/cec/index.html

HR Department Canada
451 Talbot Street, St. Thomas, Ontario N5P 3V6
Phone: 519-631-5470

Jobs? Yes
• Cost to post jobs: Free
• Cost to see jobs: Free
• Specialty: All
• Industry: All
• Country/Region/State/City: Int'l/Canada

Resumes? No
• Cost to post resumes: N/A
• Cost to see resumes: N/A

Links to Jobs? Yes

Career Advice? Yes

Employers wishing to post positions on this site need to contact their local Canadian Employment Center at 519-631-7760 or fax info to 519-631-3565. Links to Canadian newspaper classifieds. Like its US counterparts in the state employment services, they unfortunately do not get it when it comes to technology. Hopefully in the future this will change. Their e-mail is: Roshan@ein.ccia.st-thomas.on.ca

Summer Jobs

College/University
www.summerjobs.com

Donna Donovan Fishnet New Media
180 State Road, Suite 2U, Bourne, MA 02532
Phone: 508-888-3456 Fax: 508-888-3151 e-mail: fishnet@ahoy.com

Jobs? Yes
• Cost to post jobs: fee
• Cost to see jobs: Free
• Specialty: All
• Industry: All
• Country/Region/State/City: Int'l/US

Resumes? No
• Cost to post resumes: N/A
• Cost to see resumes: N/A

Links to Jobs? Yes

Career Advice? No

Site posts summer jobs around the world with search engine that makes them easy to view. Had 185 US jobs posted on our last visit with many countries also posting jobs. Tell your children to take a peek and leave you alone for the summer.

Supermarket News

Publisher/Trade
www.supermarketnews.com

Fairchild Publishing
7 East 12th Street, New York, NY 10003
Phone: 800-423-3314 Fax: 212-741-4201 e-mail: info@supermarketnews.com

Jobs? Yes
- Cost to post jobs: Fee
- Cost to see jobs: Free
- Specialty: All
- Industry: Supermarket
- Country/Region/State/City: US

Resumes? No
- Cost to post resumes: N/A
- Cost to see resumes: N/A

Links to Jobs? No

Career Advice? No

Classified ads from this trade publication. Employers pay an addition $25 to have regular and display ads posted to the internet site.

Syracuse Online

Publisher/Newspaper
www.syracuse.com

Stan Linhorst Syracuse Herald Journal
Clinton Square, Syracuse, NY 13221
Phone: 315-470-2270 Fax: 315-470-2050 e-mail: linhorst@mailbox.syr.edu

Jobs? Yes
- Cost to post jobs: Fee
- Cost to see jobs: Free
- Specialty: All
- Industry: N/A
- Country/Region/State/City: US/NE/NY/Syracuse

Resumes? No
- Cost to post resumes: N/A
- Cost to see resumes: N/A

Links to Jobs? No

Career Advice? No

Classsified ads in Sunday's paper.

Tacoma News Tribune (Help Wanted)

Publisher/Newspaper
www.tribnet.com

Tacoma News Tribune
1950 S. State Street, Tacoma, WA 98405
Phone: 509-459-5005 e-mail: bwatkins@p.tribnet.com

Jobs? Yes
- Cost to post jobs: Fee
- Cost to see jobs: Free
- Specialty: All
- Industry: N/A
- Country/Region/State/City: US/NW/WA/Tacoma

Resumes? No
- Cost to post resumes: N/A
- Cost to see resumes: N/A

Links to Jobs? No

Career Advice? No

Newspaper help wanted classifieds. Help wanted display ads are not included. No extra charges as employers must pay for advertisements in the newspaper.

Talent Hunter

Commercial Job Site/Agent
www.3dsite.com/ism/resumes/cgi-bin/talent-hunter.cgi

Charles Anthony Viviani
e-mail: cav@ax.apc.org

Jobs? Yes
- Cost to post jobs: Free
- Cost to see jobs: Free
- Specialty: All
- Industry: Graphics
- Country/Region/State/City: US

Resumes? Yes
- Cost to post resumes: Free
- Cost to see resumes: Free

Links to Jobs? No

Career Advice? No

Has an Agent that will match candidates to employer's job requirements. Site for people in the graphics industry: 3-D, artists, modeling, special effects. Could not see posted jobs as you need to register.

The Talent Network

Commercial Resume Site
talentnet.com/

Chuck O'Keefe The Talent Network
1331 Southwick Boulevard, Midlothian, VA 23113
Phone: 800-998-4044 Fax: 804-379-1215 e-mail: support@talentnet.com

Jobs? Yes
- Cost to post jobs: Free
- Cost to see jobs: Free
- Specialty: Entertainment
- Industry: Entertainment
- Country/Region/State/City: US

Resumes? Yes
- Cost to post resumes: Fee
- Cost to see resumes: Free

Links to Jobs? Yes

Career Advice? Yes

Costs applicants $20 to post their resume for three months. Employers can use the site to search resumes or post jobs for free. Focused on the entertainment community. Talentnet seeks out professional performers, models and media production professionals. Excellent source of links to entertainment industry sites.

TCM's Job Marts (HR, T&D, HRIS)

Commercial Job Site
www.tcm.com

Eric Snyder Targeted Communication Management
64 Thare Cr., Nepean, Ontario, Canada K2J 2P6
Phone: 613-825-6728 Fax: 613-825-4675 e-mail: egs@tcm.com

Jobs? Yes
- Cost to post jobs: Fee
- Cost to see jobs: Free
- Specialty: Human Resources/T&D,ER, HRIS
- Industry: N/A
- Country/Region/State/City: Int'l/Canada/US

Resumes? Yes
- Cost to post resumes: Free
- Cost to see resumes: Fee

Links to Jobs? Yes

Career Advice? No

This Canadian based supplier of training and development services has one of the efficiently designed formats for scrolling down positions listed with their site. Generalist, T&D and HRIS positions are provided on separate pages. The folks associated with this site are very active on HR Listservs and periodically send hot jobs to these professional discussion forums as an added value. Nice touch. Employers pay $200/month for posting. Site owner searches resumes for employers and charges $50 per profile.

Technology Registry

Commercial Resume Site
www/techreg.com

Peter dePenolza QuestLink Systems, Inc.
616 Carolina Street, San Francisco, CA 94107
Phone: 415-641-3838 Fax: 415-641-3188 e-mail: info@techreg.com

Jobs? Yes
- Cost to post jobs: Fee
- Cost to see jobs: Fee
- Specialty: IT/Engineering
- Industry: All
- Country/Region/State/City: US

Resumes? Yes
- Cost to post resumes: Free
- Cost to see resumes: Fee

Links to Jobs? Yes

Career Advice? Yes

Provides professional profile for candidates at $25 year. Employers currently get 5 hours free to search. Claims for this site (160,000 profiles from 40,000 companies) seems a little much. Has over 4,000 employment codes. May be worth your while for IS types.

TechWeb/TechCareers/TechHunter

Publisher/Trade Magazine
techweb.cmp.com/

Barbara Kerbel CMP Publications
600 Community Drive, Manhasset, NY 11030
Phone: 516-562-5218 Fax: 516-562-7830 e-mail: cmppr@techweb.com

Jobs? Yes
- Cost to post jobs: Fee
- Cost to see jobs: Free
- Specialty: IT
- Industry: High Technology/Agent
- Country/Region/State/City: US

Resumes? Yes
- Cost to post resumes: Free
- Cost to see resumes: N/A

Links to Jobs? Yes

Career Advice? Yes

Click on "Find a job". CMP Media Group includes Networld, EETimes and several other technology based publications. Link from this site to careers and jobs in those publications. For applicants, free agent, "TechHunter", sponsored by TechWeb and E-Span maintains a personal profile, matches jobs to the profile, e-mails job opportunities and and lets job seeker apply online. Access to career articles, advice and recruitment firms rounds out a solid site. Don't overlook salary articles and salary surveys for Network Engineers, Purchasing, IS and Engineering. Type in the search engine "jobs" and you will see over 100 articles to help you in your search.

CAREERXROADS©
Job, Resume & Career Management Sites on the World Wide Web
• The 1997 Directory •

Telecommuting Jobs

Commercial Job Site
tjobs.com/index.html

Sol Levine Levine Communications
1001 Greenbay Road, Winnetka, IL 60093
Phone: 847-835-2180 Fax: 847-835-2183 e-mail: tjobs@tjobs.com

Jobs? Yes
- Cost to post jobs: Free
- Cost to see jobs: Free
- Specialty: Telecommuting
- Industry: N/A
- Country/Region/State/City: US

Resumes? Yes
- Cost to post resumes: Fee
- Cost to see resumes: Free

Links to Jobs? No

Career Advice? No

Site specializes in positions where individuals would work remotely. Resume information is coded before supplying to employers. Employers are not charged to post a basic listing but expanded job information is fee based. Candidates are charged $10 month to post their resume in a database (a one line listing is free).

Telecommuting, Telework & Alt. Officing

Career Management
www.gilgordon.com

Gil Gordon Associates
10 Donner Court, Monmouth Junction, NJ 08852
Phone: 908-329-2266 Fax: 908-329-2703 e-mail: 74375.1667@compuserve.com

Jobs? No
- Cost to post jobs: N/A
- Cost to see jobs: N/A
- Specialty: Telecommuting
- Industry: All
- Country/Region/State/City: Int'l.

Resumes? No
- Cost to post resumes: N/A
- Cost to see resumes: N/A

Links to Jobs? No

Career Advice? Yes

Site owner is a world class expert whose home page links to a wide variety of information from around the world on the subjects of telecommuting, teleworking and alternative officing. Gil and his partner on the site, Dave Peterson, have created a "one-stop service for practitioners, researchers and policy-makers in this rapidly-evolving field." We think job-seekers and employers alike may need to consider the possibilities and this site can provide an excellent starting point.

CAREERXROADS©
Job, Resume & Career Management Sites on the World Wide Web
• The 1997 Directory •

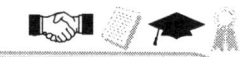

Television & Radio News Research

College/University
www.missouri.edu~jourus/

Vernon Stone Missouri School of Journalism
3805 W. Rollins Road, Columbia, MO 65203-0321
Phone: 573-882-9939   e-mail: jourus@showme.missouri.edu

Jobs? Yes
- Cost to post jobs: Free
- Cost to see jobs: Free
- Specialty: All
- Industry: Radio & Television
- Country/Region/State/City: US

Resumes? No
- Cost to post resumes: N/A
- Cost to see resumes: N/A

Links to Jobs? Yes

Career Advice? Yes

Lots of career information on the radio & television industry. Salary information on many different positions with good articles on the profession.

The Internet Career Site

Commercial Job Site/Agent
www.autorecruiter.com

David Collins Jen Chase, Inc.
Phone: 800-455-1647   e-mail: dcollins@net.master.net

Jobs? Yes
- Cost to post jobs: Fee
- Cost to see jobs: Free
- Specialty: All
- Industry: N/A
- Country/Region/State/City: US

Resumes? Yes
- Cost to post resumes: Free
- Cost to see resumes: Fee

Links to Jobs? No

Career Advice? No

Launched in September 1996, The Internet Career Site allows candidates to submit resumes and have complete control over changes, deletion, confidentiality, etc. Employers search in a relational database and have the site's agent "AutoRecruiter" immediately notify them of new candidates matching their requirements.

CAREERXROADS©
Job, Resume & Career Management Sites on the World Wide Web
• The 1997 Directory •

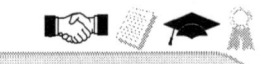

Top Jobs USA

Commercial Job Site
www.topjobsusa.com

Dynamic Information Exchange
e-mail: sales@topjobsusa.com

Jobs? Yes
- Cost to post jobs: Free
- Cost to see jobs: Free
- Specialty: All
- Industry: N/A
- Country/Region/State/City: US

Resumes? No
- Cost to post resumes: N/A
- Cost to see resumes: N/A

Links to Jobs? Yes

Career Advice? Yes

Data base containing over 40,000 current job opportunities for Professionals, Managers and Technical Specialists. Current emphasis is in the western states; however expansion into additional states and regions currently underway. Well done career information with news flashes on companies that are hiring by state and position.

Training & Devel. Resource Center

Association
www.tcm.com/trdev/nav.htm

Eric Snyder
Phone: 613-722-3751 Fax: 613-722-7981 e-mail: egs@tcm.com

Jobs? Yes
- Cost to post jobs: Fee
- Cost to see jobs: Free
- Specialty: Human Resources/T&D
- Industry: All
- Country/Region/State/City: US

Resumes? Yes
- Cost to post resumes: Free
- Cost to see resumes: Fee

Links to Jobs? No

Career Advice? No

Site has 30 listserves for T&D folks to join. Information on use net groups to learn more about training related issues. Only had 11 jobs posted with direct information. Nicely done site, easy to follow instructions for the training & development world.

TrainingNet

Commercial Job Site
www.trainingnet.com

Amar Hhaliwal
103-2609 Westview Drive, Ste 405, North Vancouver, BC V7N4N2
Phone: 604-980-0643 Fax: 604-980-4448 e-mail: info@trainingnet.com

Jobs? Yes
- Cost to post jobs: Free
- Cost to see jobs: Free
- Specialty: Human Resources/T&D
- Industry: All
- Country/Region/State/City: Int'l/US

Resumes? Yes
- Cost to post resumes: Free
- Cost to see resumes: Free

Links to Jobs? Yes

Career Advice? Yes

This is a free (employers and job seekers) jobs database specializing in training openings/resumes worldwide. Has a forum for sharing ideas.

TV Jobs

Commercial Resume Site
www.tvjobs.com

Mark Holloway Broadcast Employment Services
P.O. Box 4116, Oceanside, CA 92052
Phone: 619-754-2115 Fax: 619-754-2115 e-mail: markch@tvjobs.com

Jobs? Yes
- Cost to post jobs: Fee
- Cost to see jobs: Free
- Specialty: Communications/TV
- Industry: Entertainment/Broadcast
- Country/Region/State/City: US

Resumes? Yes
- Cost to post resumes: Fee
- Cost to see resumes: Free

Links to Jobs? Yes

Career Advice? Yes

Positions in television primarily. Good information on where to go in the industry to find a job. Links to colleges with communication programs. Internships at TV Stations also listed here. Employers place ads for free (90 days). Applicants can post a resume for 1 year for $25 that can be viewed by employers for free. Also contains a searchable index of all the TV stations in the US.

CAREERXROADS©
Job, Resume & Career Management Sites on the World Wide Web
• The 1997 Directory •

Twin Cities Job Page

Commercial
www.fentonnet.com/jobs/html

e-mail: info@fentonnet.com

Jobs? Yes
- Cost to post jobs: Fee
- Cost to see jobs: Free
- Specialty: All
- Industry: All
- Country/Region/State/City: US/MW/MN

Resumes? Yes
- Cost to post resumes: Free
- Cost to see resumes: Free

Links to Jobs? No

Career Advice? No

Resume service is free. Businesses recruiting in the Twin Cities area are charged a small fee. Direct contact information is available along with a list of newsgroups. Site keeps growing and improving as time goes on.

Have you found a site that isn't listed in CAREERXROADS?

Have you REGISTERED to receive FREE updates?

Keep us informed.

We'll keep you informed.

CAREERXROADS
Where Talent and Opportunity Connect on the Internet

CAREERXROADS©
Job, Resume & Career Management Sites on the World Wide Web
• The 1997 Directory •

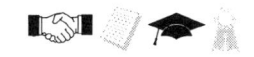

UCI Center for Int'l Education

College/University
www.cie.uci.edu/~cie

Ruth Sylte-Counselor Univ. of California, Irvine
1010 Student Services, Irvine, CA 92697-2476
Phone: 714-824-6343 Fax: 714-824-3832 e-mail: rmsylte@uci.edu

Jobs? Yes
- Cost to post jobs: Free
- Cost to see jobs: Free
- Specialty: All
- Industry: N/A
- Country/Region/State/City: Int'l/US

Resumes? No
- Cost to post resumes: N/A
- Cost to see resumes: N/A

Links to Jobs? Yes

Career Advice? Yes

Site lists short term international work assignments for students. Also links to other international job sites as well as job related list services. Great search engine that allows you to search for jobs in over 80 countries. Info also on student exchange programs around the world. Subtitle of site is Best Bets for Working Abroad. Unfortunately it looks like jobs are only for UC students.

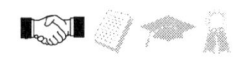

UI Design Jobs

Commercial Job Site
www.io.tudelft.nl/uidesign/jobs.html

Raghu Kolli
e-mail: uidesign@io.tudelft.nl

Jobs? Yes
- Cost to post jobs: Free
- Cost to see jobs: Free
- Specialty: IT/User Interface
- Industry: IT
- Country/Region/State/City: Int'l/US

Resumes? No
- Cost to post resumes: N/A
- Cost to see resumes: N/A

Links to Jobs? No

Career Advice? No

Site caters to user interface design techies and has jobs listed with direct contact data. Positions are posted for free for two months. Lot's of techie items on sight. Site is sponsored by 4 international research organizations/corporations.

The (National) Urban League

Association/Diversity
www.urbanleague.com

Jobs? No
- Cost to post jobs: N/A
- Cost to see jobs: N/A
- Specialty: All
- Industry: All
- Country/Region/State/City: US

Resumes? No
- Cost to post resumes: N/A
- Cost to see resumes: N/A

Links to Jobs? Yes

Career Advice? Yes

This site has a lot of potential but has decided to only link to Career Mosaic at this time. As with other diversity organizations, the Urban League can be a leader on the web and we hope that in the future they take a more active role.

US Job Network

Commercial Job Site
www.usjob.net

Michael Howard   Jaye Communications
Phone: 770-984-9444   e-mail: michael.hoeard@job.net

Jobs? Yes
- Cost to post jobs: Fee
- Cost to see jobs: Free
- Specialty: All
- Industry: N/A
- Country/Region/State/City: US/SE

Resumes? Yes
- Cost to post resumes: Free
- Cost to see resumes: Fee

Links to Jobs? Yes

Career Advice? No

This subscriber based site has nearly 250 companies posting unlimited positions, company profiles and links to their company's WWW site. All for less than $250/month. Employers are provided online forms, billing options and a password to post positions. Jobseekers can easily search by state. Jobseekers are encouraged to add their resume to the site's database which is restricted to subscribing employers.

Usjobnet K-12

Commercial Job Site
www.usjobnet.com

Mike Laverde Usjobnet
P.O. Box 60872, Sacramento, CA 95860-0872
Phone: 800-255-9807 Fax: 916-723-8660 e-mail: laverde@calweb.com

Jobs? Yes
- Cost to post jobs: Fee
- Cost to see jobs: Free
- Specialty: Teaching
- Industry: Education
- Country/Region/State/City: US

Resumes? No
- Cost to post resumes: N/A
- Cost to see resumes: N/A

Links to Jobs? Yes

Career Advice? Yes

Nice approach. Jobs are listed by function and specialty. $5 per week per ad. Direct contact information is available. Jobs are listed in alpha order which can make for a lot of work. This site continues to be a high performer in the education marketplace.

USM Resources for G/L/B Students

College/University
macweb.acs.usm.maine.edu/csce/career_glb.html

Career Services & Coop. Education Univ. of Southern Maine
100 Payson Smith Hall, PO Box 9300, Maine
e-mail: bliss@usm.maine.edu

Jobs? No
- Cost to post jobs: N/A
- Cost to see jobs: N/A
- Specialty: All/College
- Industry: All
- Country/Region/State/City: US

Resumes? No
- Cost to post resumes: N/A
- Cost to see resumes: N/A

Links to Jobs? Yes

Career Advice? Yes

Career resource links to articles for career counseling. College university links, web links as well for the gay, lesbian, bisexual community.

U. of Penn Career Services

College/University
www.upenn.edu/CPPS

U of Penn
Phone: 215-898-4381

Jobs? Yes
- Cost to post jobs: Free
- Cost to see jobs: Free
- Specialty: All
- Industry: All
- Country/Region/State/City: US

Resumes? No
- Cost to post resumes: N/A
- Cost to see resumes: N/A

Links to Jobs? Yes

Career Advice? Yes

This Career Services site is one of several models developing throughout the country to serve the needs of its graduating students at the undergraduate level as well as alumni. Site provides e-mail job posting for employers and access to career services and resources for many of the University's programs including Wharton. Nice list of career links has been added since our last visit.

Have you found a site that isn't listed in CAREERXROADS?

Have you REGISTERED to receive FREE updates?

Keep us informed.

We'll keep you informed.

CAREERXROADS
Where Talent and Opportunity Connect on the Internet

CAREERXROADS©
Job, Resume & Career Management Sites on the World Wide Web
• The 1997 Directory •

Virtual Headbook

Commercial Resume Site
www.xmission.com:80/~wintrnx/vh/virtual.html

Trevor Black Wintronix, Inc.
Phone: 801-946-8769 Fax: 801-532-10621

Jobs? Yes
• Cost to post jobs: Free
• Cost to see jobs: Free
• Specialty: Entertainment/Actors
• Industry: Entertainment
• Country/Region/State/City: US

Resumes? Yes
• Cost to post resumes: Fee
• Cost to see resumes: Free
Links to Jobs? Yes
Career Advice? Yes

The Virtual Headbook
The Vision of Wintronix, Inc.
Technology bringing casting and talent together

• A Free Resource for Casting Directors and Talent Scouts
• Actor's Headshots and Resumes Online
• Global Exposure for Actors, Models, and Other Talent
• Union and non-Union actors

Unique site for actors and directors. Registration is $60/6 months for an actor and provides access to lists of casting calls as well as a special resume bank accessible to the theatre industry. It is a free resource for Casting Directors and Talent Scouts and Agents who can submit info on-line. Actors can submit a resume, photo, sound clip and even video clips. The site does provide links to other theatre related sites. Has recently added an online tax consultant who will provide Q/A's. On our most recent visit(as this site we visit often) we learned that this site is going to merge with another. We hope the level of expertise remains the same as this is truly a top site on the web.

CAREERXROADS©
Job, Resume & Career Management Sites on the World Wide Web
• The 1997 Directory •

Virtual Job Centre

Commercial Job Site
channel.cyberiacafe.net/jobs/index.html

Jobs? Yes
- Cost to post jobs: Fee
- Cost to see jobs: Free
- Specialty: All
- Industry: N/A
- Country/Region/State/City: Int'l/UK

Resumes? Yes
- Cost to post resumes: Free
- Cost to see resumes: Free

Links to Jobs? No

Career Advice? No

Site has a form to input your resume for free. This United Kingdom site has info on jobs in IS, Education, Commerce/Finance, Media/Adv, Legal App't., Food/Catering and well as info on other areas. Simple site that is making a valid attempt: look for future updates.

A Virtual Job Fair

Job Fair/Agent
www.vjf.com

Bill Lennan West Tech
4701 Patrick Henry Drive, #1901, Santa Clara, CA 95054
Phone: 408-970-8800 Fax: 408-980-5103 e-mail: webmaster@vjf

Jobs? Yes
- Cost to post jobs: Fee
- Cost to see jobs: Free
- Specialty: YES
- Industry: All
- Country/Region/State/City: US/W

Resumes? Yes
- Cost to post resumes: Free
- Cost to see resumes: Fee

Links to Jobs? Yes

Career Advice? Yes

This site is owned by a large west coast job fair company. Technical professionals can find links to employers, a searchable job database, resume posting database and career management articles. Inofrmation on upcoming job fairs is maintained. Employers will find a number of packages for posting. Some are related to West Tech's High Technology Magazine. Search of the database by employers costs $25 per contact.

CAREERXROADS©
Job, Resume & Career Management Sites on the World Wide Web
• The 1997 Directory •

Wall Street Journal E-MART

Publisher/Newspaper
www.wsj.com

Sam Wheeler Wall Street Journal
e-mail: samuel.wheeler@cor.dowjones.com

Jobs? Yes
- Cost to post jobs: Fee
- Cost to see jobs: Free
- Specialty: All
- Industry: N/A
- Country/Region/State/City: US

Resumes? No
- Cost to post resumes: N/A
- Cost to see resumes: N/A

Links to Jobs? No

Career Advice? No

The Wall Street Journal's classified section is online and accessible to subscirbers. Should be a good place to surf for executive level positions. Employers pay space cost for the print version and get E-MART as added value.

Have you found a site that isn't listed in CAREERXROADS?

Have you REGISTERED to receive FREE updates?

Keep us informed.

We'll keep you informed.

CAREERXROADS
Where Talent and Opportunity Connect on the Internet

CAREERXROADS©
Job, Resume & Career Management Sites on the World Wide Web
• The 1997 Directory •

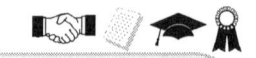

Washington Post- Career Post

Publisher/Newspaper
204.146.47.74/

Jamie Hammond Washington Post
1150-15th Street N.W., , Washington, DC 20071
Phone: 202-334-6000 Fax: 202-334-5561 e-mail: hammondj@washpost.com

Jobs? Yes
- Cost to post jobs: Fee
- Cost to see jobs: Free
- Specialty: All
- Industry: All
- Country/Region/State/City: US/E/DC

Resumes? No
- Cost to post resumes: N/A
- Cost to see resumes: N/A

Links to Jobs? Yes

Career Advice? Yes

Search the help wanted sections of the Washington Post. You can ask questions of Dick Bolles, author of "What Color Is Your Parachute," and he will respond. Nice set of career articles and links. Progressive approach for a newspaper to the web.

CAREERXROADS©
Job, Resume & Career Management Sites on the World Wide Web
• The 1997 Directory •

Web Developer's Virtual Library

Commercial Job Site
www.stars.com/

Alan Richmond CyberWeb SoftWare
7002 Kingfisher Lane, Lanham, MD 20706
Phone: 301-552-0272 e-mail: jobs@stars.com

Jobs? Yes
- Cost to post jobs: Fee
- Cost to see jobs: Free
- Specialty: IT/Web
- Industry: All
- Country/Region/State/City: US

Resumes? No
- Cost to post resumes: N/A
- Cost to see resumes: N/A

Links to Jobs? Yes

Career Advice? No

Highly specific site for techies in the virtual arena. Site is changing as several job openings are listed.

Web Dog's Job Hunt:The Best Jobs

Links/College
www.itec.sfsu.edu/students/projects/jschwartz/edtech/edtech.html
San Francisco State Career Center

Jobs? No
- Cost to post jobs: N/A
- Cost to see jobs: N/A
- Specialty: All
- Industry: N/A
- Country/Region/State/City: US

Resumes? No
- Cost to post resumes: N/A
- Cost to see resumes: N/A

Links to Jobs? Yes

Career Advice? No

A service of the California State University Employment Board, Web Dog has links for the entry level student for the San Francisco Bay area We think the Dog has taken a long nap as there are only 20 links present in a site that we all had high hopes for.

CAREERXROADS©
Job, Resume & Career Management Sites on the World Wide Web
• The 1997 Directory •

Web Engineer's Toolbox Career Center

Commercial Job Site
www59.metronet.com/dev/careers.shtml

Jobs? Yes
- Cost to post jobs: Free
- Cost to see jobs: Free
- Specialty: All
- Industry: High Technology
- Country/Region/State/City: US

Resumes? No
- Cost to post resumes: N/A
- Cost to see resumes: N/A

Links to Jobs? Yes

Career Advice? No

Allows you to list, see jobs for Web developers, CGI and Java programmers, webmasters etc. Nice list of links to industry specific publications and other sites.

Western New York Jobs

Publisher/Newspaper
www.wnyjobs.com./#anchor263367

Phone: 716-648-5658 e-mail: wnyjobs@buffnet.net

Jobs? Yes
- Cost to post jobs: Fee
- Cost to see jobs: Free
- Specialty: all
- Industry: All
- Country/Region/State/City: US/E/NY

Resumes? No
- Cost to post resumes: N/A
- Cost to see resumes: N/A

Links to Jobs? Yes

Career Advice? No

Publisher of Western NY Jobs Weekly. Ads on web site are there for 3 weeks and cost $45 per. Has direct contact info for seeing open jobs, has list of links to area employers in Western NY.

Wet Feet Press

Career Management
www.wetfeet.com

Phone: 800-926-4502 Fax: 415-826-1750 e-mail: orders@wetfeet.com

Jobs? No
- Cost to post jobs: N/A
- Cost to see jobs: N/A
- Specialty: All
- Industry: All
- Country/Region/State/City: US

Resumes? No
- Cost to post resumes: N/A
- Cost to see resumes: N/A

Links to Jobs? Yes

Career Advice? Yes

Site claims to be the information source for job seekers. Has profiles of major corporations on the site and if you want more indepth information they will obtain it for you for $25 a report.

Windows NT Resource Center

Commercial Job Site
www.bhs.com/default.asp

Dave Baker Beverly Hills Software
8845 W. Olympic Blvd., Suite 200, Beverly Hills,, CA 90211
Phone: 310-358-8311 Fax: 310-358-0326 e-mail: webmaster@bhs.com

Jobs? Yes
- Cost to post jobs: Free
- Cost to see jobs: Free
- Specialty: IT/Windows NT Users
- Industry: IT
- Country/Region/State/City: US

Resumes? Yes
- Cost to post resumes: Free
- Cost to see resumes: N/A

Links to Jobs? Yes

Career Advice? No

Not a real job service but an invaluable site for Windows developers that provides a free job/resume posting service. You can post your resume on the site but there is no mention of where it goes. Site tries to do a lot with split screen but with all of the graphics, it is very slow. With all the technology this company has, we would expect a better design.

Wisconsin Employment Bureau

Government
badger.state.wi.us/agencies/dilhr

Marty Shannon Dept. of Ind., Labor & Human Relations
201 E. Washington, P.O. Box 7946, Madison, WI 53707
Phone: 414-282-0535 Fax: 414-282-3321

Jobs? Yes
• Cost to post jobs: Free
• Cost to see jobs: Free
• Specialty: All
• Industry: All
• Country/Region/State/City: US/MW/WI

Resumes? Yes
• Cost to post resumes: Free
• Cost to see resumes: Free

Links to Jobs? Yes

Career Advice? Yes

THE WISCONSIN DEPARTMENT OF INDUSTRY, LABOR AND HUMAN RELATIONS

Providing Information about Wisconsin's Workforce and building and structure safety.

A free opportunity for employers to post jobs online, establish links and profiles, review resumes etc. Job-seekers can search by company, location, employment group and keyword as well as post resumes. Some advice and links. Excellent links to other Wisconsin sites. This site is a step ahead of many states.

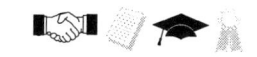

Women in Computer Science & Engineering

Association/Diversity
www.mit.edu:8001/people/sorokin/women/index.html

MIT

Jobs? Yes
- Cost to post jobs: Free
- Cost to see jobs: Free
- Specialty: IT/Engineering
- Industry: All
- Country/Region/State/City: US

Resumes? No
- Cost to post resumes: N/A
- Cost to see resumes: N/A

Links to Jobs? No

Career Advice? Yes

Limited gender- based site. Has a few helpful ideas.

Women in Higher Education

Publisher/Trade/Diversity
www.itis.com/wihe/

Mary Zenke Wenniger Company
1934 Monroe Street, Madison, Wisconsin 53711
Phone: 608-251-3232 Fax: 608-284-0601 e-mail: women@wihe.com

Jobs? Yes
- Cost to post jobs: Fee
- Cost to see jobs: Free
- Specialty: All
- Industry: Education
- Country/Region/State/City: US

Resumes? No
- Cost to post resumes: N/A
- Cost to see resumes: N/A

Links to Jobs? No

Career Advice? Yes

You can reach 12,000 women who work or have aspirations for the field of education. Cost to post a job is $340 and up. Direct contact info and detailed job descriptions are on the site. Positions run the gamut from presidents of universities to deans and faculty positions.

Women in Technology & Industry-WITI

Association/Diversity
www.witi.com

Int'l Network of Women in Technology
4641 Burnet Ave., Sherman Oaks, CA 91403
Phone: 818-990-6705 Fax: 818-906-3299

Jobs? Yes
- Cost to post jobs: Free
- Cost to see jobs: Free
- Specialty: Executive
- Industry: All
- Country/Region/State/City: Int'l/US

Resumes? No
- Cost to post resumes: N/A
- Cost to see resumes: N/A

Links to Jobs? Yes

Career Advice? Yes

The Int'l Network of Women in Technology, a non-profit organization founded in 1989, is dedicated to increasing the number of women in executive roles, helping women become more financially independent, technology-literate and to encourage young women to choose careers in science and technology. This site has the backing of some very high-tech sponsors including Microsoft. A quality feel to the site from beginning to end including an outstanding Career Center with counseling, advice articles and postings for executive jobs for women. On your visit make sure you enter the chat room where you can discuss issues that relate to opening up the glass ceiling. I wouldn't post anything short of management level positions in a technical industry.

CAREERXROADS©
Job, Resume & Career Management Sites on the World Wide Web
• The 1997 Directory •

Women Professional Directory

College/Diversity
www.womensdirectory.com

Gabriella Gillota
6440 Lusk Blvd. D209, San Diego, CA 92121
Phone: 619-643-1919 Fax: 619-543-1915 e-mail: gg@womensdirectory.com

Jobs? No
- Cost to post jobs: N/A
- Cost to see jobs: N/A
- Specialty: All
- Industry: All
- Country/Region/State/City: US

Resumes? Yes
- Cost to post resumes: Fee
- Cost to see resumes: Free

Links to Jobs? No

Career Advice? Yes

Unique site for women interested in networking. Designed to provide information that women can use to collaborate, mentor and advance their careers. Search by keywords after registering to find women with the background required. Free to use but you must register to participate.

World Hire

Career Hub/Agent
www.world.hire.com

Carrie Van Loon iDirect, Inc.
7719 Woodhollow Drive, Suite 216, Austin, TX 78731
Phone: 800-953-4473 Fax: 512-418-8851 e-mail: sales@world.hire.com

Jobs? Yes
- Cost to post jobs: Fee
- Cost to see jobs: Free
- Specialty: All
- Industry: All
- Country/Region/State/City: US

Resumes? Yes
- Cost to post resumes: Free
- Cost to see resumes: Free

Links to Jobs? Yes

Career Advice? Yes

Unique feature of job posting is that candidates must respond to employer provided qualification questions when applying for a posted job. World Hire is a Texas (Austin) based site with major supporters in the Southwest. Companies posting opportunities include Motorola, IBM, Dell Computers, Dallas Semiconductor and many more. Buttons include "Resumes" and "Jobs"," Links"," Lists" and "Career Advice". Nice design. This site plans to operate as an agent and will provide e-mail communication of openings and/or resumes. Site is free to post openings. Employers pay but the cost structure was not in place as we went to press. Definitely worth a look.

CAREERXROADS©
Job, Resume & Career Management Sites on the World Wide Web
• The 1997 Directory •

World Wide Job Seekers

Commercial Resume Site
www.cban.com/resume/

Andrew Stanley-Jones
e-mail: webmaster@cban.com

Jobs? No
- Cost to post jobs: N/A
- Cost to see jobs: N/A
- Specialty: All
- Industry: All
- Country/Region/State/City: Int'l./US

Resumes? Yes
- Cost to post resumes: Free
- Cost to see resumes: Free

Links to Jobs? No

Career Advice? No

Has large numbers of professionals posting resumes. Free for employers to view.

Worldwide Classified Database

Commercial Job Site
www.ipworld.com/classified/homepage.htm

Internet Productions Inc.
,Longwood, FL

Jobs? No
- Cost to post jobs: N/A
- Cost to see jobs: N/A
- Specialty: All
- Industry: All
- Country/Region/State/City: US

Resumes? No
- Cost to post resumes: N/A
- Cost to see resumes: N/A

Links to Jobs? No

Career Advice? Yes

Limited site as it is a Mall. Employers can post opportunities, update and delete for free. No cost for candidates. Has the new split screen look so you can obtain information faster than before.

CAREERXROADS©
Job, Resume & Career Management Sites on the World Wide Web
• The 1997 Directory •

Yahoo Job Search Services

Links

http://www.yahoo.com/business_and_economy/companies/career_and_job_search_services

Jobs? Yes
- Cost to post jobs: N/A
- Cost to see jobs: N/A
- Specialty: All
- Industry: All
- Country/Region/State/City: Int'l/US

Resumes? No
- Cost to post resumes: N/A
- Cost to see resumes: N/A

Links to Jobs? Yes

Career Advice? No

Yahoo has reorganized their employment lists at this address to include links to 2566 "Resume and Job Bank" sites, 767 "Employment Agency" sites and much more. One of the original search engines, Yahoo continues to maintain one of the most useful sites for employment information available on the Internet.

CAREERXROADS©
Job, Resume & Career Management Sites on the World Wide Web
• The 1997 Directory •

YSN Jobs Page (Young Scientists Network)

Association
www.physics.uiuc.edu/ysn/

U. of Illinois
1110 West Green Street, Laboratory of Physics, Champaign-Urbana, IL 61801
Phone: 217-333-3761 Fax: 217-333-9819 e-mail: webmaster@physics.uiuc.edu

Jobs? Yes
- Cost to post jobs: Free
- Cost to see jobs: Free
- Specialty: Science/Physics
- Industry: All
- Country/Region/State/City: US

Resumes? No
- Cost to post resumes: N/A
- Cost to see resumes: N/A

Links to Jobs? Yes

Career Advice? No

Young Scientists Network provides a simple posting of jobs updated twice a month. To find jobs, link to dept. of physics/resources/job bulletin

---

Have you found a site that isn't listed in CAREERXROADS?
Have you REGISTERED to receive FREE updates?
Keep us informed.
We'll keep you informed.

CAREERXROADS
Where Talent and Opportunity Connect on the Internet

Cross Reference Listings

AGENTS
they inform you about leads or candidates via e-mail

Imagine that you have a "Personal Assistant" to go out on the World Wide Web, find the job leads most likely to fit your skills, download them to your computer and print them out for you to review with your morning coffee and bagel. Or, consider that the same "PA" could also be your recruiting assistant to check WWW sites daily, find potential candidates that match your company openings, ask them if they are interested, collect their resumes or skill profiles and leave the results on your desk or in your e-mail "in-basket". The sites below meet the two key requirements of our definition of an agent: they will make a match AND tell you about it without your having to return to their site again and again. One or two are relatively primitive, but even so, they will save you time and provide added value to your search for talent or opportunity. Expect many more site-specific Agents in the future.

4 Work
www.4work.com
Ad One Classified Network
www.adone.com
Asia-Net
www.asia-net.com
AWWA Job Listing
www.awwa.org
Career America
www.careeramerica.com
Career Builder
www.careerbuilder.com
Career Site
www.careersite.com
Computer World's IT Careers
www.computerworld.com
E-Span (Interactive Employment Network)
www.espan.com
Global Job Services
www.indirect.com/www/dtomczyk/
HRIM Mall
www.hrimmall.com
Intellimatch
www.intellimatch.com
Job Center
www.jobcenter.com/
Job Find
www.dicwest.com/~comdata/jobfind.htm

Job Serve: IT Vacancies in the UK
www.jobserve.com
Job Smart
www.jobsmart.org
Jobs OnLine
JobsOnLine.com/emp_enter.cgi
Med Search
www.medsearch.com
Medical/Health Care Jobs Page
www.nationjob.com
The Monster Board
www.monster.com
NationJob Network
www.nationjob.com
Positions in Psychology
www.anu.edu.au/psychology/PiP/pip.htm
Real Bank
www.realbank.com
SkillBank
www.laps.com/skillbank
Talent Hunter
www.3dsite.com/ism/resumes/cgi-bin/talent-hunter.cgi
The Internet Career Site
www.autorecruiter.com
A Virtual Job Fair
www.vjf.com
World Hire
www.world.hire.com

CAREER HUBS
they offer a little of everything to job seekers and employers

Whether you are searching for talent or looking for that gem of a job, you need a place where everybody knows your name. Large multi-service career sites called Career Hubs have it all. They provide job and resume databases, career management information, company profiles, links from and to every imaginable place and some of the best search engines to quickly obtain exactly what you need. The largest sites advertise heavily to attract the level of traffic that they need to support both their claims and to increase their ability to compete for the title of "best staffing site" on the Internet...and many do succeed in drawing 10,000 and more job seekers every day. For many positions, these sites are an excellent value. The newer players on the list may have a more difficult time developing a following as corporations develop their own WWW presence. realize just how diverse the net can be, and begin to develop links to the more highly targeted sites. You can expect the Career Hubs with the greatest visibility and strongest backing to innovate with new services and experiment with their rates.

4 Work
   www.4work.com
America's Employers
   www.americasemployers.com
Career America
   www.careeramerica.com
Career City
   www.careercity.com
Career Magazine
   www.careermag.com
Career Mosaic
   www.careermosaic.com
E-Span (Interactive Employment Network)
   www.espan.com
Heart Career Connections
   www.career.com

Hyper Media Resumes & Career Center
   www.webcom.com/resumes/
Internet Career Connection
   www.iccweb.com
Job Bank USA
   www.jobbankusa.com
Job Tree
   peace.netnation.com/joblink/
The Monster Board
   www.monster.com
NationJob Network
   www.nationjob.com
Online Career Center
   www.occ.com
World Hire
   www.world.hire.com

CAREERXROADS©
Job, Resume & Career Management Sites on the World Wide Web
• The 1997 Directory •

CAREER MANAGEMENT
if you you don't know what you want

This index has something for everyone so why not browse some of the sites below to get an insight into what is going on in the "real world work place." Everything you need to explore a career is available on the Internet. Don't forget the **CAREER HUBS. They** have an enormous amount of career management information. Cross-reference our Specialty Index with the sites shown here to quickly find career information related to your area of interest. Persistence pays off, but if you get stuck, and have a specific question, send us an e-mail at mmc@careerxroads.com and we'll point you in the right direction.

About Work
  www.aboutwork.com
Career Action Center
  www.gatenet.com/cac/
Career Counseling Lite
  www.execpc.com/~cclite/
Career Crafting
  www.well.com/user/careerc/
Career Doctor
  www.career-doctor.com
Career Lab
  www.careerlab.com/clab.htm
Career Talk
  www.careertalk.com
Career Toolbox
  www.careertoolbox.com
Career Transitions
  www.bfservs.com:80/bfserv.html
Career X roads
  www.careerxroads.com
College Connection
  www.careermosaic.com/cm/cc/cc1.html
College Grad Job Hunter
  www.collegegrad.com
Decisive Quest
  www.decisivequest.com
Drake Beam Morin
  www.dbm.com/candidate
Employment Resources
  www.nova.edu/Inter-Links
  /employment.html
Entry Level Job Seeker Assistant
  members.aol.com/Dylander/jobhome.html
Finding and Getting a Job
  edie.cprost.sfu.ca/~gophers/find.html
Getting Past Go: A Survival Guide for College
  www.lattanze.loyola.edu/:80/mongen
  /home.html
GrapeVine
  jobs.index.com/gv.htm
Hard@Work
  www.hardatwork.com
Internet Career Interest Assesment
  www.ksu.edu/~dangle/icia
Job Search Materials for Engineers
  www.englib.cornell.edu//jobsearch.html
Lee Hecht Harrison
  www.careerlhh.com
National Business Employment Weekly
  www.nbew.com
Peterson's Education Center
  www.petersons.com
Princeton Review Online
  www.review.com
The Resume Hut
  www.penlan.com/penlan
Right Management Consultants, Inc.
  www.right.com
Telecommuting, Telework & Alt. Officing
  www.gilgordon.com
Wet Feet Press
  www.wetfeet.com

CAREERXROADS©
Job, Resume & Career Management Sites on the World Wide Web
• The 1997 Directory •

COLLEGE

to find that first opportunity

Everyone needs a start, a place to go that caters to the new kid on the block. These sites are definite stops for those right out of school who are looking to "jump start" their career: resume assistance, career advice, information about your first job or have some fun with a few of the wacky ideas at "The Student Center." Emory University's "Career Paradise" is one to show your parents (not really) or try Carbonate Your Brain if being a roadie for a rock band is your idea of the ideal Summer job. Don't forget to add the **CAREER HUBS** and especially JOBWEB to your tour.

Arts Net Career Services Center
   artsnet.heinz.cmu.edu/career/career.html
The Black Collegian Online
   www.black-collegian.com
Carbonate Your Brain
   www.7up.com
Career Paradise/Emory University
   www.emory.edu/Career/Links.html
Career Planning Process
   www.cba.bgsu.edu:80/class/webclass/nagye/career/
CLNET
   latino.sscnet.ucla.edu/
College Grad Job Hunter
   www.collegegrad.com
Entry Level Job Seeker Assistant
   members.aol.com/Dylander/jobhome.html
EOP
   www.eop.com
Extreme Resume Drop
   www.mainquad.com/resumedrop.html
Getting A Job
   www.americanexpress.com/student/getajob.html
Getting Past Go: A Survival Guide for College
   www.lattanze.loyola.edu/:80/mongen/home.html
Job Board
   wfscnet.tamu.edu:80/jobs.html
Job Net
   westga.edu:80/~coop/index.html
Job Net San Diego
   www.eghjobnet.com
JOB TRAK
   www.jobtrak.com
JobWeb
   www.jobweb.org/
Journalism-Related Jobs
   eb.journ.latech.edu/jobs/jobs_home.html
Kansas Careers
   www-personal.ksu.edu/~dangle/
Peterson's Education Center
   www.petersons.com
Purdue's Job List
   www.ups.purdue.edu/student/jobsites.htm
Real Jobs
   www.real-jobs.com
Resources for Students of Color
   www.alumni.wesleyan.edu/WWW/Info/CPC/soc.html
RPI Career Resource Home Page
   www.rpi.edu:80/dept/cdc
SEACnet SE Atlantic Coast Career Network
   minerva.acc.Virginia.EDU/~seacnet/
Summer Jobs
   www.summerjobs.com
Television & Radio News Research
   www.missouri.edu~jourus/
UCI Center for Int'l Education
   www.cie.uci.edu/~cie
USM Resources for G/L/B Students
   macweb.acs.usm.maine.edu/csce/career_glb.html
U. of Penn Career Services
   www.upenn.edu/CPPS
Web Dog's Job Hunt:The Best Jobs
   www.itec.sfsu.edu/students/projects/jschwartz/edtech/edtech.html

CAREERXROADS©
Job, Resume & Career Management Sites on the World Wide Web
• **The 1997 Directory** •

COUNTRY/REGIONAL

for job seekers on the move

This breakout will give you sites that focus exclusively on providing services for a specific country or region of the US. To expand this category, enter any location into a Search Engine such as "Hotbot" (http://www.hotbot.com), along with the words "jobs," "employment" or "careers." Don't forget the Career Hubs and government sites. The former will provide you with the ability to sort by city or region and the latter links to job sites by state.

(Int'l)
 ACM's Sigmod's Database
 www.acm.org/sigmod/jobs
(Int'l/Africa)
 Africa Online
  www.AfricaOnline.com/AfricaOnline/jobs.html
(Int'l/AU)
 AK Jobnet - The Big Picture
 www.ak.com.au/akjobnet.html
(Int'l/UK)
 Appointment Section
 taps.com
(Int'l/US)
 Asian Career Net
 www.rici.com/acw/index.html
(Int'l)
 Au Pair in Europe
 eidos.ca/aupair/
(Int'l/US)
 Biomedical Positions
 www.informatik.uni-rostock.de/hum-molgen/anno/position
(Int'l/Australia)
 Byron Employment Australia
 www.com.au/employment_australia/
(Int'l/Canada)
 Can Work Net
 hrdc.ingenia.com/
(Int'l/Canada)
 Canadian Job Source
 www.irus.rri.uwo.ca/~jlaw/national.html
(Int'l/China)
 Career China
 www.globalvillager.com/villager/CC.html
(Int'l/US)
 Career Exchange
 www.careerexchange.com/

(Int'l/US)
 Career Mosaic
 www.careermosaic.com
(Int'l)
 Career Opportunities in Singapore
 www.singapore-careers.com
(Int'l/US)
 Cell
 www.cell.com/cell/index.html
(Int'l/US)
 Crystallography Worldwide
 www.unige.ch/crystal/w3vlc/crystal.index.html
(Int'l/Cumbria)
 Cumbria Careers on the Net
 www.u-net.com/~c-career/
(Int'l/UK)
 Engine Room
 www.iweb.co.uk/iwsearch.html#map
(Int'lUS)
 Engineering News Record
 www.enr.com
(Int'l)
 Euro Jobs on Line
 www.belganet.be/~belganet/jobs/jobs.htm
(Int'l/US)
 Finding A Job
 www.dbisna.com/dbis/jobs/vjobhunt.htm
(Int'l/US)
 Future Business Centre On-Line
 ns.webb.com/future
(Int'l)
 Global Job Net
 riceinfo.rice.edu/projects/careersChannelsix.html
(Int'l/US)
 Global Job Services
 www.indirect.com/www/dtomczyk/

CAREERXROADS©
Job, Resume & Career Management Sites on the World Wide Web
• The 1997 Directory •

284

COUNTRY/REGIONAL
for job seekers on the move

(Int'l/Hong Kong)
Hong Kong Jobs
www.hkjobs.com
(Int'l/HongKong)
Hong Kong Standard
www.hkstandard.com/online/job/english
/engjob.htm
(Int'l/Canada)
Human Element
mindlink.net/vci/thehp.htm
(Int'l/US)
Job Listings in Academia
volvo.gslis.utexas.edu~acadres/jla.html
(Int'l/South Africa)
Job Navigator
www.jobs.co.za
(Int'l/UK)
Job Serve: IT Vacancies in the UK
www.jobserve.com
(Int'l/Canada/US)
Job Tree
peace.netnation.com/joblink/
(Int'l/US)
Jobs Mathematics
www.cs.dartmouth.edu/~gdavis/policy/
jobmarket.htmlpolicy/jobmarket.html
(Int'l/Czech Republic)
Jobs .CZ
www.cz/english_welcome.html
(Int'l/Malaysia)
Malaysia Online
www.mol.com
(Int'l/Canada)
Net Jobs Information Services
www.netjobs.com
(Int'l/US)
News Link
www.newslink.org
(Int'l/Japan)
O Hayo Sensei
www.ohayosensei.com/~ohayo/

(Int'l/Canada)
Parksville/Qualicum Career Center
qb.island.net/~careers/
(Int'l/US)
Physician Recruit Net
www.physiciannet.com/index.html
(Int'l/US)
Physics Jobs On-Line
www.tp.umu.se/TIPTOP/
(Int'l)
Plasma Laboratory Wis
plasma-gate.weizman.ac.il/jobs.html
(Int'l)
Positions in Psychology
www.anu.edu.au/psychology/PiP/pip.htm
(Int'l/Canada)
Pro Net Search
bisinc.com/pronet/ccc/
(Int'l/US)
Programmers Available
www.qldnet.com.au/web.users/
programmers
(Int'l/UK)
Recruit Net
recruitnet.guardian.co.uk/
(Int'l/Canada)
SC WIST Work Pathfinder
www.harbour.sfu.ca/scwist/pathfinder
/index.htm.
(Int'l/US)
Science Global Career Network
www.aaas.org
(Int'l/Singapore)
Singapore On Line
www.singapore.com/jobs.htm
(Int'l/Canada)
St. Thomas Human Resource Centre
ein.ccia.st-thomas.on.ca/agencies/
cec/index.html
(Int'l/US)
Summer Jobs
www.summerjobs.com

CAREERXROADS©
Job, Resume & Career Management Sites on the World Wide Web
• **The 1997 Directory** •

COUNTRY/REGIONAL
for job seekers on the move

(Int'l/Canada/US)
 TCM's Job Marts (HR, T&D, HRIS)
 www.tcm.com
(Int'l/US)
 TrainingNet
 www.trainingnet.com
(Int'l/US)
 UCI Center for Int'l Education
 www.cie.uci.edu/~cie
(Int'l/US)
 UI Design Jobs
 www.io.tudelft.nl/uidesign/jobs.html
(Int'l/UK)
 Virtual Job Centre
 channel.cyberiacafe.net/jobs/index.html
(Int'l/US)
 Women in Technology & Industry-WITI
 www.witi.com
(Int'l/US)
 World Wide Job Seekers
 www.cban.com/resume/
(Int'l/US)
 Yahoo Job Search Services
 www.yahoo.com/business_and_economy/
 companies/career_and jobsearchservices

EAST

(US/E/DC)
 Washington Post-Career Post
 204.146.47.74/
(US/E/MD)
 Life Goes On
 www.lifegoeson.com
(US/E/NC/Raleigh)
 Nando Times
 www.nando.net
(US/E/NJ)
 InJersey
 www.injersey.com

(US/E/NJ)
 NJ JOBS
 www.njjobs.com
(US/E/NJ)
 New Jersey Online
 www.nj.com
(US/E/NJ)
 Princeton 1Info (US 1)
 www.princetoninfo.com
(US/E/NJ)
 The Star Ledger
 www.nj.com
(US/E/NY)
 Western New York Jobs
 www.wnyjobs.com./#anchor263367
(US/E/NY)
 PolySort
 www.polysort.com
(US/E/NY)
 Internet Fashion Exchange
 www.fashionexch.com
(US/E/NY)
 Law Employment Center
 www.lawjobs.com/
(US/E/NY)
 New York Law Journal
 www.lextra.com/classifieds
(US/E/NY/NYC)
 New York Times
 www.nytimes.com
(US/E/NY/NYC)
 Execubank
 www.realbank.com
(US/E/OH)
 Columbus Dispatch
 www.dispatch.com
(US/E/PA)
 OnLine Opportunities
 www.jobnet.com
(US/E/PA)
 Metroworld
 metroworld.com

CAREERXROADS©
Job, Resume & Career Management Sites on the World Wide Web
• The 1997 Directory •

COUNTRY/REGIONAL
for job seekers on the move

(US/E/PA)
Job Net & Online Opportunities
www.jobnet.com
(US/E/PA)
Advance HTC
www.advancehtc.com
(US/E/PA)
Montgomery Newspapers
www.montnews.com
(US/E/PA/Phil.)
Planet Jobs-Philadelphia On-Line
www.phillynews.com/programs/ads
/SUNHLP
(US/E/VA/Norfolk)
Norfolk Virginian-Pilot Online
www.infi.net/pilot
(US/E/VA/Roanoke)
Roanoke Times Online
www.infi.net/roatimes/index.html

North East

(US/NE/Boston)
Boston Job Bank
www.bostonjobs.com
(US/NE/CT)
Hartford Courant
www.courant.com
(US/NE/MA)
Boston Herald Job Find
www.bostonherald.com/jobfind
(US/NE/MA)
Job Smart
www.jobsmart.org
(US/NE/MA/Boston)
Boston Globe
www.boston.com
(US/NE/NY/NYC)
Employment Channel
www.employ.com

(US/NE/NY/Syracuse)
Syracuse Online
www.syracuse.com

South East

(US/SE)
Medical Jobs
www.MEDJOB.com
(US/SE)
US Job Network
www.usjob.net
(US/SE/FL)
A+ On-Line Resumes
www.hway.net/olresume
(US/SE/FL/Ft. Lauderdale)
Career Spot
www.careerspot.com
(US/SE/FL/Orlando)
Orlando Sentinel
www.orlandosentinel.com
(US/SE/FL/St. Petersburg)
SPTimes
www.sptimes.com
(US/SE/GA)
Job Net
westga.edu:80/~coop/index.html
(US/SE/GA)
Georgia Job Bank
www.mindspring.com/
~exchange/jobbank/ga/jobs.html
(US/SE/GA/Atlanta)
Computer Jobs Store (Atlanta)
computerjobs.com
(US/SE/GA/Augusta)
Augusta (GA) Chronicle
www.augustachronicle.com
(US/SE/NC)
No. Carolina Career & Employment
www.webcom.com/~nccareer/

COUNTRY/REGIONAL

for job seekers on the move

South

(US/S/AL/Birmingham)
 Alabama Jobs
 www.the-matrix.com/ph/ph.html
(US/S/LA)
 Info Louisiana
 www.state.la.us/
(US/S/MS)
 Mississippi Careers Online
 www.whipcomm.com/
 whipcomm/mscareer
(US/S/TN/Chatanooga)
 Chattanooga News Free Press
 www.chatpub.com
(US/S/TN/Knox.)
 Knoxville News-Sentinel
 www.knoxnews.com

South West

(US/SW/AR)
 Arizona Careers Online
 amsquare.com/america/arizona.html
(US/SW/TX/Dallas)
 Dallas Morning News
 www.dallasnews.com/us.htm
(US/SW/TX/Dallas)
 Computer Jobs Store (Dallas)
 computerjobs.com/dallas
(US/SW/TX/Houston)
 Houston Chronicle Interactive
 www.chron.com

Mid West

(US/MW)
 Careers in Management Consulting
 www.cob.ohio-state.edu:80/dept/fin/jobs/consult.htm
(US/MW)
 American Soc. of Agricultural Eng.
 asae.org/jobs
(US/MW)
 Medical/Health Care Jobs Page
 www.nationjob.com
(US/MW/IL)
 Pioneer Press
 www.pioneerlocal.com
(US/MW/IL/Chicago)
 Career Finder
 www.chicago.tribune.com
(US/MW/IL/Chicago)
 Chicago Software Newspaper
 www.chisoft.com
(US/MW/IL/Chicago)
 Chicago Sun Times
 www.suntimes.com
(US/MW/KS)
 Kansas Careers
 www-personal.ksu.edu/~dangle/
(US/MW/MI)
 Michigan Employment
 www.mesc.state.mi.us/techjobs.htm
(US/MW/MI/Minn.)
 Minneapolis Star-Tribune
 www.startribune.com
(US/MW/MN)
 Careers On-Line
 www.disserv.stu.umn.edu/tc/grants/col/
(US/MW/MN)
 Twin Cities Job Page
 www.fentonnet.com/jobs/html
(US/MW/MN/St. Paul)
 St. Paul Pioneer Press
 www.stpaulpp.com
(US/MW/MO/KC)
 Kansas City Star
 www.kansascity.com

CAREERXROADS©
Job, Resume & Career Management Sites on the World Wide Web
• The 1997 Directory •

COUNTRY/REGIONAL
for job seekers on the move

(US/MW/MO/St. Louis)
St. Louis Area Companies on the Net
www.st-louis.mo.us/
st-louis/companies.html
(US/MW/WI)
Wisconsin Employment Bureau
badger.state.wi.us/agencies/dilhr
(US/MW/WI/Mil.)
Milwaukee Journal (Help Wanted)
www.adquest.com

North West

(US/NW)
IHRIM Chapter/Pacific Northwest
www.ihrim.org/chapters/pacificnorthwest
/index.html
(US/NW/AL/Anchorage)
Anchorage Daily News
www.adn.com
(US/NW/WA)
Doctor Link
www.doctorlink.com
(US/NW/WA/Seattle)
Seattle Times
www.seatimes.com/classified/
(US/NW/WA/Tacoma)
Tacoma News Tribune (Help Wanted)
www.tribnet.com

West

(US/W)
Colorado Online Job Connection
www.net1comm.com/~peak/
(US/W)
A Virtual Job Fair
www.vjf.com
(US/W)
OfficeNet
www.officenet1.com

(US/W)
Agricultural Job Listings
caticsuf.csufresno.edu:70/1/atinet/
agjobs
(US/West)
Abag Globe
www.abag.ca.gov/bayarea/commerce
/globe/globe.html
(US/W/CA)
San Francisco Bay Area Job Lines
www.webcom.com:80/~rmd/bay_area
/joblines.html
(US/W/CA)
Purchasing NAPM
catalog.com/napmsv/jobs.htm
(US/W/CA)
Potpourri Shoppers
www.netview.com/pp/employ/
(US/W/CA)
Saludos Career Web
www.wenet.nt/saludos/
(US/W/CA)
California Career and Employment
www.webcom.com/~career/
(US/W/CA)
CLNET
latino.sscnet.ucla.edu/
(US/W/CA)
Seamless Web: Legal Job Center
www.seamless.com/jobs/
(US/W/CA)
HRCOMM
ccnet.com/hrcomm/
(US/W/CA)
Auditions Online
www.auditions.com
(US/W/CA/LA)
Los Angeles Times
www.latimes.com
(US/W/CA/Sacramento)
Sacramento Bee
www.sacramentobee.com

COUNTRY/REGIONAL

for job seekers on the move

(US/W/CA/San Diego)
  Job Scape
  www.jobscape.com/occupational
(US/W/CA/San Diego)
  Job Net San Diego
  www.eghjobnet.com
(US/W/CA/San Fran)
  Red Guide to Temporary Agencies
  www.best.com/~ezy/redguide/intro.html
(US/W/CA/San Francisco)
  The Gate
  www.sfgate.com/
(US/W/CA/San Francisco)
  Silicon Valley Technical Employmen...
  www.sease.com/jobs.html
(US/W/CA/San Francisco)
  San Francisco Chronicle-Classified
  www.sfgate.com/classifieds/
(US/W/CA/San Jose)
  Mercury Center Web
  www.sjmercury.com
(US/W/CA/SF)
  K3 & Company
  www.k3k3k3.com/index.html
(US/W/CO)
  Denver Post
  www.denverpost.com
(US/W/CO/Boulder)
  Boulder Community Network
  www.bcn.boulder.co
(US/W/CO/Denver)
  Rocky Mountain News
  www.denver-rmn.com

DIVERSITY
is the key to the Internet. Everyone is out here.

Whoever said that the web is populated with white male techies between the ages of 25 and 30 doesn't know where to look. The sites below contain gender and minority career information and links to jobs. There are also plenty of sites with information related to disabilities, seniors (over 40) and much more. Additional information is available using our Lists & Links/Search index. The CAREER HUBS also have significant diversity information. Check out JobWeb's Catapult.

Africa Online
   www.AfricaOnline.com/
   AfricaOnline/jobs.html
Afro-Americ@: The Job Vault
   www.afroam.org/information/
   vault/afro.html
Arizona Careers Online
   amsquare.com/america/arizona.html
Asian Career Net
   www.rici.com/acw/index.html
Association for Women in Computing
   www.halcyon.com/monih/awc.html
The Black Collegian Online
   www.black-collegian.com
Black E.O.E Journal
   www.usa-ca.com/blk_blkeoe_jrnl
Careers On-Line
   www.disserv.stu.umn.edu/tc/grants/col/
CLNET
   latino.sscnet.ucla.edu/
EOP(Career Center for Workforce Diversity)
   www.eop.com
Forty Plus of Northern California
   web.sirius.com/~40plus/#contact
Frasernet
   www.frasernet.com
High Technology Careers/Links
   www.vjf.com/pub/docs/jobsearch.html
Job Scape
   www.jobscape.com/occupational
Kansas Careers
   www-personal.ksu.edu/~dangle/
Latino Web
   www.catalog.com/favision/latnoweb
Resources for Students of Color
   www.alumni.wesleyan.edu/WWW/Info
   /CPC/soc.html
Saludos Career Web
   www.wenet.nt/saludos/
Seniors On-Line Job Bank
   www.seniorsnet.com/jobbank.htm
Society of Women Engineers
   www.swe.org
The (National) Urban League
   www.urbanleague.com
Women in Computer Science & Eng.
   www.mit.edu:8001/people/sorokin
   /women/index.html
Women in Technology & Industry-WITI
   www.witi.com
Women Professional Directory
   www.womensdirectory.com

JOBS
post jobs for free and for a "fee"

Posting jobs on lots of Web Sites can add up. While many sites will initially offer free postings, you'll just as often get what you pay for. For the best return today, look for publications (Country/Region or Trade-Publications cross index) and associations (Specialty cross index) with internet components.

FREE

Abag Globe
Academic Chemistry Employment Clearinghouse
Academic Employment Network
ACM's Sigmod's Database Job Openings
Africa Online
Agricultural Job Listings
Airline Employment Ass't. Corps
America's Job Bank
Arts Net Career Services Center
Auditions Online
AWWA Job Listing
A.E.P.S.
BAMTA
Biomedical Positions
Boston Job Bank
Boulder Community Network
Building Industry Exchange
Business Job Finder Ohio State Univ.
Byron Employment Australia
California Job Bank
Carbonate Your Brain
Career Action Center
Career Builder
Career City
Career Connector
Career File's
Career Line
Career Paradise/Emory University
Career Transitions
Careers in Management Consulting
Careers On-Line
Civil Eng. & Public Works Career Paths
Clearinghouse for T&D Resources
CLNET
Computer Science Jobs in Academia
Crystallography Worldwide
Cumbria Careers on the Net
DesignSphere Online
Direct Marketing World Job Center
Disability Services at the Univ. of Minnesota
Doctor Link
Eagleview
Ed Physician
Employment Edge
Employment Opportunities in Water Resources
Engineering Jobs
The Environmental Careers Organization
Euro Jobs on Line
Execubank
FedWorld Information Network
Finishing.com
Franklin Search Group
GeoWeb for GIS/GPS/RS
Hospitality Net
HR World
HRIM Mall
ICS NY Job Listings
Impact Online
Info Louisiana
Internet Fashion Exchange
IPMA HR Job Pool
Job Board
Job Listings in Academia
Job Net
Job Net Work: Your Total Employment Connection
Job Source
Job Tree
Journalism-Related Jobs
Latino Web
Music Exchange
NAACB Job Board and Resume Bank

CAREERXROADS©
Job, Resume & Career Management Sites on the World Wide Web
• The 1997 Directory •

JOBS

post jobs for free and for a "fee"

National Diversity Journalism Job Bank
National Educators Employment Review
National Society of Professional
    Engineering HP
Netshare
News Link
NJ Job Search
NMAA'S Job Banker
O Hayo Sensei
Physics Jobs On-Line
Plasma Laboratory Wis
Positions in Psychology
Proctor & Gamble Career Center
Programmers Available
Purchasing NAPM
Radio DJ's Unemployed
Real Bank
Real Jobs
Resources for Students of Color
Right Management Consultants, Inc.
RPI Career Resource Home Page
RS/6000 Employment Page
SEACnet Southeastern
    Atlantic Coast Career Network
Seamless Web: Legal Job Center
St. Thomas Human Resource Centre
Talent Hunter
The Talent Network
Telecommuting Jobs
Television & Radio News Research
Top Jobs USA
TrainingNet
UCI Center for Int'l Education
UI Design Jobs
U. of Penn Career Services
Virtual Headbook
Web Engineer's Toolbox Career Center
Windows NT Resource Center
Wisconsin Employment Bureau
Women in Computer Science &
    Engineering
Women in Technology & Industry-WITI

YSN Jobs Page
    (Young Scientists Network)

FEE

100 Careers in Cyberspace
100 Careers in Wall Street
4 Work
AAS Career Services
Academe This Week
Ad One Classified Network
Ad Search
Adia
Advance HTC
Afro-Americ@: The Job Vault
AIP Physics Careers Bulletin Board
AJR/ News Link
AK Jobnet - The Big Picture
Alabama Jobs
Allied Health Opportunities Directory
America's Employers:
    The Job Seekers "Home"
Anchorage Daily News
Appointment Section
Arizona Careers Online
Asian Career Net
Asia-Net
Association for Women in Computing
Augusta (GA) Chronicle
A+ On-Line Resumes
Best Jobs U.S.A.
Bio Online Career Center
BioSpace Career Center
The Black Collegian Online
Black E.O.E Journal
Boldface Jobs
Boston Globe
Boston Herald Job Find
California Career and
    Employment Center
Career America
Career China

CAREERXROADS©
Job, Resume & Career Management Sites on the World Wide Web
• The 1997 Directory •

JOBS

post jobs for free and for a "fee"

Career Command Center
Career Exchange
Career Finder
Career Internet Working
Career Magazine
Career Mart
Career Mosaic
Career Network
Career Opportunities in Singapore
Career Path
Career Shop
Career Site
Career Spot
Career Surf
Career WEB
CE Weekly
Cell
Chattanooga News Free Press
Chicago Software Newspaper
Chicago Sun Times
Chronicle of Higher Education
College Connection
College Grad Job Hunter
Colorado Online Job Connection
Columbus Dispatch
Comm Careers
Communication Week
Computer Jobs Store (Atlanta)
Computer Jobs Store (Dallas)
Computer Retail Week
Computer World's IT Careers
Contract Employment Connection
Contract Employment NACCB
Contract Employment Weekly
Cool Works
Coolware Electronic Job Finder
Corporate Aviation Resume Exchange
Dallas Morning News
Denver Post
DICE
Educator's Network EDNET

Electric Power NewsLink
Emergency Medicine Practice
    Opportunity
Employment Channel
Employment Online
Engine Room
Engineering Job Source
Engineering News Record
EOP
EPage Greater NYC Classifieds
Equipment Leasing Association
E-Span (Interactive
    Employment Network)
Food and Drug Packaging
For The Record
Frasernet
Future Access Employment Guide
Future Business Centre On-Line
F-o-r-t-u-n-e Personnel Consultants
The Gate
Get a Job!
Hartford Courant
Health Careers Online
Heart Career Connections
Help Wanted
Help Wanted-USA
High Technology Career Centre
Hong Kong Jobs
Hong Kong Standard
Hot Jobs
Houston Chronicle Interactive
HRCOMM
Hyper Media Resumes & Career Center
IEEE
Imcor-Provides Top-Level Executives
InJersey
Insurance Career Center
International Dental Connection
Internet Career Connection
Internet Job Locator
iWorld

CAREERXROADS©
Job, Resume & Career Management Sites on the World Wide Web
• The 1997 Directory •

JOBS
post jobs for free and for a "fee"

JAMA
Job Bank USA
Job Center
Job Navigator
Job Net San Diego
Job Net San Diego
Job Net & Online Opportunities
Job Scape
Job Search
Job Serve: IT Vacancies in the UK
Job Smart
JOB TRAK
Job Web
Jobs OnLine
Jobs .CZ
JWT Specialized Communications
K3 & Company
Kansas City Star
Knoxville News-Sentinel
Law Employment Center
Layover
Life Goes On
Los Angeles Times
MacTemps
Malaysia Online
Manpower
MBA Employment Connection Assoc.
Med Connect
Med Search
Medical Jobs
Medical Web
Medical/Health Care Jobs Page
Mercury Center Web
Metroworld
Milwaukee Journal (Help Wanted)
Minneapolis Star-Tribune
MMWire Online
The Monster Board
Montgomery Newspapers
Nando Times
National Physician Job Listing Directory
National Society of Black Engineers

The National (Int'l) Home
   Workers Association
NationJob Network
Net Jobs Information Services
Network World Fusion
New England Journal of Medicine
New Jersey Online
New York Law Journal
New York Times
NJ JOBS
Norfolk Virginian-Pilot Online
No. Carolina Career &
   Employment Resource Center
NYC Headhunter's Mall
Oasys Network
Online Career Center
OnLine Opportunities
Orlando Sentinel
Packinfo-world
Passport Access
Perioperative Online
   Employment Opportunities
Philanthropy Journal
Physician Recruit Net
Physicians Employment
Pioneer Press
Planet Jobs-Philadelphia
   On-Line Classifieds
PolySort
Pop Jobs
Potpourri Shoppers
Princeton 1Info (US 1)
Pro Net Search
Psych
Pursuit Net Jobs
Recruit Net
Recruiters Online Network
Recruitex Technologies
Resumes on the Web
Roanoke Times Online
Rocky Mountain News
Sacramento Bee

CAREERXROADS©
Job, Resume & Career Management Sites on the World Wide Web
• The 1997 Directory •

JOBS
post jobs for free and for a "fee"

Saludos Career Web
San Francisco Chronicle-
    Classified on the Gateway
Sanford Rose Associates
Science Global Career Network
Seattle Times
Seniors On-Line Job Bank
Shawn's Internet Resume Center
SHRM HR Jobs
Singapore On Line
Snelling Staffing Services
Society of Women Engineers
The Software Jobs Home Page
SPIE's Employment Center
SPTimes
The Star Ledger
St. Paul Pioneer Press
Summer Jobs
Supermarket News
Syracuse Online
Tacoma News Tribune (Help Wanted)
TCM's Job Marts (HR, T&D, HRIS)
Technology Registry
TechWeb/TechCareers/TechHunter
The Internet Career Site
Training & Devel. Resource Center
TV Jobs
Twin Cities Job Page
US Job Network
Usjobnet K-12
Virtual Job Centre
A Virtual Job Fair
Wall Street Journal E-MART
Washington Post-Career Post
Web Developer's Virtual Library
Western New York Jobs
Women in Higher Education
World Hire

LINKS

to expand your search

Have you ever driven to a new city and gotten lost but were too stubborn to ask for directions? These are your maps and starting points to find your way to jobs on the super highway. Search engines are everywhere and while Yahoo is the only true search engine we've included (because of it's lists and links), you'll find outstanding results from altavista, excite, dejanews, webcrawler and our current favorite- hotbot. We predict the number of sites with jobs on the WWW will approach 250,000 by 1998. The lists and links to job sites shown below are maintained by various folks who want you to know their favorite places. More than 300 of the sites listed in CAREERXROADS maintain at least a few links to other job sites.

Am. Assoc. of Fin & Accounting
www.aafa.com/
Best Bets from the Net: Job Search
www.lib.umich.edu:80/chdocs/employment/
Bullseye Job Shop
interoz.com/usr/gcbristow
Canadian Job Source
www.irus.rri.uwo.ca/~jlaw/national.html
Career Network
www.careers.org
Career & Job Resources
www.goforit.com/tsunami/career.html
Connect
www.cabrillo.cc.ca.us/connect/docs/jobs.html
Cyber Hound
www.thomson.com/cyberhound/default.html
The Definitive Internet Career Guide
phoenix.placement.oakland.edu/career/internet.htm
Future Med
ourworld.compuserve.com/homepages/futuremed/main.htm
Global Job Net
riceinfo.rice.edu/projects/careersChannelsix.html
Gordon Group Home Page
www.owt.com/jobsinfo/jobsinfo.htm
Harry's BBS and Internet Job Hotlist
rescomp.stanford.edu/jobs-bbs.html
High Technology Careers/Links
www.vjf.com/pub/docs/jobsearch.html
Infoseek
www.infoseek.com
Internet Business Network
www.interbiznet.com/ibn
Internet Job Surfer
www.rpi.edu/dept/cdc/jobsurfer/joba.html

Job Hunt: On-Line Job Meta-List
www.job-hunt.org
Job Search & Employment Opps-Best Bets
www.lib.umich.edu/chdocs/employment/
JOBS
ageninfo.tamu.edu/jobs.html
Le Web Cafe Career
www.lewebcafe.com/pages/career.htm
Links on the Web
www.cob.ohio-state.edu/other/other.html#jobs
Multimedia News Stand
www.mmnewsstand.com
Open Market Comercial Sites Index
www.directory.net/
Purdue's Job List
www.ups.purdue.edu/student/jobsites.htm
Recruiting Links
www.recruiting-links.com/
Red Guide to Temporary Agencies
www.best.com/~ezy/redguide/intro.html
The Riley Guide
www.jobtrak.com/jobguide/
San Francisco Bay Area Job Lines
www.webcom.com:80/~rmd/bay_area/joblines.html
SenseMedia Job Board
sensemedia.net/getajob/
Silicon Valley Tech. Employment Agencies
www.sease.com/jobs.html
Student Center
studentcenter.com
Web Dog's Job Hunt:The Best Jobs
www.itec.sfsu.edu/students/projects/jschwartz/edtech/edtech.html
Yahoo Job Search Services
www.yahoo.com/business_and_economy/companies/career_and_job_search_services

CAREERXROADS©
Job, Resume & Career Management Sites on the World Wide Web
• The 1997 Directory •

PUBLICATIONS
to reach classifieds on-line

All publishers listed below have created a World Wide Web component for their help wanted advertising. CareerPath, SmartJobs, and AdOne represent their best (collective) foot forward. The San Jose Mercury News, Chicago Tribune and the Washington Post all have outstanding sites. As a job seeker, you cannot do better than checking out your favorite newspaper's want ads from wherever you are. Trade magazines and professional association publications are also providing web site posting (and often in advance of when the publication reaches your door). You may also want to try Newslink (http://www.newslink.org) which will take you to help wanted advertising around the world.

Academe This Week
www.chronicle.com
Ad One Classified Network
www.adone.com
Advance HTC
www.advancehtc.com
Afro-Americ@: The Job Vault
www.afroam.org/information
/vault/afro.html
Alabama Jobs
www.the-matrix.com/ph/ph.html
Allied Health Opportunities Directory
www.gvpub.com
Anchorage Daily News
www.adn.com
Augusta (GA) Chronicle
www.augustachronicle.com
The Black Collegian Online
www.black-collegian.com
Black E.O.E Journal
www.usa-ca.com/blk_blkeoe_jrnl
Boston Globe
www.boston.com
Boston Herald Job Find
www.bostonherald.com/jobfind
Brave New World
www.newwork.com
Career Center for Workforce Diversity
www.eop.com
Career Finder
www.chicago.tribune.com
Career Path
www.careerpath.com
Career Spot
www.careerspot.com

CE Weekly
www.ceweekly.com
Cell
www.cell.com/cell/index.html
Chattanooga News Free Press
www.chatpub.com
Chicago Software Newspaper
www.chisoft.com
Chicago Sun Times
www.suntimes.com
Chronicle of Higher Education
www.chronicle.com
Columbus Dispatch
www.dispatch.com
Comm Careers
www.commweek.com
Communication Week
techweb.cmp.com/cw/cw.careers
/index.html
Computer Resellers Weekly
techweb.cmp.com/crn/career/career.html
Computer Retail Week
techweb.cmp.com/crw/061996/
Computer World's IT Careers
www.computerworld.com
Contract Employment Weekly
www.ceweekly.wa.com
Dallas Morning News
www.dallasnews.com/us.htm
Denver Post
www.denverpost.com
Electric Power NewsLink
www.powermag.com
Electronic Engineering Times
techweb.cmp.com/eet/823/

CAREERXROADS©
Job, Resume & Career Management Sites on the World Wide Web
• The 1997 Directory •

PUBLICATIONS
to reach classifieds on-line

Employment Channel
www.employ.com
Employment Online
152.52.2.152/classads/employment
/careers.html
ENews
www.sumnet.com/enews
Engineering Job Source
www.wwnet.com/~engineer/
Engineering News Record
www.enr.com
EOP
www.eop.com
Federal Jobs Digest
www.jobsfed.com
Food and Drug Packaging
www.fdp.com
For The Record
www.gvpub.com
The Gate
www.sfgate.com/
Hartford Courant
www.courant.com
Hong Kong Standard
www.hkstandard.com/online/job/english
/engjob.htm
Houston Chronicle Interactive
www.chron.com
InJersey
www.injersey.com
iWorld
www.iworld.com
JAMA
ama-assn.org
Job Smart
www.jobsmart.org
Kansas City Star
www.kansascity.com
Knoxville News-Sentinel
www.knoxnews.com
Law Employment Center
www.lawjobs.com/
Life Goes On
www.lifegoeson.com
Los Angeles Times
www.latimes.com
Main Stream Work Life Center
www.worklife.com
Medical Device Link
www.devicelink.com
Mercury Center Web
www.sjmercury.com
Metroworld
metroworld.com
Milwaukee Journal (Help Wanted)
www.adquest.com
Minneapolis Star-Tribune
www.startribune.com
MMWire Online
www.mmwire.com
Montgomery Newspapers
www.montnews.com
Nando Times
www.nando.net
National Business Employment Weekly
www.nbew.com
National Diversity Journalism Job Bank
www.newsjobs.com
National Educators Employment Review
www.teacherjobs.com/
Network World Fusion
www.nwfusion.com
New England Journal of Medicine
www.nejm.org/nejm/webmate
?nejm/form/nejm/welcome
New Jersey Online
www.nj.com
New York Law Journal
www.lextra.com/classifieds
New York Times
www.nytimes.com
News Link
www.newslink.org
Norfolk Virginian-Pilot Online
www.infi.net/pilot

CAREERXROADS©
Job, Resume & Career Management Sites on the World Wide Web
• The 1997 Directory •

PUBLICATIONS
to reach classifieds on-line

O Hayo Sensei
www.ohayosensei.com/~ohayo/
Orlando Sentinel
www.orlandosentinel.com
Perioperative Online Employment Opps
www.aorn.org
Philanthropy Journal
www.philanthropy-journal.org/
Physician Recruit Net
www.physiciannet.com/index.html
Pioneer Press
www.pioneerlocal.com
Planet Jobs-Philadelphia
  On-Line Classifieds
www.phillynews.com/programs
  /ads/SUNHLP
Potpourri Shoppers
www.netview.com/pp/employ/
Princeton 1Info (US 1)
www.princetoninfo.com
Recruit Net
recruitnet.guardian.co.uk/
Roanoke Times Online
www.infi.net/roatimes/index.html
Rocky Mountain News
www.denver-rmn.com
Sacramento Bee
www.sacramentobee.com
Saludos Career Web
www.wenet.nt/saludos/
San Francisco Chronicle-
  Classified on the Gateway
www.sfgate.com/classifieds/
Science Global Career Network
www.aaas.org
Seattle Times
www.seatimes.com/classified/
SPTimes
www.sptimes.com
The Star Ledger
www.nj.com

St. Paul Pioneer Press
www.stpaulpp.com
Supermarket News
www.supermarketnews.com
Syracuse Online
www.syracuse.com
Tacoma News Tribune (Help Wanted)
www.tribnet.com
TechWeb/TechCareers/TechHunter
techweb.cmp.com/
Wall Street Journal E-MART
www.wsj.com
Washington Post-Career Post
204.146.47.74/
Western New York Jobs
www.wnyjobs.com./#anchor263367
Women in Higher Education
www.itis.com/wihe/

RESUMES
to make your point

Recruiters can search for potential applicants for free and for a fee on hundreds of sites. Most have excellent search capability. Applicants wishing to post their resumes will also find that some sites charge and others do not. Higher cost does not always mean higher value for job seekers- or recruiters. Pick the sites you want to use carefully. This is one area that may be getting crowded. Recently, more and more sites have created a skill profile for more efficient matching. Nice trend if the site's focus is a particular niche. Much more difficult to implement if you are trying to cover every discipline.

Post Resumes for Free

4 Work
Abag Globe
Appointment Section
Arts Net Career Services Center
Asian Career Net
Asia-Net
Biomedical Positions
Boston Job Bank
Building Industry Exchange
Carbonate Your Brain
Career Builder
Career City
Career Command Center
Career Exchange
Career File's
Career Magazine
Career Mosaic
Career Opportunities in Singapore
Career Path
Career Shop
Career Site
Career WEB
CE Weekly
Cell
College Connection
Computer Jobs Store (Atlanta)
Computer Jobs Store (Dallas)
Computer World's IT Careers
Contract Employment Connection
Contract Employment NACCB
Corporate Aviation Resume Exchange
DesignSphere Online

DICE
Employment Opportunities in Water Resources
Engine Room
Engineering Jobs
Entry Level Job Seeker Assistant
Execubank
Extreme Resume Drop
E-Span
Franklin Search Group
Future Access Employment Guide
Future Business Centre On-Line
Hap Hiring Assistant
Heart Career Connections
Help Wanted
High Technology Career Centre
Hong Kong Jobs
Hong Kong Standard
Hospitality Net
Hot Jobs
HR World
Human Element
International Dental Connection
Internet Fashion Exchange
Internet Job Locator
Job Bank USA
Job Navigator
Job Net
Job Net Work: Your Total Employment Connection
Job Smart
JOB TRAK

CAREERXROADS©
Job, Resume & Career Management Sites on the World Wide Web
• The 1997 Directory •

RESUMES
to make your point

Job Tree
Jobs OnLine
Jobs .CZ
K3 & Company
Law Mall
Malaysia Online
MBA Employment Connection Assoc.
Med Connect
Med Search
Medical/Health Care Jobs Page
Michigan Employment
The Monster Board
Music Exchange
NAACB Job Board and Resume Bank
National Educators Employment Review
NationJob Network
Navy
News Link
NJ Job Search
NYC Headhunter's Mall
Oasys Network
Omicron Personal Career Center
Online Career Center
Packinfo-world
Passport Access
Physics Jobs On-Line
Princeton 1Info (US 1)
Pro Net Search
Proctor & Gamble Career Center
Programmers Available
Pursuit Net Jobs
Radio DJ's Unemployed
Real Bank
Real Jobs
Recruiters Online Network
Recruitex Technologies
The Resume Hut
Resume-Link
RPI Career Resource Home Page
RS/6000 Employment Page
Saludos Career Web
 SEACnet Southeastern Atlantic Coast Career Network

Seamless Web: Legal Job Center
Seniors On-Line Job Bank
SenseMedia Job Board
SkillBank
Snelling Staffing Services
Software Contractors Guild
SPIE's Employment Center
Talent Hunter
TCM's Job Marts (HR, T&D, HRIS)
Technology Registry
TechWeb/TechCareers/TechHunter
The Internet Career Site
Training & Devel. Resource Center
TrainingNet
Twin Cities Job Page
US Job Network
Virtual Job Centre
A Virtual Job Fair
Windows NT Resource Center
Wisconsin Employment Bureau
World Hire
World Wide Job Seekers

Post Resumes for a Fee

AAA Resume Service
Acorn Career Counseling
Airline Employment Ass't. Corps
 America's Employers: The Job Seekers "Home"
Arizona Careers Online
Au Pair in Europe
A+ On-Line Resumes
A.E.P.S.
Boldface Jobs
California Career and
 Employment Center
Career America
Career China
Career Connector
Career Resumes

RESUMES
to make your point

Career Surf
Career Transitions
Colorado Online Job Connection
Contract Employment Weekly
Emergency Medicine Practice Opportunity
Employnet
Federal Jobs Digest
Forty Plus of Northern California
Frasernet
Georgia Job Bank
GeoWeb for GIS/GPS/RS
Global Job Services
Help Wanted-USA
Hyper Media Resumes & Career Center
Insurance Career Center
Intellimatch
Internet Career Connection
Internet Resume Registry
Job Center
Job Net & Online Opportunities
Job Search
Mississippi Careers Online
Net Jobs Information Services
NJ JOBS
No. Carolina Career & Employment Resource Center
Philanthropy Journal
Resumatch, Inc.
Resumes on the Web
Shawn's Internet Resume Center
The Talent Network
Telecommuting Jobs
TV Jobs
Virtual Headbook
Women Professional Directory

See Resumes for Free

AAA Resume Service
Abag Globe
Acorn Career Counseling

Airline Employment Ass't. Corps
Arizona Careers Online
Arts Net Career Services Center
A+ On-Line Resumes
A.E.P.S.
Biomedical Positions
Boldface Jobs
Boston Job Bank
Building Industry Exchange
California Career and Employment Center
Carbonate Your Brain
Career America
Career Magazine
Career Mosaic
Career Site
Career Surf
Career Transitions
Cell
College Connection
Colorado Online Job Connection
Corporate Aviation Resume Exchange
DesignSphere Online
Emergency Medicine Practice Opportunity
Employment Opportunities in Water Resources
Employnet
Engineering Jobs
Entry Level Job Seeker Assistant
Execubank
Extreme Resume Drop
Forty Plus of Northern California
Frasernet
Future Access Employment Guide
Georgia Job Bank
GeoWeb for GIS/GPS/RS
Help Wanted-USA
Hospitality Net
HR World
Hyper Media Resumes & Career Center
Internet Career Connection
Internet Fashion Exchange
Internet Job Locator

CAREERXROADS©
Job, Resume & Career Management Sites on the World Wide Web
• **The 1997 Directory** •

RESUMES
to make your point

Job Net
Job Net Work:
    Your Total Employment Connection
Job Smart
Job Tree
Lee Hecht Harrison
Malaysia Online
MBA Employment Connection Assoc.
Michigan Employment
Mississippi Careers Online
Music Exchange
NAACB Job Board and Resume Bank
National Educators Employment Review
Net Jobs Information Services
News Link
NJ Job Search
NJ JOBS
Omicron Personal Career Center
Philanthropy Journal
Physics Jobs On-Line
Princeton 1Info (US 1)
Programmers Available
Radio DJ's Unemployed
Real Bank
Real Jobs
Resumatch, Inc.
The Resume Hut
Resumes on the Web
RPI Career Resource Home Page
RS/6000 Employment Page
  SEACnet Southeastern Atlantic Coast Career Network
Seamless Web: Legal Job Center
SenseMedia Job Board
Shawn's Internet Resume Center
SkillBank
Software Contractors Guild
SPIE's Employment Center
Talent Hunter
The Talent Network
Telecommuting Jobs
TrainingNet
TV Jobs

Twin Cities Job Page
Virtual Headbook
Virtual Job Centre
Wisconsin Employment Bureau
Women Professional Directory
World Hire
World Wide Job Seekers

See Resumes for a Fee

4 Work
America's Employers:
    The Job Seekers "Home"
Appointment Section
Asian Career Net
Asia-Net
Career China
Career City
Career Command Center
Career Connector
Career File's
Career Opportunities in Singapore
Career Path
Career Shop
Career WEB
CE Weekly
Computer Jobs Store (Atlanta)
Computer Jobs Store (Dallas)
Contract Employment Connection
Contract Employment NACCB
DICE
Eagleview
E-Span
Franklin Search Group
Future Business Centre On-Line
Hap Hiring Assistant
Heart Career Connections
Help Wanted
High Technology Career Centre
Hong Kong Jobs
Hong Kong Standard
Hot Jobs

CAREERXROADS©
Job, Resume & Career Management Sites on the World Wide Web
• The 1997 Directory •

RESUMES
to make your point

Human Element
Insurance Career Center
Intellimatch
International Dental Connection
I-Search
Job Bank USA
Job Net & Online Opportunities
Job Search
JOB TRAK
Jobs OnLine
Jobs .CZ
K3 & Company
Med Connect
Med Search
Medical/Health Care Jobs Page
The Monster Board
No. Carolina Career & Employment Resource Center
Oasys Network
Online Career Center
Packinfo-world
Passport Access
Pro Net Search
Pursuit Net Jobs
Recruiters Online Network
Recruitex Technologies
Resume-Link
Saludos Career Web
Seniors On-Line Job Bank
Snelling Staffing Services
TCM's Job Marts (HR, T&D, HRIS)
Technology Registry
The Internet Career Site
Training & Devel. Resource Center
US Job Network
A Virtual Job Fair

CAREERXROADS©
Job, Resume & Career Management Sites on the World Wide Web
• The 1997 Directory •

SPECIALTY

for all the "nooks and crannies"

This "cut" will give you a breakout of sites by specialty. We tried to highlight the sites that focus only on a single discipline. Major sites offer excellent search engines and a few like NationJob have outstanding stand-alone "Pages" for industry and specialty areas.

Advertising
  Pop Jobs
  www.popjobs.com
Agriculture
  Agricultural Job Listings
  caticsuf.csufresno.edu:70/1/atinet/agjobs
Aviation
  Corporate Aviation Resume Exchange
  scendtek.com/care
Communications/Radio
  Radio DJ's Unemployed
  www.icnet.net/users/wwhite/urdjhome.htm
Communications/TV
  TV Jobs
  www.tvjobs.com
Construction/Engineering Design
  Engineering News Record
  www.enr.com
Contract/Contingent
  OfficeNet
  www.officenet1.com
Contract/Contingent
  MacTemps
  www.mactemps.com.
Crystallography
  Crystallography Worldwide
  www.unige.ch/crystal/w3vlc
  /crystal.index.html
Education (see Teaching)
Engineering
  Society of Women Engineers
  www.swe.org
Engineering
  Job Search Materials for Engineers
  www.englib.cornell.edu//jobsearch.html
Engineering
  Civil Eng. & Public Works Career Paths
  www.FileShop.COM:80/apwa/civil.html

Engineering
  Engineering Job Source
  www.wwnet.com/~engineer/
Engineering
  Engineering Jobs
  www.engineeringjobs.com
Engineering/Agricultural
  American Soc. of Agricultural Eng.
  asae.org/jobs
Engineering/Electrical/Electronic
  IEEE
  www.ieee.org
Engineering/Elect.
  ENews
  www.sumnet.com/enews
Engineering/Packaging
  Food and Drug Packaging
  www.fdp.com
Engineering/Packaging
  Packinfo-world
  www.packinfo.world.org
Engineering/PE
  National Society of Professional
  Engineering HP
  www.nspe.org
Engineering/Power
  Electric Power NewsLink
  www.powermag.com
Entertainment
  The Talent Network
  talentnet.com/
Entertainment
  Auditions Online
  www.auditions.com
Entertainment/Actors
  Virtual Headbook
  www.xmission.com:80/~wintrnx/vh
  /virtual.html

CAREERXROADS©
Job, Resume & Career Management Sites on the World Wide Web
• The 1997 Directory •

SPECIALTY

for all the "nooks and crannies"

Environmental/Water
   Employment Opportunities in Water Resources
   www.uwin.siu.edu/announce/jobs/
Finance/Accounting
   Am. Assoc. of Fin & Accounting
   www.aafa.com/
Finance/Banking
   Execubank
   www.realbank.com
Finance/Business
   Careers in Management Consulting
   www.cob.ohio-state.edu:80/dept/fin/jobs/consult.htm
Finance/Business
   Business Job Finder Ohio State Univ.
   www.cob.ohio-state.edu/~fin/jobs/jobslist.htmosujobs.htm
Finance/Business
   100 Careers in Wall Street
   www.globalvillager.com/villager/wsc
Geographic Systems
   GeoWeb for GIS/GPS/RS
   www.ggrweb.com
Government Jobs
   Federal Jobs Digest
   www.jobsfed.com
Graphic Arts
   DesignSphere Online
   www.dsphere.net/jobs.html
Health Care
   Physicians Employment
   www.physemp.com
Health Care
   Medical/Health Care Jobs Page
   www.nationjob.com
Health Care
   Hospital Web
   neuro-www.mgh.harvard.edu/hospitalweb.nclk
Health Care
   Health Careers Online
   www.healthcareers-online.com
Health Care/Physical Therapy
   PT Net (Physical Therapy)
   bob.coe.uga.edu/%7escott/pt.html
Health Care
   Future Med
   ourworld.compuserve.com/homepages/futuremed/main.htm
Health Care/Allied Health
   Allied Health Opportunities Directory
   www.gvpub.com
Health Care/DDS
   International Dental Connection
   unixg.ubc.ca:880/leighton/idc/contents.htm
Health Care/Health Information
   For The Record
   www.gvpub.com
Health Care/MD
   JAMA
   ama-assn.org
Health Care/MD
   Physician Recruit Net
   www.physiciannet.com/index.html
Health Care/MD
   Medical Web
   www.medical-web.com/med_web/medical_web.html
Health Care/MD
   Medical Jobs
   www.MEDJOB.com
Health Care/MD
   Medical Device Link
   www.devicelink.com
Health Care/MD
   Med Connect
   www.medconnect.com
Health Care/MD
   National Physician Job Listing Directory
   www.njnet.com/~embbs/job/jobs.html
Health Care/MD
   New England Journal of Medicine
   www.nejm.org/nejm/webmate?nejm/form/nejm/welcome

CAREERXROADS©
Job, Resume & Career Management Sites on the World Wide Web
• The 1997 Directory •

SPECIALTY

for all the "nooks and crannies"

Health Care/MD
  Doctor Link
  www.doctorlink.com
Health Care/MD
  Ed Physician
  www.edphysician.com/
Health Care/MD
  Emergency Medicine Practice Opportunity
  www.njnet.com/~embbs/jobjob-stat.html
Health Care/Nursing
  Perioperative Online Employment
  Opportunities
  www.aorn.org
Health Care/Physical Therapy
  APTA Home Page
  apta.edoc.com
Human Resources
  SHRM HR Jobs
  www.shrm.org
Human Resources
  IHRIM Chapter/Pacific Northwest
  www.ihrim.org/chapters/pacificnorthwest
  /index.html
Human Resources
  HR World
  www.hrworld.com
Human Resources
  HRCOMM
  ccnet.com/hrcomm/
Human Resources
  IPMA HR Job Pool
  www.ipma-hr.org
Human Resources/HRIS
  HRIM Mall
  www.hrimmall.com
Human Resources/T&D
  Training & Devel. Resource Center
  www.tcm.com/trdev/nav.htm
Human Resources/T&D
  TrainingNet
  www.trainingnet.com
Human Resources/T&D
  Clearinghouse for T&D Resources
  www.proed.com
Human Resources/T&D,ER, HRIS
  TCM's Job Marts (HR, T&D, HRIS)
  www.tcm.com
Human Resources/Recruitment
  Human Element
  mindlink.net/vci/thehp.htm
Insurance
  Insurance Career Center
  www.connectyou.com:80/talent/
International
  AK Jobnet - The Big Picture
  www.ak.com.au/akjobnet.html
IT
  Contract Employment Weekly
  www.ceweekly.wa.com
IT
  DICE
  www.dice.com
IT
  Computer World's IT Careers
  www.computerworld.com
IT
  Electronic Engineering Times
  techweb.cmp.com/eet/823/
IT
  Software Contractors Guild
  www.scguild.com/
IT
  TechWeb/TechCareers/TechHunter
  techweb.cmp.com/
IT
  Computer Jobs Store (Atlanta)
  computerjobs.com
IT
  Association for Women in Computing
  www.halcyon.com/monih/awc.html
IT
  ACM's Sigmod's Database Job Openings
  www.acm.org/sigmod/jobs

CAREERXROADS©
Job, Resume & Career Management Sites on the World Wide Web
• The 1997 Directory •

SPECIALTY
for all the "nooks and crannies"

IT
Colorado Online Job Connection
www.net1comm.com/~peak/

IT
Pro Net Search
bisinc.com/pronet/ccc/

IT
Omicron Personal Career Center
www.omicronet.com/career
/resume.htm#top

IT
Silicon Valley Technical
Employment Agencies
www.sease.com/jobs.html

IT
Job Serve: IT Vacancies in the UK
www.jobserve.com

IT
RS/6000 Employment Page
www.s6000.com/job.html

IT
Jobs OnLine
JobsOnLine.com/emp_enter.cgi

IT
Chicago Software Newspaper
www.chisoft.com

IT
Career Line
www.careerline.com

IT
Communication Week
techweb.cmp.com/cw/cw.careers
/index.html

IT
Computer Resellers Weekly
techweb.cmp.com/crn/career/career.html

IT
Computer Retail Week
techweb.cmp.com/crw/061996/

IT
Career Network
phoenix.placement.oakland.edu/career
/internet.ht

IT
MMWire Online
www.mmwire.com

IT
Advance HTC
www.advancehtc.com

IT
The Software Jobs Home Page
www.softwarejobs.com

IT
NAACB Job Board and Resume Bank
computerwork.com

IT
Comm Careers
www.commweek.com

IT
Computer Jobs Store (Dallas)
computerjobs.com/dallas

IT
High Technology Career Centre
hightechcareers.com/

IT
CE Weekly
www.ceweekly.com

IT
Contract Employment NACCB
www.computerwork.com

IT
Hot Jobs
www.hotjobs.com

IT/Engineering
Technology Registry
www.techreg.com

IT/Engineering
Women in Computer Science
& Engineering
www.mit.edu:8001/people/sorokin
/women/index.html

IT/Internet
iWorld
www.iworld.com

CAREERXROADS©
Job, Resume & Career Management Sites on the World Wide Web
• The 1997 Directory •

SPECIALTY

for all the "nooks and crannies"

IT/Multimedia
  BAMTA
  www.mlds.arc.nasa.gov:80/BAMTA/
IT/Network
  Network World Fusion
  www.nwfusion.com
IT/User Interface
  UI Design Jobs
  www.io.tudelft.nl/uidesign/jobs.html
IT/Web
  Web Developer's Virtual Library
  www.stars.com/
IT/Windows NT Users
  Windows NT Resource Center
  www.bhs.com/default.asp
Journalism
  National Diversity Journalism Job Bank
  www.newsjobs.com
Journalism
  News Link
  www.newslink.org
Journalism
  AJR/ News Link
  www.ajr.com
Law
  Law Mall
  www.lawmall.com/resumes/resumes/html
Law
  Law Employment Center
  www.lawjobs.com/
Law
  Seamless Web: Legal Job Center
  www.seamless.com/jobs/
Law
  New York Law Journal
  www.lextra.com/classifieds
Leasing
  Equipment Leasing Association
  www.elaonline.com
Marketing
  Direct Marketing World Job Center
  www.dmworld.com
Multimedia
  NMAA'S Job Banker
  www.nmaa.org/jobbank.htm
Music
  Carbonate Your Brain
  www.7up.com
Music
  Music Exchange
  www.scsn.net/~musex/
Newspapers/Publishers
  California Job Bank
  www.ccnet.com/CSNE/jobs/postings.html
Part time work.
  Programmers Available
  www.qldnet.com.au/web.users/
  programmers
Pilot
  A.E.P.S.
  www.aeps.com/aeps/aepshm.html
Psychology
  Psych
  psych.hanover.edu:80%-zfaps/
Psychology
  Positions in Psychology
  www.anu.edu.au/psychology/PiP/pip.htm
Purchasing
  Purchasing NAPM
  catalog.com/napmsv/jobs.htm
Real Estate
  Real Jobs
  www.real-jobs.com
Real Estate
  Real Bank
  www.realbank.com
Science
  Science Global Career Network
  www.aaas.org
Science
  Job Board
  wfscnet.tamu.edu:80/jobs.html
Science/Astronomy
  AAS Career Services
  www.aas.org

CAREERXROADS©
Job, Resume & Career Management Sites on the World Wide Web
• The 1997 Directory •

SPECIALTY
for all the "nooks and crannies"

Science/Biomedical/Genetics
  Biomedical Positions
  www.informatik.uni-rostock.de
  /hum-molgen/anno/position
Science/Biotechnology
  BioSpace Career Center
  www.biospace.com/sd/career
Science/Chemistry
  PolySort
  www.polysort.com
Science/Chemistry
  Academic Chemistry Employment
  Clearinghouse
  //hackberry.chem.niu.edu
  /ChemJobText.html
Science/Health Care
  Franklin Search Group
  www.medmarket.com/tenants
  /fsg/postjobs.htm
Science/Physics
  YSN Jobs Page
  (Young Scientists Network)
  www.physics.uiuc.edu/ysn/
Science/Physics
  Plasma Laboratory Wis
  plasma-gate.weizman.ac.il/jobs.html
Science/Physics
  SPIE's Employment Center
  optics.org/employment/employment.html
Scince/Physics
  AIP Physics Careers Bulletin Board
  aip.org:80/aip/careers/careers.html
Science/Physics
  Physics Jobs On-Line
  www.tp.umu.se/TIPTOP/
Sports
  Online Sports Career Center
  www.onlinesports.com:80/
  pages/careercenter.html
Sports/Outdoors/College
  Cool Works
  www.coolworks.com/showme/
Teaching
  Chronicle of Higher Education
  www.chronicle.com
Teaching
  O Hayo Sensei
  www.ohayosensei.com/~ohayo/
Teaching
  National Educators Employment Review
  www.teacherjobs.com/
Teaching
  Usjobnet K-12
  www.usjobnet.com
Teaching
  Academic Employment Network
  www.academploy.com
Teaching
  Educator's Network EDNET
  pages.prodigy.com/CA/luca52a
  /bagley.html
Telecommuting
  Telecommuting Jobs
  tjobs.com/index.html
Telecommuting
  Telecommuting, Telework & Alt. Officing
  www.gilgordon.com
Travel
  Au Pair in Europe
  eidos.ca/aupair/
Navy
  www.navyjobs.com

A Final Note for Job Seekers on Networking

All the technical wizardry in the world does you no good if your attitude about yourself, your skills and your future are not 100% positive. CAREERXROADS may have been written for folks who want to push the envelope but it's even more important to know where you want to go. If you're not there yet, start at the beginning, get the help you need from friends, family and counselors.

When you do have it together, look for support from many directions. We advocate an aggressive strategy by joining several networking groups that meet periodically and share job leads, pump each other up, and build relationships for the future. Groups from around common interests such as similar jobs or professions, gender, salary level, etc., but all are based on peer support principles. Many fail because their members forget that by truly supporting each other, they "expand the pie," rather than competing for a smaller slice.

Geoffrey Nelson, a human resource executive with more than 25 years experience, can arguably claim to have participated and started as many groups as anyone. His success in "working" the leads, networking with his associates and supporting others has always paid off by reducing his transition to a new job and finding colleagues for his network who support his long term career objectives. (Local newspapers, national publications like the "National Business Employment Weekly", community and religious groups, professional associations, colleges and outplacement firms all publicize information about networking groups. If local help is unavailable (then) online, you'll find a career forum with networking potential on just about every major Bulletin Board-Search for "career," "jobs," or "employment" and commercial World Wide Web job site.)

According to Geoff, the principles below are essential for best results.

1. Share everything. No holding back. To share a lead only after you've discovered that you are no longer a candidate is too late. Assume you are never going to be the "only" candidate and the worst case scenario - that you are helping your "competition" get in is also the worst kind of negative thinking. It's normal to be secretive, but it's not going to be successful in the long run. The "takers" of the world will seldom succeed. Even if you do help someone else get a job that you hoped would be yours, in all probability you wouldn't have gotten it anyway and you have more than likely made a friend for life. (See #2)

2. Networking Associates are as important as job leads. When someone trusts that you will share all your leads with them, they are more likely to do the same for you.

3. Your Network's "Alumni" (job-seekers who have graduate to a new position)

CAREERXROADS©
Job, Resume & Career Management Sites on the World Wide Web
• The 1997 Directory •

are an important resource even if you joined the network after they left. They are likely to provide referrals to you if you get to know them. Get in touch and stay in touch.

4. Seek out "competitors." The very best people with the same background, experience, credentials and job goals are the most important people you want to help. Refer them whenever you can and you will find a) they will return the favor, or b) you will help get them out of the market faster.

5. Use group rosters to call members in between meetings. Focus on how you can help others and you will find that it will come back to you tenfold.

6. Any job lead you submit to the network needs to be complete, current, and include any personal information you have available. Do your homework.

7. Form and lead your own mini group. (See #2 and #4 above)

8. Help recruiters by referring qualified candidates...even if they called to discuss their interest in you. Do you really think you are the only one they are going to speak with? They will appreciate your input, respect your recommendations and be more likely to remember you when it counts.

9. Two golden rules for network meeting: Be on time and do what you say.

10. Attitudes are contagious. Don't get dragged down by someone else's negativity. Their attitude is their responsibility. Avoid them like the plague they are.

Whether High Tech or Low Tech, your job search is your responsibility. Attack it with the same enthusiasm and adventure that you should be giving to every aspect of your life. We hope CAREERXROADS has added a few new ideas.

About the Authors

Gerry Crispin and Mark Mehler have each been involved in the employment field for their entire careers. Nationally recognized experts, they have pooled their knowledge of the hiring process and emerging technology to chart the developing strategies & tactics of jobs seekers and company recruiters.

Gerry Crispin, certified as a Senior Professional in Human Resources (SPHR), has been active in the Human Resource profession for more than 25 years. He has worked in career services, human resource management, organizational change and recruitment. As Vice President of Shaker Advertising Agency, Inc., a national advertising firm specializing in recruitment advertising, he creates and places thousands of help-wanted advertisements each week and consults to clients on their strategic staffing strategies. An Engineering graduate from Stevens Institute of Technology, he began his career in Human Resources with Johnson & Johnson after completing a graduate degree in Organizational Behavior. A volunteer leader with the Society for Human Resource Management, Gerry chairs their national employment practices committee and speaks frequently on the topic of emerging technology.

Mark Mehler is a highly successful consultant to major corporations on high-volume staffing with over 20 years of human resource experience. He is President of MMC Group and specializes in recruiting top talent while using emerging technology, such as the Internet, optical scanning and electronic resume databases, to reduce his client's cost-per hire. Prior to working with companies such as Johnson & Johnson, Martin Marietta, and G.E., Mark received a B.S. in Economics from Fairleigh Dickinson University and held human resource management positions with Cookson America, Millipore Corporation and Beatrice Companies.

CAREERXROADS is the result of Gerry's and Mark's volunteer involvement as contributors to a networking group of human resource professionals seeking new employment. Over the last five years, the group's meetings (every third Saturday morning) where job leads are shared, increasingly included information gleaned from the Internet. As the speed, access and accuracy of technology seemingly improved these job seekers' chance of success, Mark and Gerry began incorporating the ideas in their respective day jobs and joined forces to share what they've learned about the World Wide Web by creating a hands-on Internet Clinic for HR practitioners using university computer labs.

CAREERXROADS©
Job, Resume & Career Management Sites on the World Wide Web
• The 1997 Directory •